A SHAKESPEARE PRIMER

AMS PRESS
NEW YORK

A SHAKESPEARE PRIMER

GERALD SANDERS

Department of English, Michigan State Normal College, Ypsilanti, Michigan

New York   RINEHART & CO., INC.   Toronto

Published Pursuant to Agreement with Holt, Rinehart, and Winston, Inc.

Reprinted from the edition of 1950: New York

First AMS edition published in 1971

Manufactured in the United States of America

International Standard Book Number: 0-404-05560-5

Library of Congress Catalog Card Number: 72-175432

AMS PRESS INC.
NEW YORK, N.Y. 10003

PREFACE

This book is designed primarily for students who are beginning the study of Shakespeare in college. Instructors of Shakespeare courses usually need all their class time for the plays themselves. Yet students can read the plays more intelligently if they know something of the age in which Shakespeare lived and the conditions under which the plays were written, staged, and published. Therefore a book that conveys this information with reasonable brevity can save the instructor's time and provide the conscientious student with a background for his reading.

Through the work of devoted scholars our knowledge of Shakespeare grows with each generation. Yet since any subject so attractive as the "Shakespeare problem" cannot escape the notice of foolish as well as wise commentators, students need some orientation before they venture far into the labyrinths of Shakespearean scholarship. The aim of this book is to supply the basic information on which there is general agreement. Students who wish to explore beyond the boundaries within which I have had to keep will find titles on a variety of topics listed at the end of the volume. Some of the appendixes include material not found, so far as I am aware, in other handbooks.

I have given credit, either in the body of the work or in footnotes, to scholars on whom I have relied for specific matters. To acknowledge my indebtedness to all who have contributed indirectly to this work would be as impossible for me as it would be tedious for the reader. I record my grateful thanks to John C. Adams for the use of his floor plans of the Globe Theater and for photographs of his new model of the Globe, and to my colleagues, Hoover H. Jordan and Notley S. Maddox, for reading parts of my manuscript.

G. S.

April, 1950

CONTENTS

Preface   v

I. The Age of Shakespeare   1
II. England in the Time of Shakespeare   9
III. Shakespeare's Environment   20
IV. Shakespeare's Life   27
V. Drama and the Theater in Shakespeare's Time   39
VI. Shakespeare's Works   56
VII. Introductions to the Plays   73
VIII. Shakespearean Criticism and Scholarship   143
IX. A Note on Reading Shakespeare   154

Appendixes
A. Contemporary Comment and Praise   161
B. Early Biographical References   173
C. Shakespearean Actors and Producers   182
D. The Baconian Theory   190
E. Shakespeare's Will   194
F. Genealogy of the Houses of Lancaster and York   198

Bibliography   200

Index   215

A SHAKESPEARE PRIMER

I

THE AGE OF SHAKESPEARE

MAIN CURRENTS AND INFLUENCES. Shakespeare lived in an expansive and flowering period when the movement known as the English Renaissance reached high tide. The term "Renaissance," or "rebirth," refers in a specific sense to a rebirth of interest in classical literature and thought; but by extension it now designates in a more general sense the period itself in which the Revival of Learning took place. Whether in its specific or general meaning, the term is applicable to the age that produced Shakespeare.

In the centuries following the breaking up of the ancient Roman Empire and the triumph of Christianity, the old pagan literature was neglected; but by the thirteenth century, scholars in Italy, and later on in other European countries, began to discover and study again these ancient writings. Renewed acquaintance with the thought of Greece and Rome led to a quickening of interest in all intellectual activities and greatly expanded the intellectual horizons of medieval thinkers. Because of the long neglect of the old languages and literature, a vast amount of labor was necessary to collect, annotate, and interpret the ancient manuscripts before they could become the property of all men. This essential labor in its early stages and the poor communications of the time slowed down the spread of the movement to the north and west, so that its full impact was not felt in England until the sixteenth century. Although the early Renaissance was scholarly rather than creative, it was able—by introducing fresh standards of culture and by replacing the formalism of the medieval school system—to provide an atmosphere in which the creative artist could flourish. Thus in the wake of the movement appeared such writers and artists as Petrarch, Ariosto, da Vinci, Michelangelo, and Raphael in Italy; Rabelais, Ronsard, and Montaigne in France; Cervantes, Lope de Vega, and Velásquez in Spain; Erasmus in Holland; and scores of others hardly less important. In England the expansion of thought that came with the Revival of Learning, and the introduction of new models from Italian and classical sources, helped to develop a body of literature pre-eminent in English literary history.

In its more general sense the Renaissance may be thought of as a transitional period between the Middle Ages and the modern age. After the centuries of confusion that followed the fall of the Roman empire, more stable conditions brought a gathering of new forces, and the long stagnation gave way to a great upsurge of activity. Amid the vast changes taking place arose ideas that helped free the individual mind and spirit from subservience to old, and in many instances outmoded, institutions, and affected permanently men's concepts of their world and themselves. Among the diverse influences contributing to these changes, in addition to the Revival of Learning, were many important inventions, world discovery and exploration, new scientific theories, the Reformation, and new alignments of economic forces.

Of the inventions that helped to usher in a new age, two of the most significant were the compass and gunpowder.[1] Both of these inventions date from about the thirteenth century, but neither came into effective use until well along in the Renaissance period. Without the compass the work of the great discoverers of the fifteenth and sixteenth centuries would scarcely have been possible. The use of firearms not only changed the entire pattern of war but brought great political and social changes, first, by helping to make obsolete walled towns and castles—those medieval examples of isolationism—and, secondly, by giving greater equality to persons in possession of these arms, whatever their physical strength or rank.

---

[1] Others of less significance, yet in their several ways important, were starch, steel needles, coaches, and paper.

But important as these various inventions were, none can compare in its influence on the minds of men with the invention of printing. Hitherto the slow, laborious, and expensive process of copying manuscripts by hand had severely limited the number of literary works that any one person, however wealthy, could own. Knowledge of the best that had been preserved from the past was meager, even among the scholars who in university or monastery had access to the manuscripts gathered there. Thus for nearly all men the past was a closed book until about the middle of the fifteenth century, when the method of printing from movable type was developed in Holland and Germany. In 1476, William Caxton, who had learned the new process when he was living on the Continent, set up at Westminster the first printing press in England. During the next century, printing increased to such an extent that men of modest means could own books, both reprints of the great writings of the past and the works of contemporary authors.

For books to have value and influence, however, they must have readers; and to read books, men must have a certain amount of education. During the sixteenth century, educational facilities increased, and the educational system itself was so greatly improved that by Shakespeare's lifetime a reading and bookloving public was ready to make use of the rich treasures of the printers and booksellers. Toward the end of the fifteenth century, a band of Oxford scholars—Grocyn, Linacre, Colet, More, and others—introduced the New Learning from Italy; and their work was carried on by their followers at Oxford and by a group of Cambridge men who came under the influence of the great Dutch scholar Erasmus. Disciples of the New Learning helped formulate policies that fostered and expanded education and brought it within the reach of families of limited means. Many new grammar schools were established. Scholarships and the patronage of wealthy men assured even a university education to some of the most promising sons of poor men. The number of persons who could read and write increased greatly; and with this increase came a wider demand for books, with a consequent demand for authors and translators. Before the end of the sixteenth century, these conditions produced such professional men of letters as Thomas Kyd, Robert Greene, Christopher Marlowe, Ben Jonson, and Shakespeare.

Another highly stimulating influence on the age was world discovery. The explorations of Columbus, Vasco da Gama, the Cabots, Magellan, Drake, and others opened new continents to settlement and exploitation, brought untold wealth to Europe, and offered vast new frontiers to the adventurous spirits of the age. But more important than the economic and political changes brought on by these discoveries was the thrilling appeal to the imaginations of men as they contemplated a suddenly expanded world and speculated on the unmapped and unexplored areas of new oceans and new continents. Every tale brought back from these voyages of discovery by even the lowliest member of a ship's company furnished matter for wonder and speculation by those remaining at home. The great extension of geographical frontiers expanded also man's imagination and spirit.

Even more startling than man's new concept of his world was the new view of the universe advanced in the sixteenth century. To the medieval mind the earth, fixed and immovable, stood at the center of a universe small enough to be easily comprehended. Around the earth circled the heavenly bodies, each in its translucent sphere. Close above the visible universe was heaven, and just beneath was hell, the abodes respectively of God and Satan, each of whom took a highly personal interest in the doings of everyone. All beings and things, from God and the several orders of angels to the king and the various ranks then existing on earth, occupied a position ordained by the Creator, and every rank stood in a fixed relation to every other rank. But this view of the physical universe was challenged by the Polish astronomer Copernicus, whose book *De revolutionibus orbium coelestium* (1543) advanced the idea that the earth and other planets were satellites of the sun. Although the Copernican theory did not win immediate general acceptance, it had the effect wherever it did make its way in men's thought of upsetting the traditional theology and of helping to unsettle the old views of rank and degrees in society.

ECONOMIC AND RELIGIOUS CHANGES. Meanwhile important economic changes were taking place that affected the entire social structure. The basis of medieval society was order and tradition. From the king down, each segment held a position that seemed firmly fixed. Of these segments none exercised more power and appeared more permanent than the landed nobility, the craft guilds, and the Church. Yet by Shakespeare's lifetime all of these either had ceased to be an effective influence in national life or had undergone profound change.

The first to lose its dominant position was the landed nobility. During the Middle Ages a few great lords exercised a feudal control over large numbers of dependents. People within the domain of such a lord were in effect, although not technically, his vassals. They were destined throughout their lives to labor in his service and at need to fight under his banner in the interminable conflicts of the period. By the end of the fifteenth century, however, this system had been supplanted by more modern systems. Factors contributing to the change were war, economic trends, and the policies of the Tudor sovereigns, who ruled in the sixteenth century. A long and costly struggle between England and France, called the Hundred Years' War (1337-1453), sapped the wealth and power of the entire nation, but the burden fell most heavily on the great houses, which were weakened in resources and man power by their contributions to the prolonged warfare. Then followed the fierce and bitter Wars of the Roses (1455-1485), which involved virtually every important family of the country and all but completed the destruction of the old aristocracy. These wars ended with the ascendancy of the house of Tudor. Because of the weakened condition of the nobles, the Tudor sovereigns were able to establish a strong central government and bring the nobles into subjection to it. Early in the reign of Henry VII, the first Tudor king, laws were passed limiting the number of retainers a lord might keep and the wealth he might hold. Another Tudor policy was to foster the influence of the middle class as a counterpoise to that of the remnants of the old nobility. The former baronial regime had been based on agriculture, but as commerce and industry developed, a new group, urban rather than rural, came into prominence. All these forces were working to bring about a new economic organization of society in which the old landed nobility had a constantly decreasing importance.

Another institution which in the Middle Ages seemed an enduring part of the social structure was the guild, an association of all those having to do with a single branch of industry in a community. Every trade had its guild, the object of which was to control all work and dealings in that particular trade. So powerful were these organizations that, in effect, they ordered the life of every skilled workman, regulated the entire trade monopoly of many communities, and frequently exercised effective control over town governments. To enter any skilled trade, a man had to serve a long apprenticeship, usually seven years; and on becoming a member of a guild, he had to bind himself to contribute to its maintenance and to abide by its regulations. But the Tudor sovereigns set out to curb the guilds as they had curbed the nobles. Under Henry VII a law was passed that required the approval of a crown officer before any new ordinance of "fellowships of crafts" became effective. The greatest blow to the guilds came, however, after Henry VIII broke with the Church of Rome. The guilds had close affiliations with the Church; many of them, moreover, possessed great wealth, which was used to maintain schools, hospitals, and almshouses. Among the acts passed as a result of the break with Rome was one that appropriated to the crown all guild property held in use for religious purposes. Later on, under Elizabeth, the jurisdiction of the guilds over apprentices and journeymen was curtailed. Changing economic conditions also contributed to the decline of these organizations. Capitalism, with its emphasis on personal initiative, opposed the old system; new industries were organized on a different basis; and by the end of the sixteenth century the power and influence of the guilds were gone.

Of all the changes taking place in England in the sixteenth century, however, the most important were the religious changes. During the Middle Ages, though schisms might arise, political maneuverings threaten temporarily the papal influence, and individual churchmen attack abuses, the Church held a secure place in the national life and exerted a strong influence on everyone from king to serf. A considerable part of the population had some direct connection with the Church, and over all this group the Church exercised full jurisdiction, even in matters of crime. The Church, moreover, had a dominant position in the social economy. According to conservative estimates, the Church owned or controlled a third of the wealth of England; and churchmen also filled the highest offices in the state and helped direct state policy. But with the growth of a national spirit, a few bold leaders arose to challenge the position of the Church in secular and economic matters. In the fourteenth century, John Wycliffe had inveighed against the entire system of church policy in England; and by the next century his followers, called Lollards, had gained considerable strength. Although persecution had reduced their numbers, many Englishmen with Lollard sympathies were alive to welcome the Reformation when it began.

The movement known as the Reformation began inconspicuously enough with the demand of a German monk, Martin Luther, for church reform. But the widespread dissatisfaction among earnest churchmen over abuses that the Church seemed slow to correct, and among many of the laity over the economic power that the Church wielded, gave support and encouragement to the movement inaugurated by Luther and propelled it forward until the differences between the reforming element and the Papacy became too great to reconcile. The outcome was the establishment of the Protestant Church. In England the growing spirit of nationalism had already questioned the authority of the Church in secular affairs when the decision of Henry VIII to divorce his wife and the refusal of the Papacy to sanction the divorce brought a definite break between England and Rome, the establishment of a national church, and the alignment of England with the Protestant movement. This breaking of age-old ties between England and Rome had a profound effect on economic and political life, as well as on religious thought, in the years just before the birth of Shakespeare and during his lifetime.

The various movements and influences operative in the sixteenth century tended to have one element in common: they forced men to a greater reliance on themselves and placed greater emphasis on the individual. Their total effect was to make the age of Shakespeare one of restless activity and boundless aspiration. It was a period, in the words of one historian,[2] when men ceased looking backward to an imaginary golden age and began looking forward to a future golden age—when a long pessimistic wave died down and a shorter optimistic wave surged up. With its high challenges, its vast new frontiers, and its emphasis on the individual, it was a good age in which to be born. Even the feeling of insecurity evoked by such rapid changes had its useful purpose. Men needed a new interpretation of life, of themselves, and of their world. In Shakespeare the age found its supreme voice.

---

[2] Sir Charles Oman, *The Sixteenth Century* (New York: 1936), pp. 3, 37.

II

ENGLAND IN THE TIME
OF SHAKESPEARE

ECONOMIC FEATURES AND TENDENCIES. The England of Shakespeare's day was a sparsely populated country of perhaps five million people.[1] For the most part it was a country of rolling landscapes, wooded areas, clear streams spanned by bridges at widely separated points, and small tilled fields and pastures. Most of the people lived in hamlets and villages, but here and there rose larger towns, some still surrounded by medieval walls. Roads connecting even the more important towns were poor by modern standards, and communication was slow and difficult. The common mode of travel was by foot or horseback, though coach travel was increasing. Yet in spite of some backward conditions, the age was one of progress—of rapid internal change, of growing prosperity, and of waxing national prestige and power.

England was still principally an agricultural country, though in agriculture, as in virtually everything else, marked changes were taking place. For two or three centuries, the old feudal system—under which serfs farmed vast estates for the profit of lords whose chief interest in the soil was to wring from it enough to support their arms and maintain their power—had been slowly giving place to tenant farming. This change became noticeable after the Black Death (1348–1350), a fearful epidemic of the bubonic plague that swept away over half the population and left the surviving laborers in a favorable position

---

[1] No census was taken in those days, but careful estimates by modern scholars fix the population at between 3,500,000 and 5,000,000, with the latter the more likely figure.

to bargain with the landowners. Stringent labor laws helped defer the process of change, but the destructive wars of the fifteenth century and the general trend of economic forces operated in favor of the workers, so that by the sixteenth century tenant farming was the common practice. According to a modern historian,[2] the dominant social type in rural England in Shakespeare's day was the prosperous yeoman, or tenant farmer, who, owning or holding a hundred or more acres, supplied wool to the distant clothier, and butter, cheese, and meat to the industrial centers. Because tenant farmers themselves benefited from increased production, they introduced better strains of cattle and horses and learned to make better use of fertilizers. They also added to their income by carrying on weaving in the home and by trading in wool. The result of these innovations was an enormous increase in farm incomes, with a proportionate increase in the social, as well as the economic, status of the agricultural class. Another effect of the system was that the better rents it provided furnished capital for the landowners to build great mansions, to buy and wear rich apparel, to support themselves in town society, and to invest in commercial and manufacturing enterprises. These new uses of capital in turn contributed to the general prosperity.

Although throughout the sixteenth century agriculture remained the chief industry, trade and manufacturing began to assume importance in the national economy. Some manufacturing was carried on in the first half of the century, especially in the mining areas of the South and West, and there was also considerable commerce with the Continent; but the real expansion of both commerce and manufacturing began during the second half of the century. So rapid was the growth of both trade and manufactures during Shakespeare's life that by the time of his death England held in each a favorable position among European countries.

Of first importance among industries was the manufacture of woolen cloth. This industry, which centered at first in the

---

[2] George Unwin in *Shakespeare's England* (London: 1916), I, 325.

eastern counties, soon spread to the North and West, with the result that Manchester, York, and Halifax became manufacturing centers. With almost every farm family supplementing its income by home weaving, the total output of woolen cloth was enormous. Silk manufacture, feltmaking, straw-plaiting, and other industries were introduced, but in comparison with the manufacture of woolen cloth their roles in the national economy were minor. Meanwhile, the founding of the Royal Exchange in London (1566) was an evidence of the growing interest in commerce. London, in fact, had already attained considerable prominence as a commercial center by 1584, when an event occurred that added greatly to its importance. In this year the Spanish destroyed the great industrial city of Antwerp; in the exodus that followed, many wealthy merchants transferred their activities to London and helped to make it from this time the dominant trading center of Europe.

Adding to the wealth produced by trade was that brought in by Sir Francis Drake and other explorers and sea adventurers. In one of the political crises between England and Spain, when war appeared imminent, English privateers turned to plundering Spanish treasure ships and Spanish settlements in the New World. Thus a considerable amount of the wealth that Spain was gathering from the Americas was diverted to England. When, for instance, Drake returned in 1580 from circumnavigating the globe, his ship contained gold, silver, and precious stones to the value of a half-million pounds, all taken from the Spaniards. Yet this was but one of Drake's exploits; and Drake was but one—though the most notable and successful—of the privateers who at the expense of Spain added to the wealth of England.

Many evidences of this growing wealth became noticeable in Shakespeare's lifetime. Improved roads made travel easier. Coaches were introduced, and soon became so numerous in London that laws were necessary to regulate their use. Wealthy merchants and nobles built great mansions, and men of more moderate means began to build larger and better houses than formerly, with residences and barns separated. Glass windows replaced shutters, carpets took the place of rushes as a covering for floors, and beds and pillows came into common use instead of the pallets of a generation or two before. Tobacco—which Sir John Hawkins had introduced about 1565—was widely used, especially by the London gallants. Such common items as starch, forks, and toothpicks were introduced for the first time. A marked tendency set in among the country gentry to spend a great part of the year in London and to participate in the social life of the city. Foreign travel became more common, and with it a greater interest in the outside world and in the manners, customs, literature, and arts of other countries. The system of lending money on interest was introduced, with its attendant evils as well as its benefits to trade. Puritans might inveigh against some of these tendencies, as when Philip Stubbs named as the devouring cankers of the time dainty fare, gorgeous buildings, and sumptuous apparel, but their words did not turn men back to the more simple tastes of an earlier day. Refinements in living increased popular interest in education and in books, in the arts and in drama.

POLITICAL BACKGROUNDS AND INFLUENCES. With the growing prosperity at home came a corresponding growth in the prestige and influence of the country abroad. The shadow of approaching war with Spain, which hung over England for some years, and its removal by the destruction of the great Spanish Armada in 1588 helped to minimize religious differences at home and to effect a national unity that the growth of Puritanism did not as yet disturb. Abroad, the policies of France and Spain favored England. These two chief Continental powers were in constant conflict and were frequently at war, and each was naturally anxious to prevent England's becoming an ally of the other. Both therefore at times ignored English policies and moves that under different circumstances would probably have involved England in war. Thus, while the Continent was torn by strife, England maintained a precarious peace and was able at times to move with resolution and boldness to further its designs.

Many of the changes of the time resulted from the operation of natural processes and tendencies. One of these was the growth of democracy, for although actual democracy in the modern sense was still far distant, a tendency toward the leveling of classes had already set in and was proceeding at an accelerated pace. Others were the rising power of the middle class, which now began to make its influence felt in government as well as in business; the rise of capitalism, with its emphasis on personal initiative; and the growth of interest in science.[3] Yet while normal developments and deep-lying social and economic forces were operating to bring about vast changes in the social structure, the changes were hastened by the policies of the Tudor sovereigns, who throughout the sixteenth century occupied the English throne.

The Tudor dynasty was founded in 1485 by Henry Tudor, Earl of Richmond, who ascended the throne as Henry VII; it lasted until the death of his granddaughter, Queen Elizabeth, in 1603. For some years before Henry became king, the rival houses of York and Lancaster had engaged in a furious struggle for the crown. Henry, a Lancastrian, lacked a clear title to the crown, but he established his right to it by defeating and killing the Yorkist Richard III at Bosworth Field and then by marrying the Yorkist princess and heir, Elizabeth, thus reconciling the two warring factions. Because of the insecurity of his title, however, his right to the throne had to be confirmed by a Parliamentary election; this dependence on Parliament assured a working relationship between king and Parliament, a situation maintained in some degree by all the Tudor sovereigns.

One of Henry VII's main policies was to reduce the power of the old nobility, which was already declining, and to concentrate authority in his own hands. To achieve this purpose

---

[3] The culmination of this growing interest in science was the famous statement by Francis Bacon some years later of the inductive method of reasoning, a statement that is usually accepted as marking the beginning of modern science and therefore of the industrial revolution.

he abetted the growing influence of the middle class, which in return for royal favors was willing to further his aim. Another of his policies was to foster industry and commerce, partly because this policy brought more money to the treasury and partly because it strengthened a group that could be counted on to support his other policies. During his reign, which lasted till 1509, Henry VII was able to put down internal factions, to avoid foreign war, to build up a huge treasury, and to break the remnants of the old aristocracy and gather the controls of government in his own hands.

Henry VIII, who reigned from 1509 to 1547, carried still further his father's policies. When Henry broke with Rome over the question of his divorce from Catherine, and himself became head of the English church, he appropriated the vast holdings of land and wealth that the Church possessed, and much of this wealth he distributed among his supporters. From this redistribution of wealth arose a new aristocracy, not as yet interested in following traditions and in general opposed to the older aristocracy. In the early years of his reign, Henry VIII encouraged the disciples of the New Learning; and a number of his policies were influential in helping to establish the foundations of a new social structure, however little Henry himself may have intended such a result.

Henry VIII had three legitimate children, all of whom eventually came to the throne after him. Of these, the reigns of the first two, Edward VI and Mary, were too short—1547–1553 and 1553–1558, respectively—and too much involved with religious questions to have a marked effect on social or economic matters; but during the long reign of Elizabeth, from 1558 to 1603, the policies of the crown had considerable influence on the economic, as well as the political, status of the nation.

Elizabeth had most of the virtues and many of the faults of the Tudors. She was capricious, willful, vain, calculating, and stingy; but her love of England and her people was manifest in all her actions. When she ascended the throne, England was torn by religious strife, state finances were in a deplorable condition, the coinage had been debased until the entire national economy was on the verge of disaster, and the country had just suffered a severe blow to its pride in the loss to France of Calais, the last foothold of England on the Continent. Elizabeth's domestic policy was to restore the value of the coinage, to lessen the suffering of her most impoverished subjects, and to end religious strife by stopping persecution and by avoiding an extreme stand on the religious question. Her main foreign policy was to avoid war by using the threat of an alliance with either France or Spain, as this became necessary, in order to check a hostile move by the other. These policies and the methods she used to effect them, however much the latter may have irked her ministers, were justified by results. If she temporized on international matters, or even resorted to lying, her methods helped keep England from war; and in the peace and social order that ensued, commerce, industry, art, and letters had the chance they needed to develop. Her reign coincided closely with Shakespeare's life: it began just six years before he was born and ended only thirteen years before he died. Shakespeare, therefore, witnessed the growing prosperity that came during her reign; and before his death he witnessed two important results of Tudor policy. One was the uniting of England and Scotland under one ruler as the result of a marriage arranged long before by Henry VII between his daughter and the Scottish king, whose descendant succeeded Elizabeth on the throne. The other was the establishment of the first English settlement in the New World, a project Elizabeth had encouraged, although she did not live to see its consummation.

TRAITS AND INTERESTS OF THE PEOPLE. The England of Elizabeth is often called "merry England." Although to the modern student the time may seem merry only by comparison with the dark days of religious persecution under Mary or with the growing tensions and conflicts between Puritan and Cavalier in the following reigns, it is true that the decade following the defeat of the Spanish Armada brought an unusual sense of buoyancy and well-being to the English people. By the close of Elizabeth's reign, the effects of the New Learning on the development of printing were apparent in a widespread interest in drama, literature, and music. A literary drama was replacing the somewhat crude plays of the early part of Elizabeth's reign, prose romances were popular, criticism and realistic prose began to develop, and poetry reached a high level of attainment. A mounting interest in poetry may be traced after 1557, when Richard Tottel published *Songs and Sonnets*, a collection of poems by Thomas Wyatt, the Earl of Surrey, and others; for this volume served both to introduce new forms and themes and to show that men of the highest social rank wrote poetry. When somewhat later so popular an idol as Sir Philip Sidney appeared as a writer and defender of poetry, and when it was known that the Queen herself wrote verse, writing poetry became a mark of distinction, fit to engage the attention of everyone from Elizabeth's chief courtiers to university students.

A distinction was made, however, between writing poetry and publishing it. Since for a poet to publish his own work tended to mark him as a professional, men of high social rank and some even from the middle class were accustomed to circulate their writings in manuscript among their friends. Frequently readers into whose hands such manuscripts came made copies of the poems that appealed to them, and sometimes these private collections would fall into the hands of a printer and be published. In this way a number of anthologies made their appearance,[4] and each became a stimulus to both the reading and the writing of poetry. Meanwhile, writers who did not mind the stigma of professionalism published their own works. As a result of all this interest, the last half of the sixteenth

---

[4] Some of the early anthologies were *The Paradise of Dainty Devices*, 1576; *A Gorgeous Gallery of Gallant Inventions*, 1578; *A Handful of Pleasant Delights*, 1584 (or perhaps 1566); and *The Phoenix Nest*, 1593.

century saw a continual increase in both the quantity and the quality of English poetry.

Interest in music was even more general than interest in poetry, for whereas the appreciation of poetry was restricted to the literate, anyone might sing or play a musical instrument. In 1588, Nicholas Yonge published *Musica Transalpina*, a collection of madrigals and canzonets translated from Italian and set to music by Italian musicians; and so popular did these songs become that before the end of the century more than two dozen similar collections appeared. For ordinary folk, however, the most popular song was the broadside ballad. Hack writers composed these ballads on such themes as love, war, or a current happening. The ballads were then printed on a single sheet, or broadside, usually with a crude woodcut at the top and directions concerning the tune to which the words should be sung, and were hawked at fairs or in the streets, much as Autolycus peddles his ballads in Shakespeare's *The Winter's Tale*. When we consider the number of songbooks and broadside ballads printed, the number of songs introduced into plays to please the audiences, and the numerous references to music and singing in the literature of the time, the old saying that the England of Shakespeare's day was a nest of singing birds is hardly an exaggeration.

Helping also to make the age "merry" was the emphasis on sports and amusements. Every period, of course, has had its sports, but in the Elizabethan period the growing prosperity and freedom from war created an atmosphere especially favorable to them. In general the sports were rough, ranging from the barbarous bullbaiting and bearbaiting[5] to fencing, wrestling, and a rough sort of football. Hunting—with either hounds or hawks—was also popular, as were archery, bowling on the green, and the indoor amusements of cards, chess, and checkers; and everyone danced, from Queen to apprentice and peasant.

---

[5] In these sports the bear or bull was tethered to a long chain and was then set upon by a number of fierce dogs until it was worn out or the dogs killed.

Festival days, with their opportunity for feasting and merriment, were frequent. Markets and fairs, although existing primarily to further trade, also contributed to the social life of the time. Every town and village had its weekly market, to which farmers brought their produce and itinerant merchants their wares. Everyone attended these markets, whether or not he needed to make a purchase. Most incorporated towns, moreover, had their annual or semiannual fairs. The markets and fairs provided opportunity for everyone to visit and exchange news and gossip, as well as to carry on business, and they were thus important in the social as well as the economic life of communities where they were held.

Dire poverty still prevailed among some classes; yet for most people the standard of living rose noticeably in the latter years of the century. Food and drink were plentiful. The chief staple of food was meat, and the principal drink was ale, though men of cultivated taste preferred wine. Three or more kinds of meat were usually served at the tables of prosperous citizens, but vegetables were rare except as garnishes for meat. Breakfast was a light meal, consisting usually of bread, butter, and ale; but the two main meals—dinner at eleven o'clock and supper at five for most people, though merchants and farmers might eat later—were "so hearty that only St. George's dragon could desire anything additional." [6]

Among prosperous city dwellers, young gallants, and court attendants, dress was lavish. Both men and women wore costly and colorful attire, and small fortunes were sometimes spent on a single outfit of clothes.

On the whole, Elizabethans were a quick-tempered, impetuous, fun-loving, industrious, independent, and hospitable lot. They were fond of rough sports, and they liked gory and realistic drama and broad farce. A growing sense of nationalism among them was balanced by an increasing interest in lands and peoples beyond the boundaries of their own island. One of their most endearing qualities was their curious interest in

---

[6] W. S. Davis, *Life in Elizabethan Days* (New York: 1930), p. 68.

everything pertaining to mankind. Another was their high enthusiasm and optimism, which led them often to attempt the impossible—and sometimes to accomplish it. And seasoning all their talk and writings was a delightful humor. They could laugh not only at the foibles of mankind in general but at themselves.

III

SHAKESPEARE'S ENVIRONMENT

So far as any record shows, Shakespeare was connected during his entire life with but two places: the little provincial Midland town of Stratford-on-Avon and London, the country's metropolis, which lay some eighty miles to the southeast of Stratford. Although for nearly half his life he was closely associated with London, where as actor, playwright, and businessman he took a leading part in the theatrical life of the city, he never broke his connection with his native village. At Stratford-on-Avon he was born, grew up, married, invested much of the wealth he accumulated in London, retired to live after finishing his public life, died, and was buried. In his latter years he was recognized by the people of Stratford-on-Avon, who may have had little idea of his greatness as a poet and dramatist, as one of the town's most substantial citizens.

STRATFORD-ON-AVON. The place of Shakespeare's birth was a quiet rural market town with a population of about two thousand. It lay on the northern bank of the Avon River in the southern part of Warwickshire, a county almost in the center of England. Of the towns of this shire, only Warwick and Coventry, some ten and twenty miles respectively to the northeast, surpassed it in size and importance.

Warwickshire was principally a farming country. Its rich, loamy soil and moist climate favored agriculture. The chief farm products were grain and hay, but the rich pasturage made grazing also profitable. It was a land of small streams, rolling uplands, and forests. In the Middle Ages it had been one of the most heavily forested areas of England, but by the sixteenth century the forests were being cut down, although some heavily wooded tracts could still be found. The country was rich also in historical associations. As a child Shakespeare no doubt heard old men talk of the Wars of the Roses, in which Warwickshire played a considerable part. At Warwick, a little less than ten miles from Stratford-on-Avon, stood Warwick Castle, and a few miles farther on toward Coventry was Kenilworth Castle, both the seats of powerful lords whose ancestors had played leading roles in these wars.

The settlement at Stratford-on-Avon went back to Roman days. It probably owed its origin to the fact that here two main roads converged at a fordable spot in the river, hence its name —*straet* (road) + ford + *afon* (a Welsh word for "river"). The modern borough of Stratford was established at the end of the twelfth century by Bishop John de Coutances, who divided his estate at the ford of the Avon into quarter-acre lots of uniform frontage and depth, with provision for subdivision of the lots and of their disposition by sale or will. Toward the end of the fifteenth century, a native of the town, Hugh Clopton, who had gone to London and become wealthy, gave money to build across the Avon a fine and substantial bridge, which is still in use. A great event of the town was an annual fair, held each September, which lasted several days and drew large crowds. In Shakespeare's youth the town was important in the woolen trade, but with changing economic conditions this trade fell off and certain merchants suffered financial distress, Shakespeare's father possibly being one of those affected. The main industry was malting, and minor industries were weaving, dyeing, and tanning.

During the Middle Ages the chief institution of the town was the Guild of the Holy Cross, a sort of social-religious fraternal order that exerted a powerful influence on every department of community life. Richly endowed, it owned a beautiful chapel and guildhall, operated a grammar school and almshouse, and wielded most of the powers of government in the community. Under the Chantries Act of 1547—an act that dissolved Catholic institutions—it had been suppressed, however, and its wealth passed to the Crown. For some years thereafter the town was without a system of local government, but in 1553 it was granted a crown charter that provided for a municipal body, the Corporation, and vested in this body virtually all the rights formerly exercised by the guild. The former guild property was transferred to the Corporation, and most of the former guild officials became municipal officials, so that in the end the affairs of the town were conducted much as before the change.

Just outside the corporate limits of the town was the Stratford Parish Church, where Shakespeare was baptized and buried. Parts of this church date back to the thirteenth century, but the main structure was erected under one John of Stratford, Archbishop of Canterbury, a native of Stratford, who in the fourteenth century had it largely rebuilt. Other additions and modifications have been made since Shakespeare's time, but in its main features it is still much as it was after John of Stratford "renewyd" it.

A good description of Stratford-on-Avon as it appeared a few years before Shakespeare's birth, and no doubt as it still appeared during his lifetime, was written by John Leland, who visited the town on an itinerary he made for Henry VIII to gather data concerning ancient writers.[1] He wrote in part:

> The bridge there of late time was very small and ill, and at high waters very hard to pass by. Whereupon in time of mind [that is, within the memory of men still alive] one Clopton, a great rich merchant, and Mayor of London, as I remember, born about Stratford, having neither wife nor children, converted a great piece of his substance in good works in Stratford, first making a sumptuous new bridge and large of stone, where in the middle be a six great arches for the main stream of Avon, and at each [end] certain small arches to bear the causey [causeway], and so to pass commodiously at such times as the river riseth.

---

[1] His report was published in 1549 under the lengthy title, *The Laboryouse Journey & Serche of J. Lelande for Englands Antiquities, Geven of Hym as a Newe Yeares Gyfte to Kynge Henry the viii, with declaracyons Enlarged: by J. Bale, 1549*. A modern edition of five volumes was edited by Lucy Toulmin Smith (New York: 1907–1910).

The same Clopton made in the middle of the town a right fair and large chapel [the guild chapel] . . . . And to this chapel longeth a solemn fraternity. And at such times as needeth, the goods of this fraternity helpeth the common charges of the town in time of necessity . . . .

[The town] hath 2 or 3 large streets, beside bake lanes . . . . The town is reasonably well builded of timber . . . . The parish church is a fair large piece of work, and standeth at the south end of the town. . . . .

There is a right goodly chapel [the guild chapel] in a fair street toward the south end of the town . . . . This chapel was newly reedified in mind of man [that is, in recent memory] by one Hugh Clopton, Mayor of London. About the body of this chapel was curiously painted the Dance of Death. . . . This Clopton builded also by the north side of this chapel a pretty house of brick and timber, wherein he lay in his latter days and died [this was New Place, which Shakespeare later bought].

There is a grammar school on the south side of this chapel. . . .

There is also an almshouse of 10 poor folk at the south side of the chapel of the Trinity, maintained by a fraternity of the Holy Cross. . . .

Here in this little rural town, in many ways still medieval amid the changes taking place in England, Shakespeare grew up. With a father who held every important office in the town government and a mother who came of one of the important families of the district, he was of some consequence in his native place. His pride in it is indicated by the steps he took before he died to establish his family among the landed gentry there and by his never transferring his allegiance wholly to London. Such records as come down to us show that in London he preferred to be "William Shakespeare, gentleman, of Stratford-upon-Avon." As a boy he absorbed the life of the village, and he came to know, perhaps as well as any English poet, the countryside and the beauties of rural England. Later it all somehow got into his plays and poems.

LONDON IN SHAKESPEARE'S TIME. Just when and how and why Shakespeare went to reside in London is not known, but such a move was certainly not uncommon among intelligent and ambitious young men of the time. London then as now was the heart of England. With a population of little more than 100,000, it was small compared with the modern megalopolis. Moreover, it was dirty, unsanitary, afflicted with epidemics of the more virulent diseases, and infested with pickpockets, confidence men, and other types of criminals. But it was also the seat of government, the busy center of commercial activity, and the home of arts and letters. Here the Queen lived and kept her court, writers congregated, and drama flourished. It was a place of intense activity, both commercial and intellectual—a place calculated to arouse to their fullest the perceptions of a countryman of much duller parts than those possessed by William Shakespeare.

The city proper extended along the north bank of the Thames River for about two miles and back from the bank for a half mile. The river itself formed the southern boundary of the city, and the medieval wall, then still intact, inclosed the city on its other sides. The wall ran in a rough semicircle from the Thames near the Tower—an ancient castle popularly believed to have been built by Julius Caesar—to a place some two miles west on the bank, where a brook, called the Fleet, emptied into the river. The population was increasing at such a rate, however, that the space between the wall and river could not accommodate everyone. Flourishing suburbs were therefore growing up outside the walls to the north and across the river to the south. Entrance to the city was gained on the land side by seven gates, and on the river side by one bridge or by boat. The river then was not the muddy, dirty stream it is today, but was clear and sparkling, with swans on the surface, and hundreds of boats plying up and down and across it. It was the main avenue of traffic in London. Stairs led down to it, at the foot of which boatmen waited to transport passengers to their destinations.

The brick or timber houses were crowded together. Each story overhung the one below, so that on the narrower streets the top stories almost touched, shutting out much of the light; and from the upper windows slops were emptied on the streets and sometimes on the heads of unwary pedestrians who did not keep near the wall. The streets for the most part were narrow and crooked and were choked with dirt and filth. Open sewers provided what drainage there was. Hawkers were everywhere, crying their wares, such as "Small coals!" "Hot peas!" "Hot fine oatcake!"; and adding to the din were the cries of shopkeepers, who accosted all passers-by with the shout, "What do ye lack?" and an enumeration of their goods. Later on, coaches—which had been introduced in England in 1564—and other kinds of carriages were so abundant that they became a traffic hazard, and their numbers had to be restricted.

The most common buildings after the houses and shops were churches and taverns. Within the city were over a hundred churches, chief among them St. Paul's Cathedral—not the modern classic pile, but a Gothic structure destroyed in the Great Fire of 1666. St. Paul's, indeed, was the chief edifice of the city, and in addition to its use as a place of worship it served as a town meeting place. Here gallants went to display their fine clothes, lawyers met their clients, merchants gathered to arrange trades, and everyone strolled to dispense and pick up gossip. In its neighborhood were most of the bookshops of the city. Of taverns the number was legion, and to them resorted men of every class. Some of these taverns—the Mermaid, for example—live in history as the meeting places of poets and men of letters. Because houses were not yet numbered, taverns, as well as business establishments in general, were distinguished by painted signs—such as the Mitre in Bread Street, the Pegasus in Cheapside, and the like. Other important places in the city were the Royal Exchange and the Inns of Court—the former, the center of business and trade; the latter, England's law schools, where young men of rank prepared themselves for careers in law and government and occupied their abundant spare time by patronizing the drama and trying their hand at writing.

In so crowded a city and in an age when the knowledge of sanitation and medicine was so primitive, the wonder is that the entire population did not succumb to the frequent epidemics. The average Londoner of the time was not noted for his cleanliness. The city had no great baths, such as the Romans were fond of constructing, and a person rarely had a complete bath. Instead, those who were prosperous enough used scent to hide offensive odors. The same practice was used also in the home, for though carpets were replacing rushes as a covering for floors, their use was far from universal; and to cover the scent of mildewed and decaying rushes, perfumes were widely employed. Dirt and vermin were commonplace, and disease was prevalent. The plague and smallpox were the worst killers among contagious diseases, but fevers and other diseases took a large toll. Epidemics of the plague were frequent, often driving great numbers from the city in fright and causing thousands of deaths. During Shakespeare's residence in London, especially bad epidemics occurred in 1593 and 1603, and the city was subject to recurring epidemics of this dread disease until the Great Fire of 1666 destroyed its breeding places and doubtless the rats that transmitted it.

The picture that comes down to us from Shakespeare's day is of a people intensely patriotic, fond of rough sports and of gambling, greatly interested in music and drama, quick of temper and ready for a fight, and fond of display and lavish dress. But those who provide this picture were the well to do. Thousands of hard-working artisans and sober citizens went along their industrious way, little affected by the world of books and drama or by activities at Court. Among these latter, a decided trend toward Puritanism was setting in, and by the time of Shakespeare's departure from London, the city was predominantly Puritan. All this diversity made an ideal laboratory for Shakespeare to work in. He was above it all, viewing it with Olympian detachment; but he was of it too, and much of it lives in his plays.

IV

SHAKESPEARE'S LIFE

FAMILY BACKGROUND. The first record of the name "Shakespeare" that has been discovered so far is of one William Saksper of Gloucestershire who in 1248 was hanged for robbery. Before the end of the thirteenth century four other records of the name have been found, and in the fourteenth century eleven, three of these in Warwickshire. During the fifteenth and sixteenth centuries, the name appears frequently in Warwickshire records, most of the persons mentioned being shoemakers, brewers, weavers, tenants, or from similar ranks.

Shakespeare's own line has not been traced beyond his grandfather, Richard Shakespeare, who lived at Snitterfield, a hamlet four miles northeast of Stratford-on-Avon. Richard apparently owned no land but was a fairly prosperous tenant farmer on the estate of Robert Arden. In spite of the assertion by some writers that he had several children, of only two do we have any reliable evidence. These are John, the poet's father, and Henry, an elder son, who all his life was a farmer in or near Snitterfield.

Because records of baptisms and burials were rarely kept before 1558, especially of those of the lower classes, the date of John Shakespeare's birth is not known; but on the basis of the few facts that we know about him, it is conjectured that he was born between 1530 and 1535. Our first actual glimpse of him is of his being assessed a fine on April 29, 1552, for violating a sanitary ordinance of Stratford-on-Avon by allowing a pile of filth to accumulate before his house in Henley Street. As the records show that most citizens of the community were fined at one time or another under this ordinance and as the violation of the law appears to have been about the equivalent of overparking in our time, this record does not impugn the character of John Shakespeare. Its value for us is that it shows him as already the owner of the Henley Street property and as being a businessman of the town. By trade he was a glover, and since he was a member of the glovers' guild, which would have required his serving an apprenticeship of about seven years, he may have been living in Stratford for a number of years before we hear of him. About 1557 he married Mary Arden, daughter and chief heir of his father's landlord. For many years he was connected with the affairs of Stratford-on-Avon, being in turn aletaster (1556), burgess (1557), constable (1558), affeeror—one who decided fines in cases for which the statutes made no specific provision—(1559), chamberlain (1561–1562), alderman (1565), high bailiff (1568–1569), and chief alderman (1571).

Shakespeare's mother was the youngest of eight children of Robert Arden of Wilmcote, a hamlet about three miles from Stratford. The family was of ancient lineage, tracing its descent from Rohan the Saxon, Earl of Warwick, in the time of Alfred the Great, and, according to some scholars, from Alfred himself. Robert Arden was a prosperous farmer and landholder. At his death in 1556 he left to his daughter Mary, with other property, the freehold of the estate of Asbies, which consisted of nearly sixty acres. Shortly thereafter she married John Shakespeare. Records indicate that she and her husband lived the remainder of their lives in one house in Henley Street, Stratford-on-Avon. They had eight children: Joan, who was baptized September 15, 1558, and who died in infancy; Margaret, who was baptized December 2, 1562, and died the following April; William, who was baptized April 26, 1564; and thereafter, Gilbert (October 13, 1566–February 3, 1612),[1] Joan (April 15, 1569–November 4, 1646), Anne (September 28, 1571–April 4, 1579), Richard (March 11, 1574–February 4, 1613), and Edmund (May 3, 1580–December 31, 1607). Except

---

[1] The dates are of baptism and burial, the only dates recorded in the parish registers.

for the records concerning her children, a few relating to her property, and that of her death in September, 1608, nothing is known of Shakespeare's mother.

John Shakespeare's ownership of two properties and his participation in public affairs indicate that he was a substantial and fairly well-to-do citizen in Stratford-on-Avon. In public records he is listed as "yeoman," the class just below that of "gentleman," and in 1596 he was granted a coat of arms and raised to the latter rank. On the ground that he was excused after 1578 from paying certain assessments, and on other somewhat questionable premises, certain scholars hold that he fell into financial difficulties in his latter years. Because he is known to have dealt in wool—as appears to have been the custom of glovers—and Stratford had declined as a woolen center by 1590, and because he had a large family to support, it is possible that in his old age he was in straitened circumstances. But of this there is no positive proof, for important men were sometimes excused from assessments, and even at the time when he was supposed to be in difficulties, the records show him making important purchases of property.

SHAKESPEARE'S YOUTH. Biography in the modern sense was unknown to the Elizabethans. Of the nobility and important statesmen some records would be kept; but about a man of the middle class, an actor and writer of plays, nothing would be written with an eye to enlightening future generations. It is therefore surprising that we know as much as we do of such writers as Shakespeare, Spenser, and Ben Jonson. Although no modern biography can really make these men live again—as Samuel Johnson, for instance, lives in Boswell's great biography—from contemporary records and allusions we can reconstruct their lives in a general way. The indefatigable labor of scholars provides us with more information about Shakespeare than we usually have about commoners of his day.

Because in those days a record was kept only of baptisms, marriages, and burials, we do not know even the exact date of Shakespeare's birth. He was baptized on Wednesday, April

26, 1564. The custom, frequently disregarded, was to baptize a child on the first Sunday or holy day after its birth. In any event, it would be baptized as soon after birth as possible. An eighteenth-century guess that Shakespeare was born on April 23 is now popularly accepted.

What appears to be unquestionably true, despite the lack of actual records, is that young Shakespeare grew up in his native town, the eldest of the six surviving children of a respectable businessman who was important enough to become high bailiff, or mayor, of the town, and that he attended the Stratford Grammar School. This grammar school had been maintained by the Guild of the Holy Cross; but by the crown charter of 1553 it became a responsibility of the Corporation of Stratford, its foundation and revenues were restored, and the salary of the schoolmaster was set at twenty pounds a year—double that paid at such schools as Eton. During the time Shakespeare would have attended the school, the masters were Walter Roche (1567–1571), Simon Hunt (1571–1577), and Thomas Jenkins (1577–1579), all B.A.'s of Oxford. According to the usual curriculum of the time, a child first learned his letters in a hornbook,[2] then studied a primer, and shortly began the study of Latin. The last would include William Lyly's *Grammatica Latina, Sententiae pueriles,* Cato's *Maxims,* and such authors as Virgil, Ovid, and Horace. In the fifth form he would begin to study Greek; and he would study the Bible in the Geneva version. If Shakespeare followed the normal course, he probably attended the school from 1571 to 1578. According to reports gathered long after his death by Aubrey and Rowe,[3] Shakespeare, on leaving school, at first entered the employ of his father or was apprenticed to a butcher, and later was for a while a schoolmaster in the country.

The next actual record of Shakespeare after that of his baptism is of his marriage. About this marriage only three

---

[2] A leaf containing the alphabet, religious texts, and the like, covered with transparent horn and held in a frame to which a handle was attached.
[3] See Appendix B, pp. 175, 178.

actual facts are known, in spite of the most diligent search for other records; but of conjecture, much of it palpably absurd, a great many volumes have been written. The facts are, first, that on November 27, 1582, a marriage license was issued by the Bishop of Worcester, in whose diocese Stratford lay, to "Wm. Shaxpere and Anne Whateley of Temple Grafton," permitting their marriage after a single asking of the banns; second, that on November 28, 1582, a bond was furnished by two Stratford farmers, Fulke Sandells and John Richardson, to protect the Bishop of the diocese should there appear later any impediment to the marriage of "Willm Shagspere . . . and Anne Hathwey of Stratford"; and third, that on May 26, 1583, a daughter, Susanna, was born to William Shakespeare.

At the time of his marriage, Shakespeare was not quite nineteen, and his bride was twenty-six. In spite of the different names of the bride in the documents, and the different places of residence attributed to her, all evidence supports the assumption that Shakespeare married Anne Hathaway, daughter of Richard Hathaway, a well-to-do farmer of the neighboring hamlet of Shottery, who had died the previous July.[4] Where no contemporary evidence exists, it is impossible to be positive in an interpretation of every element relating to Shakespeare's marriage. Yet there is no need to suppose William a wild youth and Anne a woman of lax morals, for at that time trothplight marriage was commonplace. Such a marriage was roughly equivalent to a civil marriage today, but it was not recognized by the Church in matters of dowry rights or the legitimacy of children. In the same diocese are many records of church marriages shortly before the birth of a child to insure the child's being recognized as legitimate by the Church. In this it seems probable that Shakespeare was following a recognized

---

[4] For the best conjectures about the marriage and comment on all the matters involved, see J. W. Gray, *Shakespeare's Marriage and Departure from London* (London: 1905); J. Q. Adams, *A Life of William Shakespeare* (Boston: 1923), pp. 65–78; E. K. Chambers, *William Shakespeare* (London: 1930), II, 41–52; and B. R. Lewis, *The Shakespeare Documents* (Stanford, Calif.: 1940), pp. 160–176.

custom of the time. The most likely conjectures about the marriage appear to be that Richard Hathaway was contemplating the marriage of his daughter at the time of his death; that Anne, who was Richard's daughter by a former marriage, left her stepmother to live with relatives at Temple Grafton, some five miles distant; that she and Shakespeare made a trothplight marriage; that the approaching birth of a child made it expedient to have a church ceremony, and since a "closed season" was approaching, during which the Church forbade marriages except by special dispensation, there was time for only one asking of the banns before the ceremony; and that, since William as a minor could not furnish the bond himself and it was not the custom for the groom's father to furnish it, two neighbors of Anne's family provided bond to protect the bishop if it should appear afterward that some impediment to the marriage existed.

After the birth of Susanna, twins were born to Shakespeare on February 2, 1585. At that time he was almost twenty-one. The next we hear of him is at London seven years later, when he had already made some stir in dramatic circles. Of the intervening years we have no verifiable record. What seems to be the most authentic report was told to Aubrey by William Beeston, a theatrical manager whose father was a member of Shakespeare's company—namely, that in his younger years Shakespeare was a schoolmaster in the country. Other traditions—such as the one that he stole Sir Thomas Lucy's deer and ran away to London to escape prosecution—date from the eighteenth century and are based on the most flimsy evidence, or none at all. How he became interested in the stage, therefore, can only be conjectured. Aubrey in his biographical sketch reports merely that "being inclined naturally to poetry and acting, [he] came to London." This inclination may have been fostered in a number of ways. Latin plays, or English plays modeled after them, were often performed in grammar schools, and he may well have developed his first interest in drama by taking part in some of these performances. Many references in his plays show his familiarity with the old guild plays, and it is not at all unlikely that he witnessed performances of these plays at the neighboring town of Coventry, which had one of the most famous cycles. Furthermore, bands of traveling players, under the patronage of certain great noblemen, often acted at Stratford-on-Avon. In 1573, for instance, the Earl of Leicester's Players performed there; in 1576, the Earl of Worcester's and the Earl of Warwick's; and these or other companies were there at various other times. It is a plausible conjecture that Shakespeare met these players and thus made some sort of contact with the professional troupes. However it happened, in some manner he became connected with the stage, and by 1592 held a position of some importance in theatrical circles in London. It is in no way mysterious that we lack information about how this connection was made. Rather it would be the sheerest accident if records were extant of the beginnings of a professional career by an unknown provincial youth of that day.

SHAKESPEARE IN LONDON AND HIS LATER LIFE. In September, 1592, shortly after the death of the poet and playwright, Robert Greene, a pamphlet entitled *Greene's Groatsworth of Wit, Bought with a Million of Repentance,* purportedly written by Greene but prepared for the press by Henry Chettle, was published in London. In it, Greene, addressing his fellow playwrights Marlowe, Peele, and Nashe, warned them against writing for the stage because others would obtain fame through their labors. He then adds: "Yes trust them not: for there is an upstart Crow, beautified with our feathers, that with his *Tygers hart wrapped in a Players hyde,* supposes hee is as able to bombast out a blanke-verse as the best of you: and beeing an absolute *Iohannes fac totum,* is in his own conceyt the onely Shake-scene in a countrey." The "tygers hart" phrase, which is an allusion to *Henry VI, Part III,* I, iv, 137, and the sneering reference to "Shake-scene in a countrey" seem too specific to refer to any save Shakespeare. Because Shakespeare, an actor and not a university man at that, was invading successfully the field hitherto occupied by a group of university men, Greene—or Chettle, using Greene's name—obviously was jealous of the new writer. Chettle later offered a handsome apology for his part in the attack on the "upstart Crow," and the attack appears not to have harmed Shakespeare. Its importance is the proof it offers that by 1592 Shakespeare was so well established in London as actor and playwright that he aroused the jealousy of other writers for the stage.

Meanwhile further events were taking place that would bring Shakespeare to the notice of the reading public. A riot of apprentices on June 11, 1592, led the Privy Council to close all theaters for three and a half months, and before this period was up an epidemic of the plague made it necessary to keep them closed. They reopened on December 29, but in February, 1593, a recurrence of the epidemic closed them again and kept them closed till June, 1594. During this period of enforced idleness, Shakespeare, instead of joining a group of the actors who went on a tour of the provinces, apparently spent his time writing two long poems and possibly some plays. The first of the poems, *Venus and Adonis,* which he dedicated to the young Earl of Southampton (b. 1573), was entered in the Stationers' Register on April 18, 1593. The second, *The Rape of Lucrece,* also dedicated to Southampton, was entered in the Stationers' Register on May 9, 1594. Both were published by Richard Field, a native of Stratford-on-Avon of about Shakespeare's own age, who had gone to London and after serving his apprenticeship as a printer had married the widow of his former employer and established his own business. To the dedicatory epistle of each of these poems Shakespeare signed his name, and thus made his first public appearance as an author.

Whatever Shakespeare's early connection with the theater, by the end of 1594 he was one of the leading members of the dramatic company whose patron was Henry Carey, then Lord Chamberlain, the company therefore being known as the Lord Chamberlain's Servants. His membership in this company is shown by a document, dated March 15, 1595, that records a payment to three members of the company, of whom Shakespeare was one, for performing two comedies at Court during the previous Christmas season. Since only the chief members of a company were mentioned in records of such payments, it is clear that by this time Shakespeare held a secure position with the group. Henceforth to the end of his public life his connection with this company under its various patrons may be traced in many records. He became its chief playwright, a full-sharing member, and later part owner of the Globe and Blackfriars Theaters in which the company played.

The story of his last twenty years is one of growing recognition as a writer and of increasing wealth and position. The recorded facts relating to these years may be summarized briefly. On August 11, 1596, his son Hamnet, one of the twins, was buried at Stratford-on-Avon. In that year also, Shakespeare's father applied for and was granted a coat of arms, thus raising himself, and of course his son, to the rank of gentleman. On May 4, 1597, Shakespeare bought New Place, one of the largest and finest houses in Stratford, for which he paid £60. This house, of brick and timber, stood opposite the Guild Chapel on nearly an acre of ground. Tax records indicate that before 1596 Shakespeare lived in London in St. Helen's parish, Bishopsgate, inside the city, and that from about 1596 to 1608 he lived across the river in the Clink on the Surrey Bankside. From the records of a lawsuit in which one Stephen Belott sued his father-in-law, Christopher Mountjoy, for a dowry and had Shakespeare called as a witness, it appears that in 1604 he lived, perhaps temporarily, in the Mountjoy home in Cripplegate Ward. In May, 1602, he bought, for £320, 107 acres of arable land near Stratford-on-Avon; and in September of the same year he bought another house and quarter-acre of ground near New Place. Then on July 24, 1605, he purchased for £440 the lease of a portion of the tithes of grain and hay of Old Stratford, Bishopton, and Welcombe, and the small tithes—of wool and lamb and privy tithes—of the entire parish of Stratford.[5] He also was part owner of the Globe and Blackfriars Theaters in London; and in March, 1613, he bought a house in London in the fashionable district of Blackfriars, for which he paid £140 and gave a mortgage for a balance of £60. These various transactions indicate that although he did not acquire great wealth he did become a man of substance and that he left his heirs well off when he died.

Shakespeare's father died in 1601 and his mother in 1608. On June 5, 1607, his elder daughter, Susanna, married John Hall, a physician of Stratford-on-Avon; and on February 21, 1608, a daughter named Elizabeth was born to the Halls. Shakespeare's younger daughter, Judith, on February 10, 1616, married Thomas Quiney, son of an old friend of the family. Because this marriage took place during Lent, when a special license to marry was required, and because for some reason the couple failed to obtain the license, Judith and her husband were excommunicated. The reason for the failure to procure a license is not known, but since Shakespeare died just ten weeks later, and his will, made shortly after the marriage, settled certain matters about Judith's dowry, it seems reasonable to infer that his illness may have had something to do with the hasty marriage.

The date of Shakespeare's Last Will and Testament was March 25, 1616. In it, after making minor bequests and providing for Judith, he left the bulk of his property to Susanna during her life, then to her eldest male heir, or if she had no son, to his granddaughter Elizabeth and her male heirs; if Elizabeth had no male heirs the property was to go at Elizabeth's death to Judith and her male heirs.[6]

---

[5] The nature of this investment was somewhat like that of buying a mortgage today. By paying £440 outright, Shakespeare obtained the right to collect these tithes for himself or heirs for thirty-one years. When in 1625 his heirs sold their interest in the tithes, the annual value of the tithes was £90. Although the return was considerably less than this at first, it was nevertheless a good investment for Shakespeare.

[6] Susanna's only child was Elizabeth, who was twice married but had no issue. Judith had three sons: Shakespeare (November 23, 1616–May 8,

Shakespeare was buried on April 25, 1616, his death having occurred, according to the statement on his monument, on April 23. As owner of a part of the Stratford tithes, he had the privilege of burial inside the Stratford Parish Church, and the place selected was inside the chancel rail before the high altar. Over the grave is a stone slab without name or date, on which is engraved the following epitaph:

> Good friend, for Jesus' sake forbear
> To dig the dust enclosed here.
> Blest be the man that spares these stones,
> And curst be he that moves my bones.

The original stone has been replaced by the one now over the grave, but records of the original stone indicate that the present one is an exact replica of the original.

Sometime before 1623 a monument to Shakespeare was set up on the north wall of the chancel, to the left of the tomb as one faces the high altar. It carries the following inscription:

> Judicio Pylium, genio Socratem, arte Maronem:
> Terra tegit, populus maeret, Olympus habet.[7]
>
> Stay, Passenger, why goest thou by so fast?
> Read if thou canst whom envious Death hath placed
> Within this monument: Shakespeare, with whom
> Quick nature died; whose name doth deck this tomb
> Far more than cost: since all that he hath writ
> Leaves living art but page to serve his wit.
>   obiit ano do[i] 1616
>   Aetatis · 53 die 23 Apr.

The Reverend John Ward, vicar of Stratford from 1662 to 1681, kept a diary in which, under the date 1661–1663, he

---

1617); Richard (February 9, 1618–February 26, 1639); and Thomas (January 23, 1620–January 28, 1639). Susanna was buried July 16, 1649, having survived her husband by nearly fourteen years. Judith died February 9, 1662. Shakespeare's direct line ended with the death of Elizabeth Hall (then Lady Barnard) in 1670.

[7] A Nestor in judgment, a Socrates in wit, a Virgil in art: the earth encloses, the people mourn, Olympus keeps [him].

wrote this note about Shakespeare: "Shakespear, Drayton, and Ben Jhonson had a merry meeting, and itt seems drank too hard, for Shakespear died of a feavour there contracted." Since in Ward's time men would still be living who had known Shakespeare, the report may contain some truth.

Shakespeare's widow lived till August 6, 1623. His sister Joan, who married William Hart, survived him many years, and through her descendants the Shakespeare line is still extant. His direct line, however, ended with the death of his granddaughter, Elizabeth Hall.

V

DRAMA AND THE THEATER

IN SHAKESPEARE'S TIME

Shakespeare began his theatrical career at a favorable time. The first theaters in England had only recently been built; several companies were organized to perform plays; a theater-going public had grown up; and a group of writers had brought the drama to a level of literary excellence never before reached in English dramatic history. Drama was just entering on a period of great development in both the quality and quantity of plays—a period that would be rich in dramatic achievement even without the works of Shakespeare. "There is a tide in the affairs of men which taken at the flood leads on to fortune," Shakespeare had one of his characters say.[1] Such a tide was running when he began his dramatic career, and it was the good fortune of both Shakespeare and English literature that he arrived in London at a time to take it at the flood.

I

THE DEVELOPMENT OF DRAMA IN THE SIXTEENTH CENTURY. At the beginning of the sixteenth century several types of dramatic representation existed, but there was nothing that could be called a literary drama. The most spectacular of the several types was the GUILD PLAYS—a series of episodes on Biblical themes, performed by the craft guilds at great yearly festivals. These originated centuries earlier in the church liturgy and were taken over for performance by the guilds. Many English towns had a cycle of these plays, those of York, Chester, Coven-

---

[1] *Julius Caesar*, IV, iii, 218.

try, Wakefield, and London being especially notable. They retained their popularity until after the middle of the sixteenth century, when the decline of the guilds and a growing interest in a more secular form of drama marked their end. In structure they were more like pageants than plays, and their primary aim was to teach rather than to entertain; yet their introduction of such homely realistic details as a fight between Noah and his wife, or the raging of Herod when the Wise Men left without informing him of the whereabouts of the infant Jesus,[2] indicates an interest in purely dramatic representation, apart from spectacle or didactic aim.

Another type was the MORALITY PLAY, which evolved in the fifteenth century and continued popular through the early decades of the next century. In it the characters personified abstractions—usually, but not always, virtues and vices fighting for man's soul. This appears to have been the first type of play to be acted professionally in England, for when strolling entertainers first conceived the idea of giving plays, the allegory was popular, and they adapted it to their use. But since they were more interested in entertaining their audiences than in teaching moral lessons, they added modifications that contributed to the growth of a drama whose main purpose was to amuse rather than teach.

Another type that became popular in the early sixteenth century was the INTERLUDE, a form evolved by noblemen's servants whose function was to entertain their masters and guests at banquets. Such entertainment consisted at first of telling stories, but ultimately someone hit on the idea of adding a plot in which there would be a contest over whose story was best. From here it was only a step to real drama. Because these interludes were played during banquets, when wine was flowing freely, they were light and comic, and relied on broad farce and physical action for their appeal. The performers in these plays were required to serve their masters only in the winter; hence they

---

[2] For this scene the guild treasurer methodically records the sum spent for soap "to make Herod foam at the mouth."

were free in the summer to travel from town to town and give their plays before public audiences. Since the sole purpose of such tours was to make money, these noblemen's servants were in a real sense professionals and were forerunners of the later professional companies.

All this drama—guild plays, morality plays, and interludes—made use of homely realism in portraying character and action. Save for a few of the episodical scenes in the guild plays, it relied on broad farce to catch and hold the interest of its audiences, which consisted largely of uneducated rustics. Its plots were crude and usually rudimentary, its dialogue simple, and its most popular character the Vice, a buffoon whose part was to involve the other characters in difficulties and thus to complicate the action.[3] A good example of the native drama in its later development is *Cambises* (c. 1560), a "tragedy with mirth." A study of *Cambises* and similar plays indicates that this old native drama owed little or nothing to classical drama. If the authors of such plays ever heard of the "classic unities,"[4] they paid no heed to them. The plots resembled those of the poorest modern motion pictures, with a great deal of extraneous matter mixed with the main story, and with serious and farcical themes vying for attention. Yet all this was what the audiences wanted, and in time these plays—essentially outgrowths of the earlier interludes—displaced the guild plays and the moralities in public favor. From such crude dramas performed by strolling players, came the main design of the literary works of a later day.

Meanwhile in the grammar schools and universities a dif-

---

[3] In the early "immoral morality," *Mankind,* for instance, just as the devil—the Vice in that play—is about to appear, the actors stop the play and announce that a collection will be taken and that unless the amount meets their expectations the devil will not appear.

[4] Unity of action, of time, and of place. Aristotle had laid down the principle of unity of action and had given the hint for unity of time by saying that tragedy, so far as possible, endeavors to confine itself to a single revolution of the sun. The unity of place, limiting the action to one place, was added later. Classical dramatists generally adhered to these unities.

ferent type of drama was developing. By at least the second quarter of the century, some schools were giving Latin plays—usually the comedies of Plautus and Terence and the tragedies of Seneca. Next they performed original plays written in Latin, and finally plays in English modeled on the classics. This SCHOOL DRAMA was constructed much more expertly than was the native drama. It usually adhered to the classic unities and made use of good plots, interesting situations, and clever dialogue, especially in comedy.[5]

For many years the native and the school drama developed independently, neither having much, if any, influence on the other; but as each type had something to contribute, a fusion of the two sooner or later was natural, and it actually came about in the 1580's through the conscious efforts of a group of young playwrights now usually called the University Wits. The young men comprising this group—Christopher Marlowe, Robert Greene, George Peele, Thomas Lodge, and Thomas Nashe—came down to London from the universities to earn a living and, finding that they could make money by writing for the stage, turned their talents in this direction. Because they had school and university backgrounds, it was natural that their favorites—Plautus, Terence, Seneca, and Italian Renaissance dramatists—should influence their writings. Nevertheless, as it was also necessary to please a public brought up to like the native drama, they effected a compromise by combining elements from each type. Slightly antedating this group were two other writers, John Lyly and Thomas Kyd, who also made noteworthy contributions to the drama. These seven men, Shakespeare's immediate predecessors, were chiefly responsible for molding the new drama—by fusing the homely realism of the native drama, the superior construction of the classical drama, and new romantic elements from pastoral and Renaissance sources—into a form ready for the master hand of Shakespeare.

---

[5] Good examples of the school drama are the comedy *Gammer Gurton's Needle* (1552), by William Stevenson, and the tragedy *Gorboduc* (1562), by Sackville and Norton.

JOHN LYLY (c. 1554-1606) after attending Oxford became a member of the household of Lord Burleigh, Elizabeth's chief minister. There he learned enough of courtly life to write two popular works of fiction, *Euphues, the Anatomy of Wit* and *Euphues and His England*. Later he entered the service of Burleigh's son-in-law, the Earl of Oxford, who was patron of a company of boy actors. His success as a writer of fiction led Oxford to set him to writing plays for the boys. In such dramas as *Campaspe* and *Endymion,* Lyly reflected the tastes of his audience, which was made up of courtiers and sophisticated members of the court circle. His plays therefore were free from the coarseness and vulgarity so much a part of the native drama. His themes dealt with romantic love; and he introduced a new type of heroine, an idealized woman, modest, refined, and beautiful, in marked contrast to the shrewish types of both the native and school drama. He wrote witty dialogue and developed interesting plots, and probably because his chief skill lay in writing prose he established prose as a vehicle of dramatic expression.[6]

THOMAS KYD (1558-1594) attended the Merchant Tailors' School and then took up his father's occupation of scrivener, or law clerk; but finding the copying of law papers irksome, he turned to translating and to writing dramas. Perhaps he was influenced by the publication of *Seneca: His Ten Tragedies* (1581), for he modeled his plays on Seneca's. He wrote several plays of blood and revenge, among them probably an early version of *Hamlet*. The most popular was *The Spanish Tragedy*, with a plot that included ghosts, madness, a letter written in blood, and several murders. Kyd used blank verse effectively, taught succeeding playwrights the value of strong dramatic situations, made such types as the ghost and madman popular in English tragedy, and with his sensational themes and bombas-

---

[6] Because the boy actors came from the royal choirs and were therefore good singers, Lyly also introduced many songs in the plays; but some scholars believe that Oxford himself, who is known to have been a good poet, wrote all or most of these. This use of song was not an innovation, however, as the older school dramas often contained songs.

tic speech won the favor of theater audiences so completely that tragedy henceforth became an important element of English drama. He also helped demonstrate that one could live as a professional writer.

Of the University Wits, the greatest, and the one who contributed most to the evolution of the drama, was CHRISTOPHER MARLOWE (1564–1593). In a succession of plays—*Tamburlaine, Parts I* and *II; Faustus; The Jew of Malta; Edward II*—he focused attention for the first time in English drama on character rather than event, and he wrote so eloquently that Peele declared him "fit to write passions for the souls below." His use of blank verse—what Ben Jonson called "Marlowe's mighty line"—with its resonant phrases and occasional run-on lines, showed for the first time how effective in drama this form could be. More than anyone before Shakespeare, he helped to create the type of drama in which a single powerful character becomes the center of attention throughout a play.

ROBERT GREENE (1558–1592) next to Marlowe was the most important of the University Wits. He was the first of the group to make a profession of writing. His early work was prose fiction, imitative of Lyly's *Euphues;* but following Marlowe's success as a playwright, he turned to drama. Most of his plays were inferior to Marlowe's, but in *Friar Bacon and Friar Bungay* and *James IV* he approached in some respects the work of his great contemporary. The rivalry, for instance, between Friar Bacon and Friar Bungay, a native and a foreign necromancer, makes for a better plot than the theme of Marlowe's *Faustus,* and the humor in Greene's play is superior. Greene's chief contributions to drama were a romantic love theme, romantic heroines, and a wholesome, pleasant background of English life.

The other University Wits—THOMAS NASHE (1567–*c.* 1601), GEORGE PEELE (*c.* 1558–1597), and THOMAS LODGE (*c.* 1558–1625)—though less important than Marlowe and Greene, made noteworthy contributions to the formation of a literary drama. Peele, the first of the group to write for the stage, experimented with a number of forms: pastoral comedy in *The Arraignment* of *Paris,* the chronicle play in *Edward I,* the melodrama of blood in *The Battle of Alcazar,* and the play based on a Biblical theme in *David and Bethsabe.* Of his extant plays the best is *The Old Wives' Tale,* in which he made clever use of folk themes to create a satire on romantic drama. Nashe, a pamphleteer and novelist, was chiefly important in drama as a satirist. Lodge was skillful in evolving good plots, and he collaborated in the writing of a number of plays before he ceased writing for the stage in order to become a physician.

This group, with middle-class backgrounds and a university education, went down to London between 1580 and 1590 to become free-lance men of letters. They were a small group and were little more than youths when they arrived in London; yet their contributions to English drama were great. In a remarkably short time they replaced the "jigging rime" of the old plays with forceful, beautiful blank verse. They created characters that for the first time in English drama gave the exceptional actor a chance to display his ability. Though they were scholars with university backgrounds, they lacked the reverence for tradition that would have made them force on English audiences a form of drama that had flourished in a different age and setting. Their knowledge of classical drama enabled them to construct better plots, to create more interesting situations, and especially to better the quality of their verse; but they were not such pedants as to wish to preserve everything from the classical drama and to scorn everything in the native drama. Instead, they utilized the best elements of both types. As pioneers they had their faults: their plays were often episodical, the plots lacking in continuity. But by providing a better vehicle of expression for the actors, by treating themes of more intrinsic worth than were customarily treated in the old native drama, and by creating interesting situations and characters they produced a drama that not only appealed to the public taste but had intrinsic merit as literature. Their work was an effective preparation for the appearance of Shakespeare on the theatrical scene.

II

DRAMATIC COMPANIES IN SHAKESPEARE'S TIME. By the time Shakespeare became connected with the stage, the method of organization and conduct of theatrical companies was well established.

These companies had their origin in the groups kept in service by the king and nobles to entertain their household and guests at banquets and on other special occasions. When they were not required for that purpose, they were free to travel and to perform for any audience that would contribute to their maintenance. In time, as the size of the groups increased, with a consequent increase in the costs of their maintenance, and as the public demand for drama grew, public performances occupied an increasing portion of their time. Because of a law, however, that classed actors as rogues and vagabonds, subject to arrest by any petty law official unless they could show that they were the servants of some lord, it was still necessary that they be under the patronage of a nobleman powerful enough to protect them. Also because the Court favored drama, noblemen were encouraged to become patrons of acting companies. Hence was established a working relationship whereby a group of actors, under the patronage of a leading noble or member of the Court, was granted a license or patent that allowed the group to give public performances. In order to maintain strong and responsible groups, the tendency was to limit the number of companies, with the result that those to whom licenses were issued came to enjoy the privilege of monopolies. During Shakespeare's time, the number of acting companies permitted in London was usually no more than five, and for a while there were only two, of which his company was one.[7]

---

[7] In addition to the professional companies, there were also companies of children actors. They were made up of choir boys from the royal chapels and St. Paul's whose main occupation was singing but who in their spare time performed plays, as did the boys in grammar schools. These children were nonprofessionals for whom acting was a secondary occupation; yet

A professional company consisted of full members, hired men, and apprentices. The full members, to whom the license or patent was issued, were the important personnel of a company. In addition to producing plays of an acceptable standard of excellence, they were responsible for maintaining a stable organization and for conducting all the business affairs of a company. The standard number of full members in a company was twelve, though at times it might be fewer or, more rarely, more. Since a group of this size could not perform all the tasks involved in staging and acting plays, the company augmented the staff with hired men. These "hirelings" received a straight salary and usually had secondary roles or performed the more menial tasks in connection with the productions; yet they often remained with one company throughout their careers, just as the full members were likely to do. Finally, a company would have several apprentices—usually boys, though instances are recorded of grown men who became apprentices. Since women were not used on the English stage until after 1660, the apprentices usually played female parts as well as parts of children and youths. The entire company—full members, hirelings, and apprentices—usually comprised from twenty to thirty-five people.

The custom in Elizabethan theaters was to charge general admission, collected at the door, and then to rent seats in the galleries to those who did not wish to stand in the "yard," or pit, to see the play. Most companies rented the theaters in which they played, the customary rent being half the proceeds from the sale of gallery seats. From its income, the company had to pay the salaries of the hirelings, the maintenance of the apprentices, the cost of furnishings, and all general expenses. What remained was the members' profit. They would also receive all special fees, such as those for performance at Court,

---

they often played at Court and before semipublic audiences, which paid to see them. At times they enjoyed great popularity, and some of the best plays of the period were written for them. Since Shakespeare had no connection with them, however, they are not considered here.

Inns of Court, and special parties. In normal years, when the theaters were not closed by epidemics, the members had a lucrative profession. Many of them, including Shakespeare, became well to do and were able to buy estates and to make profitable investments.

The company with which Shakespeare was affiliated from at least 1594 to the end of his public career appears to have been reorganized in June, 1594, when the theaters reopened after the severe plague epidemic of 1593–1594. Its patron was Henry Carey, Lord Hunsdon, a cousin of Queen Elizabeth. As he was Lord Chamberlain, the company was known until his death in July, 1596, as the Lord Chamberlain's Men. His son succeeded him as patron of the company, which was then known as Lord Hunsdon's Men until he, like his father, became Lord Chamberlain, in March, 1597. Thereupon the company again became known as the Lord Chamberlain's Men, a title it retained till May, 1603, when the new sovereign, King James, took it under his own patronage. Thereafter it was called the King's Men.

According to the letters patent issued when King James became patron of the company, the full members at that time were Laurence Fletcher, William Shakespeare, Richard Burbage, Augustine Phillips, John Heminges, Henry Condell, William Sly, Robert Armin, and Richard Cowley. By the following year the number had increased to twelve and thereafter remained constant, new members being admitted only as old ones died or resigned. The number probably had been nine from the time the company was reorganized in 1594 until the increase near 1604.[8]

Since no record identifies Shakespeare with any company before December, 1594, it is not necessary to summarize the conjectures about his early affiliations with a specific company. That he was already connected with the stage in some way and

---

[8] For a full consideration of this matter, see T. W. Baldwin, *The Organization and Personnel of the Shakespearean Company* (Princeton, N. J.: 1927), pp. 82–83.

was important enough to attract notice is apparent from Greene's attack on him, but whether he was with Pembroke's Men, Lord Strange's Men, or another company, or was a freelance writer, all of which beliefs have been maintained, cannot be demonstrated with finality.[9]

III

THEATERS IN SHAKESPEARE'S TIME. The first playhouse in England built for the specific purpose of giving dramatic performances was erected in 1576 and was called the Theater. Its builder was James Burbage, a leading member of the Earl of Leicester's Men. For its location he chose a site just north of the London corporate limits in the liberty[10] of Holywell, near Finsbury Field. Within a year a second theater, the Curtain, was built near the Theater, and soon there were others: Newington Butts (in use by 1580), south across the Thames, a mile from London Bridge; and the Rose (in use by 1588), also across the Thames on the Bankside. Thus by the time Shakespeare began his public career several theaters existed that had been built especially for theatrical performances.

Before the erection of these theaters the players had to perform in town halls, guildhalls, schoolhouses, even churches—places often unsuitable to their purpose. Gradually, however, the custom had grown up, especially in London, of using innyards. The inns were built around a court or yard to which access was gained from one or more streets by archways. From the yard, stairs led to galleries, which extended around the four sides of the yard and overlooked it. Actors found several ad-

---

[9] For such conjectures, see Adams, *Life*, pp. 130–135; and Chambers, *Elizabethan Stage*, II, 128–131, and *William Shakespeare*, I, 57–62; and compare Baldwin, *op. cit.*, pp. 290–292.

[10] A "liberty" was a district formerly under the jurisdiction of the Church. After the break with Rome, these districts came under the direct jurisdiction of the Crown. Because the Crown favored theaters and drama, whereas the city authorities, with Puritan tendencies, opposed them, the location of playhouses in a liberty was necessary if the theater was to have reasonable freedom from interference.

vantages in using these inns: they could prepare a stage quickly by laying boards across the tops of barrels or carts; they had a tiring room available in which to change costumes; and they could station "gatherers" at the archways to collect admission fees. The innkeepers, in turn, also profited from the arrangement by the extra sales from persons attending the plays, by renting rooms, and perhaps by collecting a special fee from those who preferred to see the play from one of the galleries. As interest in the drama grew, certain innkeepers, in fact, found it more profitable to rent their premises to acting troupes than to run them as inns, so that by 1575 at least five inns in or near London were being used as theaters,[11] and several of them remained in use for years after the first regular theaters were built.

This use of innyards affected greatly the architecture of the first playhouses, for when Burbage built the Theater he modeled its main features on those of the innyards, and his plan was followed by other early builders of theaters. Although no Elizabethan theater has survived to modern times, and plans, or even exact descriptions, of the earliest theaters are lacking, a brief description and drawing of the Swan Theater—made by a Dutch priest, Johannes de Witt, on a visit to London about 1596—a contract for the building of the Fortune Theater in 1600, and many references in plays and elsewhere have enabled scholars to reconstruct the general features of the Shakespearean playhouse.[12]

The playhouses for the most part were made of timber, set on

---

[11] These were the Red Lion in Stepney, a parish in Middlesex; the Bull in Bishopsgate Street; the Bell and the Cross Keys, both in Gracechurch Street; and the Bel Savage on Ludgate Hill, the last four inside the city. There may have been others concerning which we lack records.

[12] The following description is a composite one. Where records are so scanty, an attempt to give a precise description of a specific theater would be futile. All the evidence indicates that this is a reasonably close picture of the general features of an Elizabethan playhouse. There were some exceptions, however: the Fortune was square; some late theaters were roofed all over; and there were differences in size and probably in many minor characteristics.

brick foundations, and were finished outside with laths and plaster. They were large enough to accommodate an audience of perhaps two thousand. In general design they were polygonal on the outside and round, or almost so, on the inside, and were tall enough for three galleries.[13] The galleries extended from one side of the stage around the entire inside of the building to the opposite side of the stage. They were supported by columns, which were carved for decorative purposes, and they were divided into "rooms," somewhat in the manner of boxes in modern theaters. The rooms were supplied with seats, some of which were cushioned. Access to the lowest gallery was by stairs on each side of the stage, and to the upper galleries by stairs at the back of each lower gallery. The galleries and part of the stage were roofed with thatch or tile, but the center of the building—"the yard"—had no roof, no seats, and perhaps only a dirt floor. The building had two doors, one on the side opposite the stage, by which the audience entered, and one behind the stage for the use of the personnel of the theater.

The stage was a large platform, 3 or 4 feet in height, which extended into the middle of the yard.[14] This outer stage had no curtain. Over part of it was a projection, called "the heavens" or "shadow," which was supported by columns. The shadow contained machinery for lowering and raising properties and actors who took the part of gods, fairies, and similar creatures. The stage had a trap door through which properties and actors could be brought on the stage or be made to disappear quickly. Behind the stage was a tiring house, where the actors dressed, and where such helpers as the prompter, make-up man, and stagekeeper could stay. On each side of the tiring house, near the edges of the stage, were exit doors; and between these doors was an alcove, used for staging interior scenes. Curtains or

---

[13] At the Fortune Theater the galleries, beginning with the lowest, were 12, 11, and 9 feet high, and were 12 feet in depth. Each of the two upper galleries protruded 10 inches beyond the one below.

[14] The stage of the Fortune Theater was 43 feet wide and 27½ feet deep.

an arras, used both for decoration and in staging the interior scenes, separated the alcove from the outer stage.[15] Above the alcove was a gallery that projected beyond the alcove. This was used when the play called for balcony scenes; at other times it apparently was let to important persons, as we have mention of "lords' rooms" in this location. Above the stage roof and extending higher than the gallery roof was a small penthouse, called the hut, from the top of which floated a flag bearing the sign of the theater—such as a swan at the Swan Theater and Hercules holding up the earth at the Globe Theater. From the door of the hut a bugler announced the beginning of a play, and the hut may have served as a storage room or a supplementary tiring house.

These theaters made a brave showing in Shakespeare's London. Many references testify to their beauty, luxury, and sumptuousness. The columns, said de Witt, resembled marble so closely as to deceive the most cunning. Nothing so fine could be found on the Continent, said Thomas Coryat, a widely traveled Englishman. And the Puritans often exclaimed against them as examples of ostentation and lavish show.

For the most part the theaters were built by businessmen and rented to dramatic companies as business ventures. The owners, called housekeepers, received as rent half the proceeds from the sale of gallery seats, and this seems to have been a profitable arrangement for them. Only the Globe among the public playhouses appears to have been owned by the members of a dramatic company. Cuthbert and Richard Burbage, sons of the builder of the Theater, owned a half interest in it, and the other half was owned in equal shares by five other members of the company—Shakespeare, Heminges, Phillips, Pope, and Kempe.[16]

---

[15] Chambers conjectures (*op. cit.*, III, 82–83) that the alcove may have extended into—and thus have been part of—the tiring house, so that when an interior scene was not required, the entire space would be a tiring house, and that therefore only curtains separated the tiring house from the outer stage.

[16] This group, with one or two changes in personnel, leased and operated the Blackfriars Theater in 1608. But the Blackfriars was a different type

In addition to the playhouses already mentioned as being in use by the time Shakespeare began his public career, other public theaters built during his lifetime were the Swan (1595), located on the Bankside, across the Thames south of London; the Globe (1599), located on the Bankside; the Fortune (1600), located in the northwest part of London in the liberty of Finsbury and the parish of St. Giles; the Red Bull (*c.* 1605), in St. John Street, the parish of St. James, Clerkenwell; the Hope (1613), on the Bankside; and Porter's Hall (1615), in Blackfriars. Shakespeare's company gave most of its performances at the Theater, the Curtain, the Globe, and the private theater, the Blackfriars. The two with which it was most intimately connected were the Theater and the Globe. Of these, the Theater was torn down in 1599 and its materials used in building the Globe. The latter was destroyed on June 29, 1613, when a cannon which was shot off during a performance of Shakespeare's *Henry VIII* set fire to the thatch roof, but it was rebuilt the next year.[17]

IV

THE AUDIENCE AND STAGING. Plays began at 2 o'clock in the afternoon and lasted about two hours. As there were no reserved seats, the audience tended to gather early in order to get the best places to stand or sit. At the outer door, each paid his penny—or two pennies if it were the first performance of a new play. Those willing to stand in the yard paid nothing further, but those who wished gallery seats had to pay another fee— usually the equivalent of that collected at the door—to gatherers stationed at the gallery stairs. Wealthier patrons could pay still more for admission to the two–penny and gentlemen's

---

of theater: it was enclosed, and it had a history entirely different from that of the public theaters discussed here. For its history, see J. Q. Adams, *Shakespearean Playhouses* (Boston: 1917), pp. 182–233.

[17] Shakespeare owned a tenth part of the Globe, but as no mention of this ownership is made in his will, it is probable that when the sharers were called on for funds to rebuild the theater he did not comply and so ceased to be a sharer.

rooms. They could even buy seats on the stage itself; but the custom of sitting on the stage seems to have been limited to youthful gallants who wished to cut a public figure.

The audience was a cross section of all London: apprentices, servants, artisans, substantial middle-class citizens, courtiers, and lords; men and women, the latter, especially if from the better classes, wearing masks; pickpockets and harlots; young and old. Hawkers went up and down, selling books and other wares. Many of the audience brought refreshments, such as cakes and ale. While waiting for the play to begin, some settled down to card games. There was much good-natured raillery—as at our ball games—and occasional fights. The scene, in fact, resembled more nearly that at one of our outdoor games or boxing matches than the more decorous scene at a modern theater.

When the time came for the play to start, the trumpeter appeared at the door of the hut and gave three "soundings"; then, until the practice became old-fashioned and was abandoned, a prologue came out in his long black cloak and gave a preview of the play, sometimes also taking the occasion to advertise the next play. There were no programs, and though sometimes a placard on the stage may have announced the scene of action, this information was given usually through the dialogue. The outer stage customarily had no properties, except a stool, table, and similar simple objects, although when a play demanded a spectacular scene that could not be staged in the alcove, machinery was available to let down elaborate properties from the "heavens" or raise them through the trap door. If properties were required, as in a bedroom scene, the action usually took place in the alcove, so that when the scene was over the curtain could be drawn and the play continue on the outer stage without interruption. The action proceeded without intermission, as in moving-picture theaters today. Most of it took place on the outer stage, with the alcove being used for interiors or for properties when they were required, and the balcony for certain settings. Since the outer stage had no curtains and the action was continuous, a playwright often marked the end of a scene with a couplet; the actors for this scene then left the stage in one direction while those who were to begin the next entered from another direction.

Because the groundlings stood around the stage on three sides and gallants often sat on the stage, the action took place close to the audience. Thus asides and soliloquies were more natural than they are today. That a large part of the audience stood to see the play had an effect on the play itself: more action was required to hold the attention of the audience, songs and witty repartee or melodramatic episodes had to be introduced, and the language had to be effective to keep interest from flagging.

To put all that we have been saying another way, Shakespeare's plays are what they are in part because a great dramatist and poet wrote them, but in part also because of the conditions under which they were staged and the audience for which they were written.

VI

SHAKESPEARE'S WORKS

Surviving literary works attributed to Shakespeare comprise two long narrative poems, a group of sonnets, and thirty-five complete plays and parts of three others. He may also be the author of a few minor poems and have had a hand in a very few other plays. This output may not seem large in comparison with the more than two hundred plays of his contemporary, Thomas Heywood, but if we consider the quality of much of it, Shakespeare's other duties as actor and member of his company, and his death at the relatively early age of fifty-two, we must credit him with being a reasonably prolific writer. His first published work over which no question of authorship arises appeared in 1593, and he continued to write for approximately the next twenty years, his most productive period being from 1594 to 1608. He wrote his dramas for the stage, and apparently did not set great store by them as enduring literature.[1] Whether he saw through the press any of those published before his death is uncertain. At least he gave to none the careful supervision that he gave to the publication of his two long poems. As his reputation grew, unscrupulous publishers did not hesitate to ascribe to him work demonstrably not his. Some of his plays were stolen and published in garbled editions without his consent or that of his company. As a result, despite his faring better than most of his contemporaries in the matter of publication, it has taken the devoted efforts of scholars for two and a half centuries to establish the Shakespeare canon, to

---

[1] See, for instance, Sonnets lxii and cxi. See also *Shakespeare's Producing Hand* (London: 1948), by Richard Flatter, who marshals an array of evidence to support his theory that when Shakespeare wrote his plays he had in mind principally the actors and the stage performance of the plays.

settle approximately the order and dates of his plays, and to reproduce with reasonable fidelity the text of the plays. And work yet remains to be done on most of these problems.

Customs regarding the writing and ownership of plays in Shakespeare's time were altogether different from those in practice now. When a modern author writes a play, he rarely has in mind a specific set of actors to perform it. In Shakespeare's day the playwright usually wrote with one company in mind, and he tried to provide parts for at least the leading members of the company. Shakespeare wrote all his plays, except perhaps the earliest ones, for one company, that known as the Lord Chamberlain's and, later, as the King's Men. The personnel of this company is so well known that one scholar[2] has been able to conjecture the parts taken in the various plays by its members. In our time, furthermore, the playwright usually owns his play, and an acting company or a publisher may not change it without his permission. If it is published, it remains his property, and he alone receives royalties from it. In Shakespeare's day, though, when a play was accepted by a company, the company and not the author owned it thenceforth, and could revise or publish it without the author's permission.

Methods of publication then and now were also different. No copyright laws existed like those under which we operate; and unscrupulous printers and publishers were often able to obtain a manuscript by unlawful means and to publish it without the consent of either the author or the company that owned it. Some protection was afforded by an arrangement of the London Company of Stationers, which included both manufacturers and sellers of books, whereby the printer or publisher would enter on the public register-book of the Company— called the "Stationers' Register"—the title of a play or other work he intended to publish; he would then be considered to

---

[2] T. W. Baldwin, *Organization and Personnel of the Shakespearean Company* (Princeton, N. J.: 1927), pp. 229–283, and the charts preceding that chapter.

have the sole right to publish the work. But this arrangement gave no protection against unethical printers and publishers, and many plays got into print without the consent of the rightful owners.

Because a dramatic company derived its income from acting plays that were popular and because the publication of a play would make it available to dishonest troupes that would not scruple to appropriate it, the tendency was to withhold publication of a popular play—and of course publishers would have little interest in one that was not popular. A company, however, sometimes published a "true copy" of a play to prevent its being issued in a mangled edition or to replace such an edition already published. It might also sell a play if the company was breaking up or if the theaters were closed by the plague or for some other reason, and the company was in need of money. Editions of plays published with the consent of the owners are known as *legitimate* editions, and those stolen and published surreptitiously as *illegitimate*. Because a piratical publisher had to secure copy for his edition by hiring someone to attend the theater and memorize what he could of the play or take it down in the primitive shorthand of the time, or by bribing some hireling to write out his own part and devise the parts of other actors as well as he could, it is obvious that the illegitimate editions are poor and unreliable copies of what an author actually wrote.

THE QUARTOS AND FOLIO. Nineteen of Shakespeare's plays were published singly, eighteen during his lifetime and one—*Othello*—six years after his death; and thirty-six, including eighteen of those published singly, were published in a collected edition in 1623. *Pericles,* the one published singly and not included in the collected edition, was added to the latter in 1664. The remaining play in which he had a hand, *The Two Noble Kinsmen,* is usually included among the works of his collaborator, John Fletcher.

The plays that were published singly are referred to as "quartos"—"quarto" being a printer's term for the page size resulting from folding twice the sheets on which the book was printed, thus making four leaves. A first edition is referred to as "Q1," a second edition as "Q2," and so on. The quartos were small books of from sixty to ninety pages, the number of pages depending on the length of the play. They were about 7 by 8 inches in size, had paper backs, were poorly printed as a rule, and sold for about sixpence. Because they were cheaply made and each copy was likely to be read by many people, few copies have been preserved.[3] Quartos published with the consent of the owners, and therefore without much change from the original manuscript, are termed "good" quartos; and those that were unauthorized, and therefore usually full of errors, are termed "bad" quartos. Of the known first quartos of Shakespeare's plays, eleven are good, six are bad, and scholars are in disagreement about two. There were several quartos of some of the plays. Those appearing before the collected edition, with their dates, and with the bad quartos starred, are as follows:

Titus Andronicus	1594 (Q1), 1600 (Q2), 1611 (Q3)
Henry VI, Part II	*1594 (Q1), *1600 (Q2), *1619 (Q3)
Henry VI, Part III	*1595 (Q1), *1600 (Q2), *1619 (Q3)
Richard II	1597 (Q1), 1598 (Q2, Q3), 1608 (Q4), 1615 (Q5)
Richard III	1597 (Q1), 1598 (Q2), 1602 (Q3), 1605 (Q4), 1612 (Q5), 1622 (Q6)

---

[3] For instance, only one copy of *Titus Andronicus* Q1 has so far come to light—a copy now in the Folger Shakespeare Library, Washington, D. C.; and only two copies of *Hamlet* Q1—one now in the Huntington Library, San Marino, California, and one in the British Museum, London. Of some quartos that scholars conjecture, no copy has been found. Of most, however, a few copies still exist. For a list of extant quartos and where they may be found, see Henrietta C. Bartlett and A. W. Pollard, eds., *A Census of Shakespearean Plays in Quarto*, rev. ed. (New Haven, Conn.: 1939).

Romeo and Juliet	*1597 (Q1), 1599 (Q2), 1609 (Q3), no date (Q4)
Henry IV, Part I	1598 (Q1), 1599 (Q2), 1604 (Q3), 1608 (Q4), 1613 (Q5), 1622 (Q6)
Love's Labour's Lost	1598 (Q)
Henry V	*1600 (Q1), *1602 (Q2), *1619 (Q3)
Henry IV, Part II	1600 (Q)
Much Ado about Nothing	1600 (Q)
Merchant of Venice	1600 (Q1), 1619 (Q2)
Midsummer-Night's Dream	1600 (Q1), 1619 (Q2)
Merry Wives of Windsor	*1602 (Q1), *1619 (Q2)
Hamlet	*1603 (Q1), 1604 (Q2), 1605 (reissue of Q2), 1611 (Q3), no date (Q4)
King Lear	1608 (Q1), 1619 (Q2)
Troilus and Cressida	(*?) 1609 (Q1, two issues)
Pericles	(*?) 1609 (Q1, Q2), 1611 (Q3), *1619 (Q4)
Othello	1622 (Q)

The collected edition of 1623 is known as the First Folio, "folio" being a printer's term for the page size resulting from folding once the sheets on which the book was printed, thus making two leaves. There were three subsequent editions—in 1632 (F2), 1663 and a second issue in 1664 (F3), and 1685 (F4). The First Folio, in spite of typographical and other errors, was a well printed and substantial volume. The plays were arranged under three headings—comedies, histories, tragedies—with separate pagination for each section, the total numbering 908 pages. The largest extant copy measures 13⅜ x 8¾ inches. A copy sold for about one pound. The number of copies printed is conjectural, but as a sale of probably a thousand was needed to defray the expense of publication, unless someone underwrote the project, and as some 180 copies are still in existence, the size of the edition must have been large. In addition to the plays previously published in quartos—except *Pericles*, which was added to the second issue of F3—the First Folio contained eighteen plays for which it is our only source. The list of plays in the order of their arrangement, with those starred that had not been published previously, is as follows:

Comedies: **The Tempest; *The Two Gentlemen of Verona; The Merry Wives of Windsor; *Measure for Measure; *The Comedy of Errors; Much Ado about Nothing; Love's Labour's Lost; A Midsummer-Night's Dream; The Merchant of Venice; *As You Like It; *The Taming of the Shrew; *All's Well That Ends Well; *Twelfth Night; *The Winter's Tale.*

Histories: **King John; Richard II; Henry IV, Parts I and II; Henry V; *Henry VI, Part I; Henry VI, Parts II and III; Richard III; *Henry VIII.*

Tragedies: *Troilus and Cressida; *Coriolanus; Titus Andronicus; Romeo and Juliet; *Timon of Athens; *Julius Caesar; *Macbeth; Hamlet; King Lear; Othello; *Antony and Cleopatra; *Cymbeline.*

Before the publication of the First Folio, Ben Jonson had published a selection of his plays, and other playwrights had published some of their works, but this was the first publication of a collected edition of the dramatic works of any English author. The undertaking seems to have been partly a business venture by a group of printers and publishers, and partly a memorial to Shakespeare by John Heminges and Henry Condell, the two survivors among the older members of the company with which he was so long affiliated. The printers and publishers involved in the undertaking were William and Isaac Jaggard, father and son, who were both printers and publishers; Edward Blount, stationer and publisher; John Smethwick, publisher, and formerly printer for a brother of William Jaggard; and William Aspley, publisher. There is some evidence that the printing, which was done at the establishment of the Jaggards, was in process for more than two years before the Folio was issued. Because William Jaggard died in the autumn of 1623, the entry in the Stationers' Register for the plays not entered previously was made to Isaac Jaggard and Blount. Smethwick and Aspley were doubtless associated with the venture because they owned the copyright of several of the plays previously issued.

Heminges and Condell included in the Folio a dedicatory epistle to two brothers, the Earls of Pembroke and Montgomery, sons of the Countess of Pembroke, Sir Philip Sidney's sister, and both high in the esteem of King James, Pembroke at the time being Lord Chamberlain. Other inclusions were an address by Heminges and Condell, written in a rather light tone, "to the great variety of readers," urging them to buy the book; a fine, deeply serious commendatory poem to Shakespeare by Ben Jonson; three commendatory poems by lesser poets; an engraving of Shakespeare's portrait by Martin Droeshout, a young artist of Flemish descent; and a "list of the principal actors in all these plays."[4]

In spite of the boast of Heminges and Condell in their address to the readers that they presented the plays "cured and perfect of their limbs; and all the rest, absolute in their numbers, as [Shakespeare] conceived them," the Folio contained a great variety of errors. Some of these resulted from the illegibility of the manuscript and from miscellaneous errors in the copy, some from the carelessness of the compositors, and some from the sort of copy furnished the printers. Because the last is the most difficult to deal with, scholars have been assiduous in their efforts to determine the source of the copy for each play. Although in so conjectural a matter they have not reached universal agreement, they have been able to throw a great deal

---

[4] For the dedication, the address to the readers, and Jonson's poem, see Appendix A of this volume; and for a full consideration of all matters concerning the Folio, see E. K. Chambers, *William Shakespeare* (Oxford: 1930), I, 137–167, and B. R. Lewis, *The Shakespeare Documents* (Stanford, Calif.: 1940), pp. 547–582.

of light on the problem. Nearly all the plays that had already been published were set up from the quartos, usually the latest quarto, so that the Folio repeated the accumulated errors of the various editions and added others of its own. As copy for the remaining plays, Heminges and Condell apparently supplied playhouse manuscripts. These may have been the author's original manuscripts, or they may have been the acting versions used in staging the play—called in the theatrical jargon of the time the "books." Each actor also of course had a copy of his part, and it is possible that a few of the plays were set from copy made by assembling these parts. Because of the tediousness of assembling the various parts, however, this method would be used only if no other copy were available.

Whether some quartos and some parts of the Folio were set from Shakespeare's own manuscript is a question difficult to answer, since no direct evidence exists to prove that they were.[5] The condition of the text of a number of the plays, however, supports the assumption that the printers had the original copy. For other plays they clearly did not have it. Next to the original manuscript, the best source would be the "book," the authoritative stage-copy, though this would doubtless contain cuts and would therefore differ to some extent from the author's manuscript. A play assembled from actors' parts might also contain cuts, as well as minor additions, such as gags. Obviously, therefore, the plays in the Folio vary in their fidelity to the original manuscript. For those first published in the Folio, modern editors have little leeway in conjecturing what the variations were; but for a few, by using a good quarto—as, for instance, *Hamlet* Q2—along with the differing Folio version, they can come close to the original. We must bear in mind, however, that although the plays as we have them may not be in every detail as they came from Shakespeare's pen; yet if two of Shakespeare's oldest companions and fellows in the theatrical business assure us—as they do—that they have made every

---

[5] Flatter, *op. cit.*, offers strong arguments that they were. See especially his statements about the text of *Macbeth*.

effort to present accurate versions of his plays and that they were satisfied with the Folio—as apparently they were—it is not likely to contain marked departures from the plays as he wrote them.

CHRONOLOGY OF THE PLAYS. The Folio offers no evidence of the time of composition and almost none of the order in which Shakespeare wrote his plays. The quartos merely fix a terminal limit for the plays published in that form. By painstaking research and the marshaling of an increasing body of evidence, however, scholars have done a good deal in the matter of dating the plays. In this work they have made use of three kinds of evidence: external, internal-external, and internal.

External evidence, which often does no more than fix terminal dates, but sometimes fixes the actual or approximate date of composition, comes from allusions to a play in other books that are dated, from entries in the Stationers' Register, and from letters, diaries, and other sources. Thus in his *Palladis Tamia: Wits Treasury* (1598), Francis Meres praises Shakespeare for his *Two Gentlemen of Verona, Comedy of Errors, Love's Labour's Lost, Love's Labour's Won*,[6] *Midsummer-Night's Dream, Merchant of Venice, Richard II, Richard III, Henry IV*,[7] *King John, Titus Andronicus*, and *Romeo and Juliet*. Obviously, therefore, these plays were written before 1598, when Meres made up his list. And in the *Gesta Grayorum*, a chronicle history of Gray's Inn, is a statement that on December 28, 1594, "a Comedy of Errors (like to Plautus his *Menechmus*) was played by the players." This statement, supported by other evidence, apparently refers to Shakespeare's *Comedy of Errors*, and thus fixes a terminal date as early as late 1594 for this play.

Internal-external evidence is that derived from allusions in a

---

[6] No play of Shakespeare's entitled *Love's Labour's Won* has survived, but most scholars agree that this reference is to *The Taming of the Shrew*.

[7] We cannot tell whether Meres had in mind both parts of *Henry IV* or only *Part I*.

play to events or writings outside for which we have dates. An example of such evidence is a reference in *Henry V*, V, Prologue, 28-34, to an expedition to Ireland led by the Earl of Essex. As the Earl was absent on this expedition between April 15 and September 28, 1599, the lines must have been written at that time. Evidence of this sort, when the allusion is unmistakable, fixes an initial date for a play. The chief trouble with it as evidence is that what we may take as a clear allusion may be accidental or may have been added during a revision; hence such evidence is valid only if the reference appears conclusive or if other evidence strongly supports it.

Internal evidence comes from studying an author's style and noting changes in his manner of writing, his use and treatment of themes, and similar tendencies. Shakespeare, for instance, used the feminine ending and the run-on line much more frequently in his late than in his early verse.[8] Other tendencies at different stages of his career have also been carefully noted. Such evidence is an aid in assigning a play to a particular period, but it is involved in too many subjective features—the character speaking, the special requirements of a scene, and the interpretations of the editor—to make for more precise dating. As further evidence, plays that conform in theme and method of treatment may also be assigned with some confidence to the same period. Help also comes from examining the plays for changes in staging and theatrical practices and in comparing these with changes in practice that we can learn from other sources. No conclusive answer to the question of just when a play was written can be arrived at from internal evidence alone, but it is valuable in establishing limits and in providing for a general arrangement. On the basis of themes employed, treatment of themes, style, and methods of staging, scholars have usually agreed in distinguishing four stages in Shakespeare's

---

[8] By "feminine ending" is meant the closing of a line of verse with an extra unstressed syllable after the stressed syllable; and by "run-on line" is meant the continuing of a line of poetry into the next line without grammatical or rhetorical pause. Both devices tend to make the poetry less stiff and rigid, and therefore more like normal speech.

career: that of experimentation and apprenticeship, lasting up to about 1594; that of the histories and "joyous" comedies, from 1594 to about 1600; that of tragedies and "bitter" comedies, from 1600 to about 1608; and that of romances and tragicomedies, from 1608 until he ceased to write. Although these divisions are arbitrary and have no rigid boundaries, they are helpful in establishing general groupings of the plays. By taking note of the internal evidence and by using all available external evidence and such internal-external evidence as appears valid, scholars have been able to establish a reasonably accurate chronology for the plays.

In a matter that must depend to some extent on conjecture and the interpretation of evidence, we cannot expect absolute agreement among authorities. The following table gives the dates assigned to each play by several eminent authorities: E. K. Chambers,[9] J. Q. Adams,[10] and the editors of the Oxford edition[11] of Shakespeare, whose list is a composite one of the opinions of "modern critics." Because new interpretations and occasionally new bits of evidence throw more light on problems of chronology, the later a list is made—assuming it to be by a competent scholar who is seeking truth instead of pursuing a pet theory—the more accurate it is likely to be.

	Chambers	Adams	Oxford eds.
Henry VI, Part II	1590–1591	c. 1592	1592?
Henry VI, Part III	1590–1591	c. 1592	1592?
Henry VI, Part I	1591–1592	1592 (rev. 1598)	1592
Richard III	1592–1593	by 1595	c. 1593
Comedy of Errors	1592–1593	before 1592	c. 1591
Titus Andronicus	1593–1594	1592	1594

---

[9] Chambers, *op. cit.*, I, 270–271. The table is reproduced by permission of the publishers.

[10] J. Q. Adams, *A Life of William Shakespeare* (Boston: 1923). See his index.

[11] *Complete Works of William Shakespeare* (London: 1919), p. 1351. The table is reproduced by permission of the publishers.

SHAKESPEARE'S WORKS

	Chambers	Adams	Oxford-eds.
Taming of the Shrew	1593–1594	by 1594 (rev. 1597)	c. 1596
Two Gentlemen of Verona	1594–1595	1593–1594	c. 1592
Love's Labour's Lost	1594–1595	1592	c. 1590
Romeo and Juliet	1594–1595	1596	c. 1593
Richard II	1595–1596	1595	c. 1594
Midsummer-Night's Dream	1595–1596	1596	c. 1594
King John	1596–1597	1595	c. 1594
Merchant of Venice	1596–1597	1597	c. 1595
Henry IV, Part I	1597–1598	1597	1597?
Henry IV, Part II	1597–1598	1597	1598?
Much Ado about Nothing	1598–1599	1599	c. 1599
Henry V	1598–1599	1598	1599
Julius Caesar	1599–1600	1598–1599	1599
As You Like It	1599–1600	1599	c. 1600
Twelfth Night	1599–1600	1599–1600	c. 1600
Hamlet	1600–1601	1601	c. 1602
Merry Wives of Windsor	1600–1601	1598	1599?
Troilus and Cressida	1601–1602	1602	c. 1602
All's Well That Ends Well	1602–1603	1596 (rev. 1600–1601)	c. 1602
Measure for Measure	1604–1605	1603–1604	c. 1604
Othello	1604–1605	1604	c. 1604
King Lear	1605–1606	1605–1606	1605?
Macbeth	1605–1606	1606	1606?
Antony and Cleopatra	1606–1607	1607	1607?
Coriolanus	1607–1608	1608–1609	c. 1608
Timon of Athens	1607–1608	1607	c. 1608
Pericles	1608–1609	1607	c. 1608
Cymbeline	1609–1610	1609–1610	1610?
Winter's Tale	1610–1611	1610–1611	1610?
Tempest	1611–1612	1611	1611?
Henry VIII	1612–1613	1613	c. 1611
Two Noble Kinsmen	1612–1613	1613	—

68 A SHAKESPEARE PRIMER

NONDRAMATIC WORKS. *Venus and Adonis,* the first of two long narrative poems by Shakespeare, was entered in the Stationers' Register on April 18, 1593, and was published before June of that year by Shakespeare's fellow townsman, Richard Field, who had migrated to London and had taken up the trade of printer and publisher. It was an amorous poem of a type then much in vogue,[12] and employed a richly decorative and ornate style. It was written in iambic pentameter in stanzas riming *ababcc,* and contained 1,194 lines. The main source of the poem was Ovid's *Metamorphoses,* Books IV, VIII, and X, although Shakespeare derived ideas for his version from other sources and was influenced in his style by Renaissance writers. He apparently saw the book through the press himself, for of all his works it is the most free of errors. He dedicated it to the young Earl of Southampton (b. 1573) in a brief formal epistle:

> Right Honorable, I know not how I shall offend in dedicating my unpolished lines to your Lordship, nor how the world will censure me for choosing so strong a prop to support so weak a burthen; only if your Honor seem but pleased, I account myself highly praised, and vow to take advantage of all idle hours till I have honored you with some graver labor. But if the first heir of my invention prove deformed, I shall be sorry it had so noble a godfather: and never after ear so barren a land for fear it yield me still so bad a harvest. I leave it to your Honorable survey, and your Honor to your heart's content, which I wish may always answer your own wish, and the world's hopeful expectation.
>
> Your Honor's in all duty,
William Shakespeare.

In 1594, Shakespeare published his second long poem, *The Rape of Lucrece,* apparently the "graver labor" that he had promised the Earl of Southampton, to whom this poem also was dedicated. It was printed by Field but was published by John Harrison, who had acquired from Field the copyright of *Venus*

---

[12] Other examples of about the same date are Marlowe's *Hero and Leander,* Lodge's *Glaucus and Scilla,* Daniel's *Complaint of Rosamund,* and Drayton's *Endimion and Phoebe.*

and Adonis. For his theme, Shakespeare again went to Ovid, this time to his *Fasti,* but the evidence indicates that he had also read the story in a prose version by Livy and in Chaucer's *Legend of Good Women.* He also used a Chaucerian verse form, the rime royal stanza—a seven-line stanza in iambic pentameter riming *ababbcc.* The poem was considerably longer than *Venus and Adonis,* as it ran to 1,855 lines. It tells the story of the rape of Lucrece, a chaste Roman matron, by Sextus Tarquinius. The emphasis, however, is less on the narrative element than on the impact of the deed on Lucrece and on Tarquin himself.

Both of these poems became very popular, *Venus and Adonis* running into ten editions and *Lucrece* into six in Shakespeare's lifetime. Meres, in his *Palladis Tamia* (1598), wrote: "As the soul of Euphorbus was thought to live in Pythagoras, so the sweet, witty soul of Ovid lives in mellifluous and honey-tongued Shakespeare: witness his *Venus and Adonis,* his *Lucrece,* his sugared Sonnets among his private friends, &c." [13]

Meres speaks of Shakespeare's "sugared Sonnets among his private friends." In 1609, *Shakespeare's Sonnets* was issued in quarto, apparently without Shakespeare's permission, certainly without his supervision. The volume was entered in the Stationers' Register on May 20, 1609, by Thomas Thorpe, a publisher of a somewhat shady reputation. It was printed for Thorpe by George Eld, a reputable printer who also printed Shakespeare's *Troilus and Cressida* and some important works by other writers. The book was sold by two stationers, John Wright and William Aspley, the latter of whom was later associated in the publication of the First Folio.

The *Sonnets* has raised more questions than has any other work by Shakespeare. The copy for Thorpe's edition was in all probability a manuscript made for private circulation. But beyond this, all is question. From Meres's reference we know that at least some of the sonnets were in circulation by 1598; and from internal evidence and from the fact that the writing

---

[13] For other comments, see Chambers, *op. cit.,* II, 189–199.

of sonnet sequences was then at high tide, scholars agree in assigning the sonnets to the period of the long narrative poems. Thorpe placed the following dedication in the quarto:

> TO · THE · ONLIE · BEGETTER · OF ·
> THESE · INSVING · SONNETS ·
> MR · W · H · ALL · HAPPINESSE ·
> AND · THAT · ETERNITIE · ·
> PROMISED ·
> BY ·
> OVR · EVER-LIVING · POET ·
> .WISHETH ·
> THE · WELL-WISHING ·
> ADVENTVRER · IN ·
> SETTING ·
> FORTH ·
> T · T ·

Who the "Mr. W. H." is, whether he was the "begetter" in the sense that Shakespeare wrote the sonnets about him or that he procured them for Thorpe, and whether a typographical error was made in printing the initials "W. H." are questions over which scholars have argued endlessly without supplying any final answer. But these are minor questions compared with those raised by the sonnets themselves: To whom in the first place were they written? Are they to be taken literally, or was Shakespeare merely following the popular fad of writing in the Petrarchan vein? Who was the "dark lady"?[14] The Quarto contained 154 sonnets, nearly all written in the form invented by the Earl of Surrey (four quatrains and a couplet, in iambic pentameter, riming *abab cdcd efef gg*), and a poem of 329 lines entitled "A Lover's Complaint," which some scholars doubt is Shakespeare's work.

OTHER WORK. Except for the sonnets, the preservation of which

---

[14] For summaries of the sonnet sequence and a good discussion of the problems involved, see Adams, *op. cit.*, pp. 160–181 (summary, pp. 173, 175–178), and Chambers, *op. cit.*, I, 559–576 (summary, pp. 559–560).

SHAKESPEARE'S WORKS 71

we owe apparently to Thorpe, and for the two long narrative poems, which he had published himself, all of Shakespeare's work of any consequence is preserved in the Folio; and this we owe to his old theatrical companions, Heminges and Condell. A few other items, however, merit brief consideration.

Preserved in the British Museum is a play in manuscript entitled *Sir Thomas More* in which at least one scene (II, iv, 1–172) is ascribed to Shakespeare by some scholars. The play is mainly the work of Anthony Munday, a minor playwright of the time, twenty-six of the forty-two pages being in Munday's handwriting. The remaining pages are in various hands. The scene previously referred to, in which More quells a riot, was long thought to be by Shakespeare because of its high quality and certain resemblances to his style. More recently this view has been supported—but not unanimously—by handwriting experts.[15]

On the basis of resemblances of certain lines to lines in his sonnets and to his early style, some scholars ascribe to Shakespeare most of the first two acts of *Edward III,* a chronicle play, which was published in 1596 after having been "sundry times played about the City of London." The play, however, has no great merit, whatever its authorship.

In 1599, William Jaggard, later an associate in the Folio project, published *The Passionate Pilgrim* as "By W. Shakespeare." This seems to have been a commonplace book, somewhat like a modern scrapbook, in which someone collected twenty short pieces, mostly on love. Two of these are variants of two of Shakespeare's sonnets, and three other pieces are variants of passages from *Love's Labour's Lost.* There is no evidence that any of the others are by Shakespeare, and some are known to be by other writers.

In 1601, Robert Chester, a minor poet, published *Love's Martyr,* a collection of his own work, to celebrate the wedded

---

[15] Incidentally, if the handwriting is Shakespeare's, it is the only bit of manuscript in his hand that has come down to us. Some signatures survive—in the will and in one or two other places.

love of his patron, Sir John Salisbury. He included in the volume poems by Jonson, Chapman, Marston, and Shakespeare. The single poem ascribed to Shakespeare, "The Phoenix and Turtle," a poem of sixty-seven lines, is a lyric of high merit.

Shakespeare's name has been connected with a few other poems and with a number of plays, but the evidence of his authorship in any of these instances is extremely tenuous; and even if his authorship could be proved, it would neither enhance his fame nor detract from it. He lives chiefly in the plays gathered in the Folio and in the Sonnets and the two long narrative poems. If other works of his survive, their existence is a matter of interest but not of high importance.

VII

INTRODUCTIONS TO THE PLAYS

FIRST PERIOD: APPRENTICESHIP AND EXPERIMENTATION

HENRY VI, PARTS I, II, and III

Philip Henslowe recorded in his diary the performance by Lord Strange's Men on March 3, 1592, of a "new" play, *Harey the vi*. The view of scholars that this was *Henry VI, Part I*, is supported by a statement of Thomas Nashe in his *Pierce Penniless*, which was entered in the Stationers' Register on August 8, 1592, concerning the triumph on the stage of "brave Talbot," one of the main characters in *Henry VI, Part I*. In September of that year, Greene in his attack on Shakespeare in his *Groatsworth of Wit* parodied *Henry VI, Part III*, I, iv, 137. A plausible inference from these references is that by the autumn of 1592 all three parts of the *Henry VI* trilogy were being acted in London theaters.

On March 12, 1594, Thomas Millington entered in the Stationers' Register "a booke intituled, the firste parte of the Contention of the twoo famous houses of York and Lancaster with the deathe of the good Duke Humfrey and the banishement and Deathe of the Duke of Suffolk and the tragicall ende of the prowd Cardinall of Winchester, with the notable rebellion of Jack Cade and the Duke of Yorkes ffirste clayme vnto the Crowne"; and later in the year he issued the play in quarto. In 1595, Millington published, without having entered it in the Stationers' Register, *The true Tragedie of Richard Duke of Yorke, and the death of good King Henrie the Sixt, with the whole contention betweene the two Houses Lancaster and Yorke*. These were both bad quartos. On April 19, 1602, Thomas Pavier, who had acquired the copyright from Millington, entered these in the Stationers' Register as *The firste and Second parte of Henry the vi,* but he did not print them until 1619, when he published a quarto under the title *The Whole Contention* . . . . "Diuided into two Parts: And newly corrected and enlarged. Written by William Shakespeare, Gent." These were included in the Folio as *Henry VI, Parts II* and *III,* and the old *Harey the vi* was first published in the Folio, where it became *Henry VI, Part I.*

Because the quartos of *The Contention* and *The True Tragedy* differ widely from the Folio versions of *Henry VI, Parts II* and *III,* and because of Greene's reference to "an upstart Crow, beautified with our feathers," these plays until lately were attributed to Marlowe, Peele, or some other author or group of authors, and it was thought that Shakespeare merely reworked them. But as a result of more information about the publication of the bad quartos and of a searching study within recent years of the different versions,[1] opinion has veered, and it is now the more generally accepted view that Shakespeare wrote all three parts.

For his plays dealing with English history, Shakespeare relied chiefly on Raphael Holinshed's *Chronicles of England, Scotland, and Ireland* (1577, enlarged 1586–1587); but he used also Edward Hall's *The Union of the two noble and illustrate famelies of Lancastre & Yorke, etc.* (1542 and later), John Stowe's *Chronicles of England from Brute until this present yeare of Christ* (1580), and Sir Thomas More's *History of King Richard the thirde* (1543). His main source for *Henry VI* was Holinshed. As he grew up in a county rich in memories of the Wars of the Roses, his interest in the theme, and

---

[1] Madeleine Doran, *Henry VI, Parts II and III: Their Relation to the Contention and the True Tragedy* (Iowa City: 1928); Peter Alexander, *Shakespeare's Henry VI and Richard III* (London: 1929); W. W. Greg, *The Editorial Problem in Shakespeare* (London: 1942), pp. 52–61; and others.

something of the atmosphere and general tone of the plays, doubtless came from the talk of old people to whose tales he had listened as a boy.

The three parts of *Henry VI* deal with the evil that results from disunity among the nobles, who instead of being allied for the country's good are grasping for power and position. *Henry VI, Part I,* considers Henry's life from the death of his father, Henry V, to the time of his marriage to Margaret of Anjou, daughter of the titular King of Naples. The scenes alternate between England and France, those in England having to do mainly with political, and those in France mainly with military, events. The character most carefully delineated and best calculated to arouse the interest of Shakespeare's audience is Talbot, an English military leader who dies in France because two political rivals bicker instead of going to his aid. Joan of Arc is introduced and appears in several scenes, where she is portrayed as a witch and strumpet, the view of her held by most Englishmen of Shakespeare's time.

Henry VI, Part II, begins with the arrival of Margaret to become Henry's queen. The nobles, still jockeying for power, destroy, first, Gloucester—"the good Duke Humfrey"—and then Suffolk, who helped plot Gloucester's murder. As the play ends, the Duke of York, now openly challenging Henry's right to the crown, is victorious in a battle between the York and Lancaster factions. Some of the most powerful scenes of this part of the trilogy are those in which Jack Cade, a laborer, arouses the people against Henry. These passages are also important as showing Shakespeare's first treatment of mob scenes.

Henry VI, Part III, carries the grim plot to a violent conclusion in the deaths of Henry, his young son, and Warwick "the kingmaker," who aids first one faction and then the other. Early in the play, the forces of the faction supporting Henry meet and defeat the Yorkist forces, and the Duke of York is slain. Thereafter the fortunes of war favor first one side and then the other, but gradually the Yorkist faction gains the ascendancy. Henry is slain by Richard, Duke of Gloucester, one of the three surviving sons of the Duke of York; and the eldest son, the Earl of March, is crowned as Edward IV. Richard of Gloucester is introduced as a diabolical plotter and murderer, and the way is thus prepared for Shakespeare's next play, *Richard III*.

The plays are written largely in blank verse. *Part II* contains 448 lines of prose; the other two parts of the trilogy, none. Each part contains a small number of pentameter lines that rime—fewer than 600 in the three plays. The blank verse of *Part I* is less rigid than that of the other two parts, a circumstance that some authorities believe points to its being written later than *Parts II* and *III*. The descriptions in *Part I*, the references to classical mythology, the learned quotations, and the general style indicate an affinity with the narrative poems that Shakespeare dedicated to the Earl of Southampton. Though these are the plays of an apprentice, they contain elements that appear in the mature plays of later periods.

RICHARD III

The first reference to *Richard III* is an entry in the Stationers' Register on October 20, 1597. A quarto, which differs considerably from the Folio text, but which was probably set up from a copy prepared for acting rather than from a stolen copy, was published in 1597. Meres lists *Richard III* among the tragedies that he ascribes to Shakespeare (1598). Internal evidence places it among the earliest of Shakespeare's works. Since it is a continuation of the events treated in *Henry VI*, it probably was written soon after the Henry plays. It proved to be immensely popular, six quartos being called for before the publication of the Folio. The Folio version contains 230 lines not in the quartos, and the latter have some lines not in the Folio text.

Because Marlowe's influence is discernible in *Richard III*, some scholars have held that it was written by Marlowe and revised by Shakespeare; but this view was more common when the last two parts of *Henry VI* in their original form were attributed to other authors. Its ascription to Shakespeare by Meres, by Q2, and by the Folio seems preponderant evidence in favor of Shakespeare's authorship. Scholars generally agree that Shakespeare's early style was influenced by Marlowe; and this explanation is sufficient to account for the Marlowean tone here.

Shakespeare's source was mainly Holinshed's and Hall's *Chronicles*. He may also have used Sir Thomas More's *History of King Richard the thirde,* and possibly an old play, *The True Tragedy of Richard the Third,* of which we have record before 1588.

Richard III deals with the final events of the Wars of the Roses, but the emphasis is less on these events than on the character of Richard III, a subtle and unprincipled villain who employs his devilish gifts to obtain the crown for himself. The action follows immediately on that of *Henry VI, Part III*. Edward IV, eldest of the three sons of the Duke of York, Henry VI's old foe, has just succeeded Henry on the throne. Richard, Duke of Gloucester, youngest of the three sons, initiates a plot against the second son, the Duke of Clarence, who in the event of Edward's death would stand between Richard and the crown. Also in furtherance of his scheme, Richard woos and wins the widow of Henry VI's son, whom he had helped to murder. Shortly after the murder of Clarence, at Richard's instigation, Edward IV dies; and by masterly deceit, Richard has himself made king. Next he has Edward's two young sons murdered. But by now his wickedness has alienated many of the nobles, among them the Duke of Buckingham, who had been his chief supporter. When, therefore, Henry, Earl of Richmond, of the Lancastrian faction, arrives from abroad to prosecute his claim to the crown, the nobles flock to Henry's support. The forces meet at Bosworth Field, where Richard, fighting valiantly, is defeated and slain. The play ends with the Earl of Richmond ascending the throne as Henry VII.

The influence of Marlowe is evident in the emphasis on one

main character, the villain-hero, in the static quality of the main character, and in the type of blank verse, the long speeches, and the soliloquies. The influence of Thomas Kyd may possibly be seen in the revenge motif, the ghost scenes, and the use of dreams, for though these elements are found in More's life of Richard, Kyd had already popularized their use in drama. As his vehicle of expression, Shakespeare employed blank verse almost exclusively. The verse lacks the ease and freedom of that in his later plays; it contains few run-on lines and is formal and rhetorical. The delineation of Richard's character, however, foretells the master who was later to create Iago and Macbeth.

THE COMEDY OF ERRORS

The first mention of *The Comedy of Errors* is in a report of a performance at Gray's Inn, one of the societies of lawyers and law students in London, on December 28, 1594. The style and treatment attest its early date among Shakespeare's works, and Adams[2] conjectures that he wrote it when a schoolmaster in the country and used it to gain his first connection with the London theater. It was first printed in the First Folio.

The idea for the plot came from Plautus's *Menaechmi*, with a further suggestion from the same author's *Amphitruo;* and the tragic undertone came from the tale of *Apollonius of Tyre*. Shakespeare improved on his sources by having two sets of twins, instead of the one set in Plautus, and by heightening the intrigue and adding a romantic love element.

The play is a farce-comedy, but suspense is gained by a threat of tragedy. A feud between Syracuse and Ephesus has caused both towns to impose the death penalty against a citizen of either place found in the other unless he can pay a huge ransom. Aegeon, a merchant of Syracuse, is caught in Ephesus and cannot meet the ransom terms. But the Duke of Ephesus, on hearing Aegeon's story of how he and one of his twin sons

---
[2] J. Q. Adams, *A Life of William Shakespeare* (Boston: 1923), pp. 132–133.

had been separated years before from his wife and the other twin as the result of a shipwreck, and of his being caught at Ephesus during a search for the lost wife and son, defers the execution of Aegeon for a day to allow him time to raise the ransom. Meanwhile, unknown to Aegeon, the son whom he had saved and who for some years had been searching for his brother arrives in Ephesus; and the twin who had been with the mother has become a citizen of Ephesus, is married, and lives near by. As they are now both in the same neighborhood, each twin is mistaken for the other; and to complicate matters each is served by a twin servant. Errors of identity among the two sets of twins create a great deal of mirth; and as the action proceeds, the situations become more involved and more farcical until the last act brings the discovery of the true relationship of all the members of the group. Aegeon, moreover, discovers his wife, who had been separated from the twin who was with her in the shipwreck. The entire family is thus reunited, and the Duke remits Aegeon's ransom.

Some evidences that the play was the work of an apprentice are the doggerel verse, of which there is considerable, the balance among the groups and the speeches among members of the groups, and the alternate puns, quibbles, and similar artificial devices. Its brevity[3] may be another evidence that it was a very early work.

TITUS ANDRONICUS

On January 23, 1594, Henslowe recorded in his diary a performance of *Titus Andronicus* by the Earl of Sussex' Men, marking the play as new. Yet, because Henslowe sometimes listed a revised play as new and occasionally called an old play new when it was played for the first time by a new company, little reliance can be placed on his notation. Some schol-

---

[3] It is the shortest of Shakespeare's plays, having only 1,778 lines. Some authorities have conjectured, however, that certain scenes may have been lost or dropped before the copy for the Folio was procured.

ars believe the play to be a slightly revised version of *Titus and Vespasian*, which was acted by Lord Strange's Men in 1592; and there is some slight evidence to support this belief.[4] It was entered in the Stationers' Register on February 6, 1594; and the quarto, issued shortly after this entry, states that it had been played by the Earl of Derby's, the Earl of Pembroke's, and the Earl of Sussex' Men. This would indicate that it had been on the boards for some time. If Shakespeare wrote the original version, internal evidence points to its being one of his very early plays.

Because it contains such an unrelieved succession of horrors, many authorities have been loath to believe that Shakespeare wrote it. The only external evidence against his authorship is extremely late. In 1687, Edward Ravenscroft in the "Address" to a play adapted from *Titus Andronicus* said, "I have been told by some anciently conversant with the Stage, that it was not Originally his, but brought by a private Authour to be Acted, and he only gave some Master-touches to one or two of the Principal Parts or characters." Against this late statement, we have Meres's ascription of the play to Shakespeare in his *Palladis Tamia* (1598) and its inclusion by Heminges and Condell in the Folio. The probability appears to be, therefore, that it is by Shakespeare, and that in trying his 'prentice hand at tragedy he out-Heroded Herod at a time when the horror and revenge play was highly popular on the Elizabethan stage.

No specific source for the plot has been found. Some of the themes are very old in literature, and the author—whether Shakespeare or another—blended them and added touches of his own.

It is a revenge play, in the tradition of Kyd. A noble Roman, Titus Andronicus, comes home a hero after conquering the Goths. Offered the throne, he refuses it and supports the claim of Saturninus, son of the dead emperor, who desires to marry Titus's daughter, Lavinia. Bassianus, younger brother of Saturninus, however, claims Lavinia and with the aid of her

---

[4] E. K. Chambers, *William Shakespeare* (London: 1930), I, 319.

brothers abducts her. Saturninus, having become emperor with Titus's help, marries Tamora, captured queen of the Goths, whom Titus had brought to Rome. She and her Moorish paramour, Aaron, perform or instigate a succession of revolting deeds: the murder of Bassianus, the rape of Lavinia by Tamora's sons, who then tear out her tongue and cut off her hands to prevent her informing on them, and the execution of Titus's sons for the supposed murder of Bassianus. The plot thereafter deals with the effort of Titus to avenge the rape of his daughter and the judicial murder of his sons. In this he is successful, but he, too, dies in the general destruction. Another of Titus's sons, who had been exiled, returns with an army of Goths, is proclaimed emperor, and vindicates his father's reputation. The Moor, Aaron, is a prototype of such later villains as Iago, without any of the latter's outward charm.

Except for fewer than two hundred lines, the play is written in blank verse. The style is rhetorical and declamatory, rather than conversational. Most of the lines are end stopped, and Latin tags are frequent. The play is Senecan in theme and development. Titus himself, by wrong decisions, starts the chain of events that engulf his house. Even thus early in his plays, Shakespeare apparently was probing human motives and trying to see why the best of motives often lead to tragedy. At that time he had not learned to give adequate expression to his ambitious aim of analyzing character and showing its operation in human affairs and its influence on events; but as an early instance of his interest in this problem, *Titus Andronicus* is a highly important laboratory specimen. The revolting plot should not prevent the student of Shakespeare from considering the play carefully in order to study the first tentative gropings of the great dramatist toward an adequate statement of the influence of character on action. He had far to travel before giving his great demonstration of Cordelia's rightness when she said, "We are not the first who, with best meaning, have incurr'd the worst"; but it is a reasonable assumption that without a *Titus Andronicus* we might not have had a *Lear*.

THE TAMING OF THE SHREW

Authorities are in wide disagreement over both the date and the extent of Shakespeare's hand in *The Taming of the Shrew*. An older play, *The Taming of A Shrew*, was entered in the Stationers' Register on May 2, 1594, and was published in a quarto edition in that year with a statement that it had been "sundry times" acted by the Earl of Pembroke's Men. Subsequent quartos of this play were issued in 1596 and 1607. The first publication of *The Taming of* THE *Shrew* as we have it was in the First Folio. Yet the history of the various publications, including that of the Folio version and of a quarto issued in 1631, indicates that *A Shrew* and *The Shrew* were considered by publishers to be the same play, in spite of marked differences in the text. The problem of dating arises over the relationship of the two plays and over the question of authorship. If Shakespeare merely revised *A Shrew*, the date of his participation is late, perhaps as late as 1598, but if he wrote the play in its original form, it belongs, on both internal and external evidence, to an early period of his work.

Some scholars believe that Shakespeare wrote the play and that the differences between the quartos of *A Shrew* and the Folio *The Shrew* may be explained by *A Shrew's* being a stolen copy. To support them is the apparent identification of the two titles with the same play and the ascription of the play to Shakespeare by the Folio editors. Meres in his list of Shakespeare's plays in *Palladis Tamia* (1598) mentions *Love's Labour's Won*, and since no play bearing that title has been found, some scholars believe it refers to *The Shrew*. If this conjecture could be proved, evidence of Shakespeare's authorship would be stronger. Yet such sane and competent scholars as Adams and Chambers attribute to Shakespeare only the part of reviser in this play.[5] Certainly Shakespeare's hand is

---

[5] Adams, *op. cit.*, pp. 223–225, and Chambers, *op. cit.*, I, 323–328. Professor Hardin Craig, in *Elizabethan Studies and Other Essays in Honor of George F. Reynolds* (Boulder, Colo.: 1945), pp. 150–154, and in *An Interpre-*

evident in the main plot. Except for evidences of hurry and carelessness—faults not always lacking in plays we know to be Shakespeare's—no substantial reason has been offered against his authorship of the play.

No specific source has been found for the main plot—the Petruchio–Katharine action that has to do with the taming of the shrew. This is an old folk theme, and it may have been found in many sources. The subplot, dealing with the Lucentio–Bianca intrigue, comes from Ariosto's *I Suppositi,* probably in George Gascoigne's translation. The Induction was probably suggested by a tale from the *Arabian Nights,* "The Sleeper Awakened."

The main plot, in which Petruchio "tames" the shrew, Katharine, is a comedy of character, and the subplot, in which Lucentio schemes to win Bianca, is a comedy of intrigue; but many elements of the play are farcical. Baptista, a rich merchant of Padua, has two daughters, the elder, Katharina, being as shrewish as the younger, Bianca, is sweet and winsome. Bianca has several suitors, but her father will not allow her to marry till her elder sister has a husband. The suitors therefore hunt for someone to court Katharina, and find Petruchio ready to assist them when he hears of the size of Katharina's dowry. His wooing is stormy; he outdoes Kate in shrewishness and sets the wedding date, and then appears for the wedding in disreputable apparel. He pretends such ill temper that Kate has no chance to be shrewish and instead sets herself to make him more agreeable. Meanwhile, the wooers of Bianca get into various difficulties because of their rivalry for her; but finally Lucentio gets her, another of her suitors marries a widow, and the play ends with a wedding feast at which Petruchio demonstrates that

---

tation of Shakespeare (New York: 1948), pp. 89–94, argues strongly for a theory advanced by Bernhard ten Brink, a nineteenth-century German scholar, that an original play on the theme existed at least as early as 1589 (when it was mentioned in Robert Greene's *Menaphon*), and that this old play was the original of both *A Shrew* and *The Shrew,* the former being a bad quarto of the original and the latter a rewriting of the old play by Shakespeare.

he alone has a sweet and obedient wife. The Induction, one of the most charming parts of the play, presents a tinker who is found while dead drunk by a nobleman and taken into the latter's house, dressed in rich garments, put into a fine bed, and told when he becomes sober that he is a lord who has been insane for fifteen years and has just recovered his sanity. The play, *The Taming of the Shrew*, is then presented for him. This sets up an interesting situation that demands a conclusion, but in our version of Shakespeare's play nothing further is made of the tinker, and after the second act he is not mentioned. In all likelihood a concluding scene was written for this part of the play, and was lost before copy was provided for the Folio.

According to the tables made by Fleay and corrected by Furnivall, the play has 2,649 lines, of which 516 are prose, 1,971 are blank verse, and 169 are rimed pentameter lines. Most of the blank-verse lines are end stopped, and there is some doggerel in the play, both evidences of early writing. Yet some parts are in the manner of the late second period. These differences in style may be the result of a revision by Shakespeare of his own work some years after the play was first written. The integration of the main plot and the subplot is well managed.

THE TWO GENTLEMEN OF VERONA

The first reference so far discovered to *The Two Gentlemen of Verona* is its listing as one of Shakespeare's plays by Francis Meres in his *Palladis Tamia* (1598). The first publication of the play was in the First Folio. Its theme, treatment, and style mark it as early, as do certain echoes of the Sonnets and a number of experimental features. Some authorities, indeed, have placed it among the very earliest of Shakespeare's plays; yet Adams conjectures that it was written in the period of enforced idleness resulting from the closing of the theaters in 1592–1593, when Shakespeare wrote his long narrative poems; and Chambers states that "a single date, early in the season of 1594–1595, really meets all the conditions" necessary to explain its characteristics.

INTRODUCTIONS TO THE PLAYS 85

As with other early plays attributed to Shakespeare, certain scholars see in it the work of other hands because it is below the standard of his later work. Such reasoning, of course, is based on the questionable assumption that a great master requires no period of apprenticeship but is great from the time of his earliest work. The play indeed shows the influence of Greene and Lyly, but other early plays by Shakespeare reflect the work of his contemporaries; and its inclusion by Meres and the Folio editors is a strong argument for Shakespeare's sole authorship.

The main plot was probably based on the story of Don Felix and Felismena in Jorge de Montemayor's *Diana Enamorada*, or possibly on an old play, now lost, *The History of Felix and Philiomena*, which the Queen's Men performed at Court in 1585. The theme, however, was common in Renaissance literature, and Shakespeare may have come on it elsewhere. He derived suggestions from Lyly's *Euphues* and his play *Endymion*.

The Two Gentlemen of Verona was Shakespeare's first attempt at writing a drama of romantic love. It is in the tradition of the comedies of Greene and Lyly, with additional elements from Renaissance literature. The "two gentlemen" are Valentine and Proteus, intimate friends, who find their friendship threatened when Proteus, forgetting a former sweetheart, falls in love with Silvia, Valentine's sweetheart, and resorts to treachery against his friend to win her. But their friendship survives the test imposed on it, and in the end Valentine gets his Silvia, Proteus returns to the love of his former sweetheart, and the friendship of Valentine and Proteus is firmly re-established. In this play for the first time Shakespeare introduces a number of elements that he used frequently in later plays: romantic greenwood scenes in which Valentine becomes chief of a band of outlaws; low-comedy scenes in which Launce and his dog provide the humor; and a girl disguised as a page in order to be near her lover.

The play is full of puns, quibbles, *double-entendres*, and

artificialities of style. Either a careless adaptation of a source in which the scenes of action were by the sea or a considerable ignorance of Italian geography led Shakespeare to show Valentine and Proteus traveling from Verona to Milan, both inland cities, by ship.[6] More lines are written in prose in this play than in any of the plays previously discussed. About two thirds of the play is in blank verse; but in spite of the fact that the verse is less formal and rhetorical than that of the early histories, it can hardly be called distinguished. The chief importance of this comedy is its introduction of new romantic elements that point directly to the great comedies of the next period.

LOVE'S LABOUR'S LOST

The first reference to *Love's Labour's Lost* so far discovered is that by Meres in his *Palladis Tamia* in 1598. A quarto was published in 1598, with the notation on the title page, "As it was presented before her Highnes this last Christmas. Newly corrected and augmented By W. Shakespeare." Scholars are in considerable disagreement over the date of the play, some considering it one of the earliest plays and some placing it as late as 1597. Chambers considers the versification too adroit for an early date, and he places it at the end of the first period,[7] but most authorities place it early in the first period. Perhaps the best explanation is that advanced many years ago by H. D. Gray,[8] that the play was written originally as early as 1590, or shortly after, and that the augmentations noted in the quarto were rather thorough and were made for the court performance. Such an explanation would account for a number of repetitions

---

[6] Perhaps this was one of the instances Ben Jonson had in mind when in answer to the statements of Shakespeare's fellows that his copy came to them with scarcely a blot on it, Jonson said he could have wished that a thousand lines had been blotted. See Appendix A.

[7] Chambers, *op. cit.*, I, 333-338, where also he discusses the identification of the characters and other controversial points.

[8] See H. D. Gray, *The Original Version of "Love's Labour's Lost"* (Stanford, Calif.: 1918).

Mr. WILLIAM SHAKESPEARES

COMEDIES, HISTORIES, & TRAGEDIES.

Published according to the True Originall Copies.

Courtesy of the Folger Shakespeare Library

WARWICKE

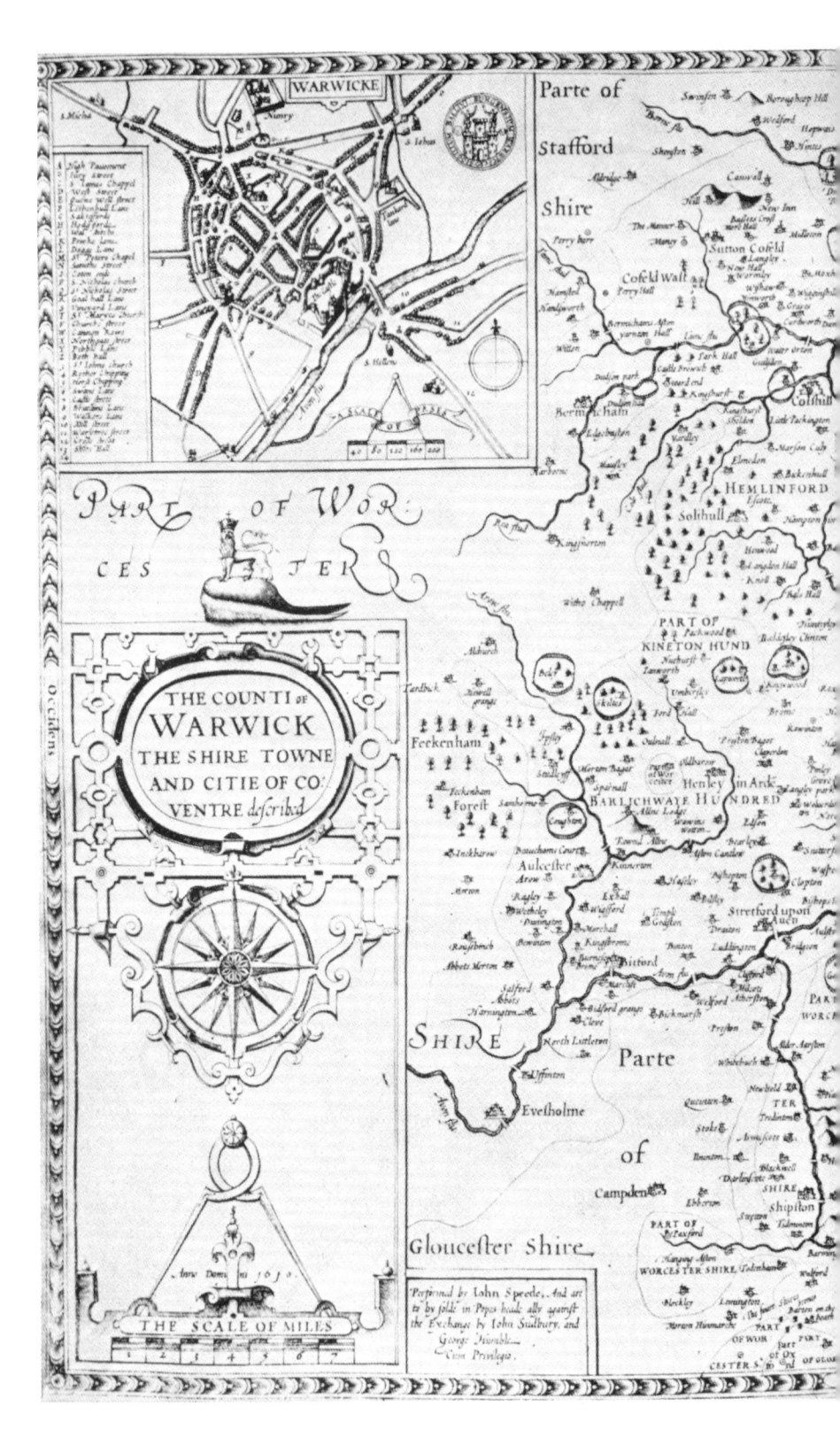

A High Pauement
B Iury ſtreet
C Iames Chappell
D Weſt ſtreet
E Quines Will ſtreet
F Liſten hull Lane
G Sadiersſtreet
H Horſefaire
I War. Birche
K Pinche Lane
L Dogg Lane
M S. Peters Chapel
N Smiths ſtreet
O Caten croſſe
P S. Nicholas church
Q S. Nicholas ſtreet
R Gaol hull Lane
S Vineyard Lane
T S. Maries Church
V Church yarde
W Commō Rowe
X Northgate ſtret
Y Puble Lane
Z Bath hall
1 S. Iohns church
2 Butcher chopping
3 hard chopping
4 Swane Lane
5 Bowlinge Lane
6 Walkers Lane
7 Mill ſtreet
8 Warwicks ſtreet
9 Croſſe hole
10 Abot Hall

Parte of Stafford Shire

PART OF WOR: CESTER

THE COUNTI OF WARWICK THE SHIRE TOWNE AND CITIE OF CO: VENTRE deſcribed

Anno Domini 1610

THE SCALE OF MILES

Performed by Iohn Speede, And are to be ſolde in Pops head alley againſt the Exchange by Iohn Sudbury, and George Humble.
Cum Privilegio.

Gloucester Shire

Courtesy of the Folger Shakespeare Library

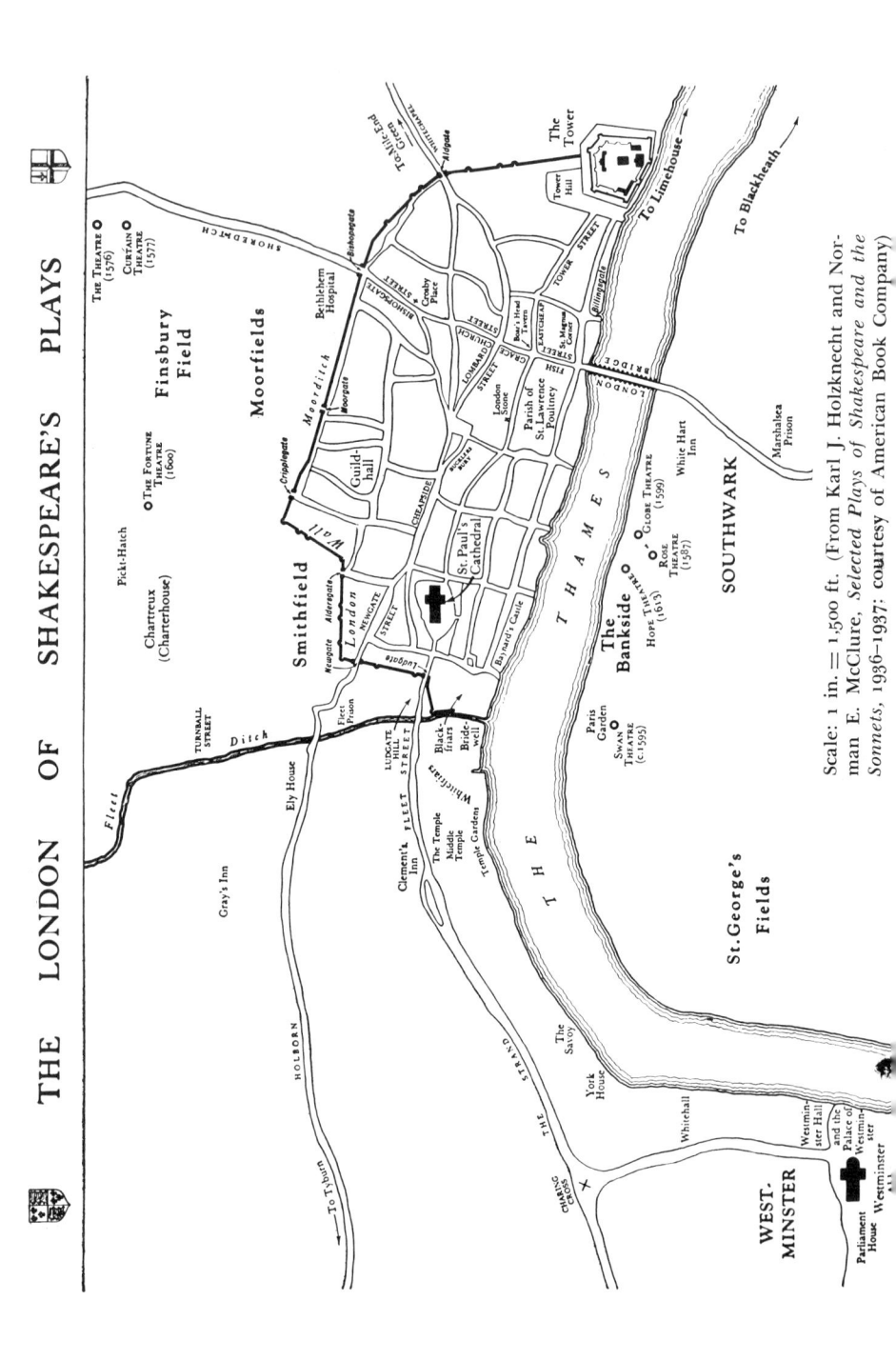

THE LONDON OF SHAKESPEARE'S PLAYS

Scale: 1 in. = 1,500 ft. (From Karl J. Holzknecht and Norman E. McClure, *Selected Plays of Shakespeare and the Sonnets*, 1936–1937: courtesy of American Book Company)

Herald Tribune—Ted Kell

Close-up, exterior, and cross section of a scale model of the Globe Theater by President John C. Adams of Hofstra College

Herald Tribune—Ted Kell

FIRST LEVEL

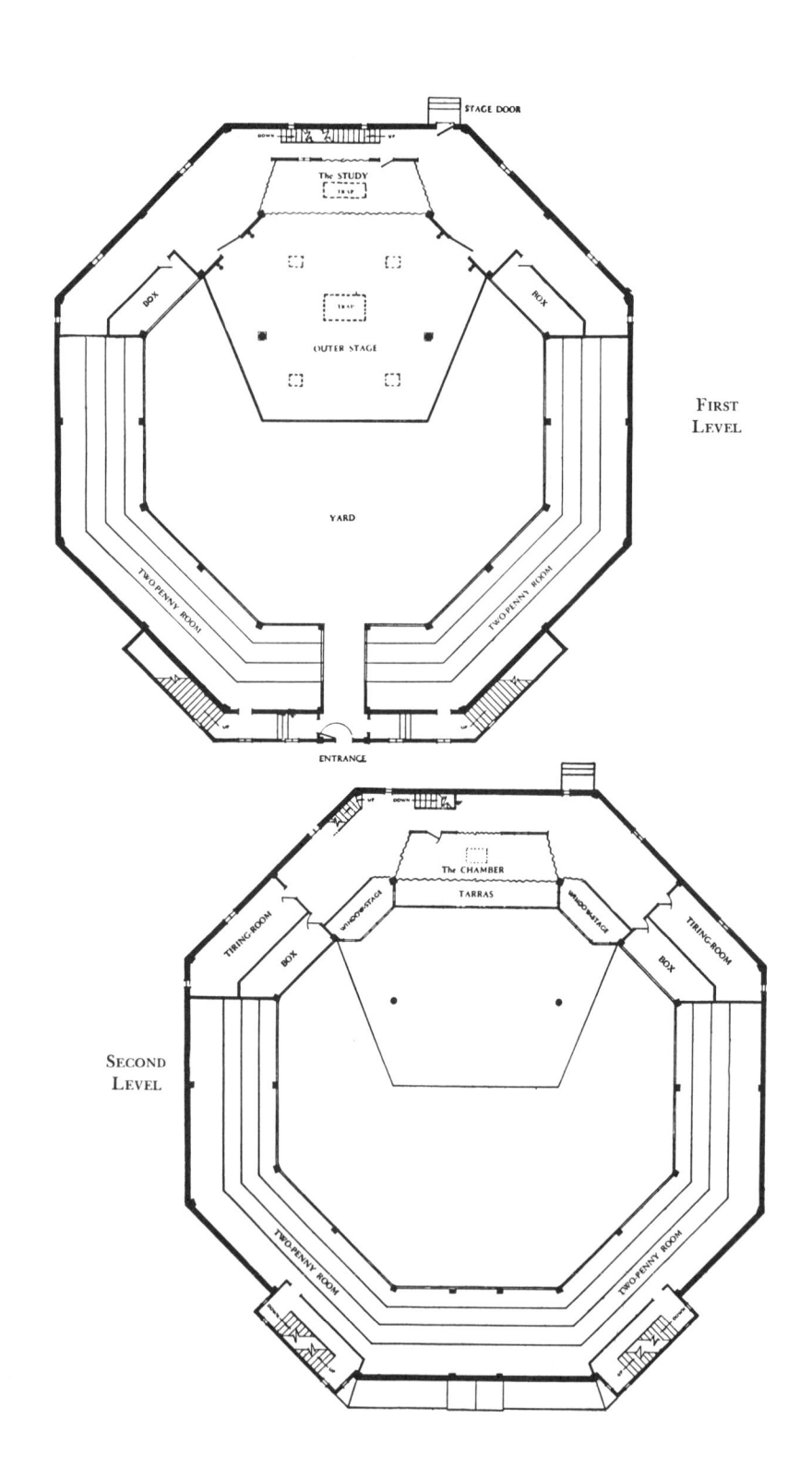

STAGE DOOR
The STUDY
TRAP
BOX
BOX
TRAP
OUTER STAGE
TWO-PENNY ROOM
TWO-PENNY ROOM
YARD
ENTRANCE

SECOND LEVEL

The CHAMBER
TARRAS
WINDOW-STAGE
WINDOW-STAGE
TIRING-ROOM
TIRING-ROOM
BOX
BOX
TWO-PENNY ROOM
TWO-PENNY ROOM

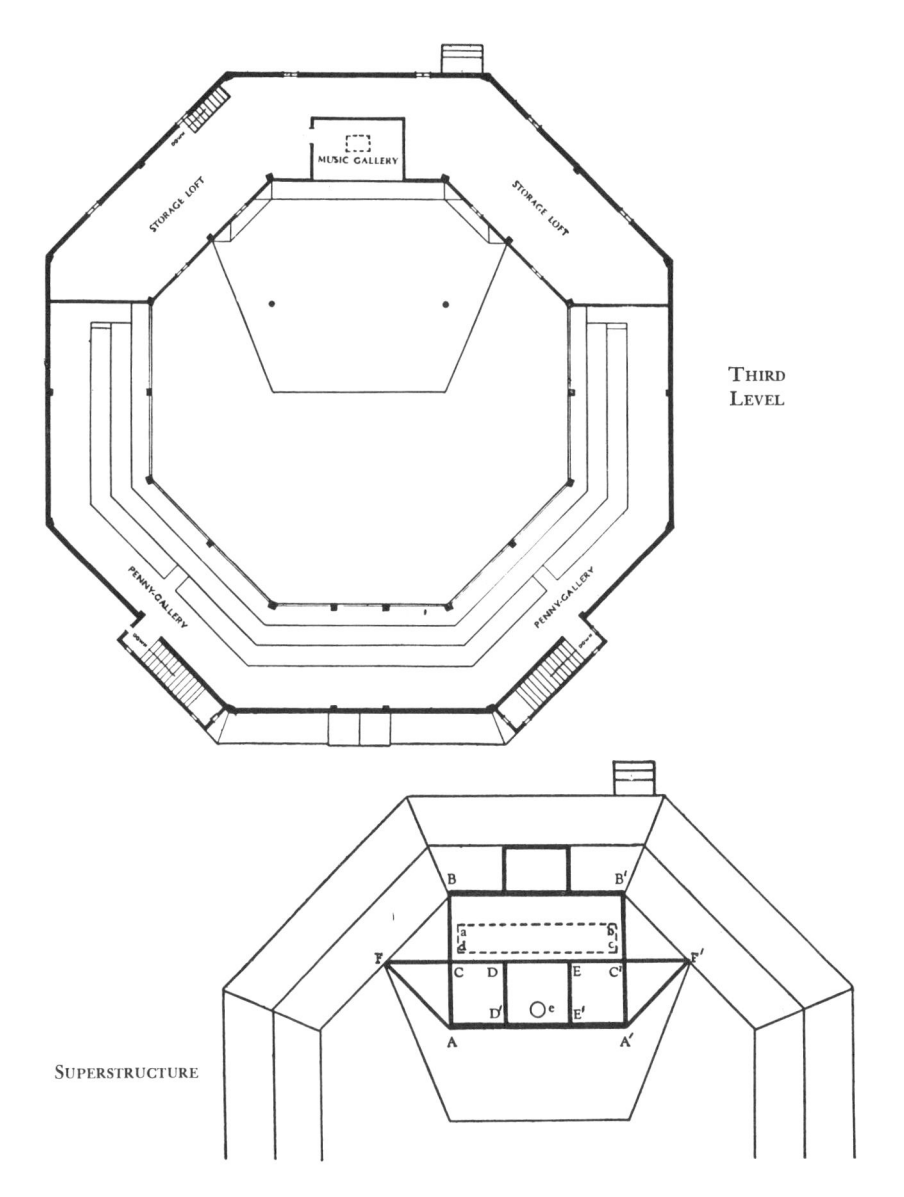

RECONSTRUCTED PLANS OF THE GLOBE THEATER
(*Approximate scale: 1 in. = 24 ft.*)

First, second, and third levels, and superstructure. Superstructure: stage posts, A and A'; corner posts, B and B'. Base of stage heavens on rectangle A, A', B', and B (24×17 ft.). Secondary beams, as sills for huts, $C-C'$, $D-D'$, $E-E'$; bracing beams, $A-F$, $A'-F'$. Transverse hut on rectangle B, B', C' and C, with trap opening a, b, c, and d, used for descents; forward hut on rectangle D, E, E' and D', with trap opening e, used for pyrotechnical displays. (From *The Globe Playhouse,* Harvard University, 1942; courtesy of the author, John C. Adams, and the publishers)

[Illustrations on first and last pages of insert are from the First Folio, 1623.]

THE TRAGEDIE OF
HAMLET, Prince of Denmarke.

Actus Primus. Scœna Prima.

Enter Barnardo and Francisco two Centinels.

Barnardo.
Ho's there?

Fran. Nay answer me: Stand & vnfold your selfe.

Bar. Long liue the King.

Fran. Barnardo?

Bar. He.

Fran. You come most carefully vpon your houre.

Bar. 'Tis now strook twelue, get thee to bed *Francisco*.

Fran. For this releefe much thankes: 'Tis bitter cold,
And I am sicke at heart.

Barn. Haue you had quiet Guard?

Fran. Not a Mouse stirring.

Barn. Well, goodnight. If you do meet *Horatio* and *Marcellus*, the Riuals of my Watch, bid them make hast.

Enter Horatio and Marcellus.

Fran. I thinke I heare them. Stand: who's there?

Hor. Friends to this ground.

Mar. And Leige-men to the Dane.

Fran. Giue you good night.

Mar. O farwel honest Soldier, who hath relieu'd you?

Fra. Barnardo ha's my place: giue you goodnight. *Exit Fran.*

Mar. Holla *Barnardo*.

Bar. Say, what is *Horatio* there?

Hor. A peece of him.

Bar. Welcome *Horatio*, welcome good *Marcellus*.

Mar. What, ha's this thing appear'd againe to night.

Bar. I haue seene nothing.

Mar. Horatio saies, 'tis but our Fantasie,
And will not let beleefe take hold of him
Touching this dreaded sight, twice seene of vs,
Therefore I haue intreated him along
With vs, to watch the minutes of this Night,
That if againe this Apparition come,
He may approue our eyes, and speake to it.

Hor. Tush, tush, 'twill not appeare.

Bar. Sit downe a-while,
And let vs once againe assaile your eares,
That are so fortified against our Story,
What we two Nights haue seene.

Hor. Well, sit we downe,
And let vs heare *Barnardo* speake of this.

Barn. Last night of all,
When yond same Starre that's Westward from the Pole
Had made his course t'illume that part of Heauen
Where now it burnes, *Marcellus* and my selfe,
The Bell then beating one.

Mar. Peace, breake thee of: *Enter the Ghost.*
Looke where it comes againe.

Barn. In the same figure, like the King that's dead.

Mar. Thou art a Scholler; speake to it *Horatio*.

Barn. Lookes it not like the King? Marke it *Horatio*.

Hora. Most like: It harrowes me with fear & wonder

Barn. It would be spoke too.

Mar. Question it *Horatio*.

Hor. What art thou that vsurp'st this time of night,
Together with that Faire and Warlike forme
In which the Maiesty of buried *Denmarke*
Did sometimes march: By Heauen I charge thee speake.

Mar. It is offended.

Barn. See, it stalkes away.

Hor. Stay: speake; speake: I Charge thee, speake. *Exit the Ghost.*

Mar. 'Tis gone, and will not answer.

Barn. How now *Horatio*? You tremble & look pale:
Is not this something more then Fantasie?
What thinke you on't?

Hor. Before my God, I might not this beleeue
Without the sensible and true auouch
Of mine owne eyes.

Mar. Is it not like the King?

Hor. As thou art to thy selfe,
Such was the very Armour he had on,
When th'Ambitious *Norwey* combatted:
So frown'd he once, when in an angry parle
He smot the sledded *Pollax* on the Ice.
'Tis strange.

Mar. Thus twice before, and iust at this dead houre,
With Martiall stalke, hath he gone by our Watch.

Hor. In what particular thought to work, I know not:
But in the grosse and scope of my Opinion,
This boades some strange erruption to our State.

Mar. Good now sit downe, & tell me he that knowes
Why this same strict and most obseruant Watch,
So nightly toyles the subiect of the Land,
And why such dayly Cast of Brazon Cannon
And Forraigne Mart for Implements of warre:
Why such impresse of Ship-wrights, whose sore Taske
Do's not diuide the Sunday from the weeke,
What might be toward, that this sweaty hast
Doth make the Night ioynt-Labourer with the day:
Who is't that can informe me?

Hor. That can I,

At

and other inconsistencies and for the difference in style between parts of the play.

Meres lists the play as by Shakespeare, and the quarto ascription of the play to him supports Meres. It is, in fact, the only early play except *The Comedy of Errors* in which a part of the work is not ascribed by some authorities to another writer. The plot apparently is Shakespeare's own, as no source has been found, but it is based on common political talk of the time. Some of the characters, perhaps most of them, represent actual persons, but who these were is now beyond identification, save in a few instances. The influence of Lyly is clearly evident in the scenes of wit combat and in the introduction of songs, but Shakespeare satirizes many of the courtly conventions that Lyly treated seriously.

The play is a satire on the social customs and personal affectations of the time. Ferdinand, King of Navarre, and his three closest friends swear to spend three years in study and meditation, during which time they will avoid the society of women. But a visit to his Court by the Princess of France and her three ladies in waiting upsets this scheme. Each of the men proceeds to fall in love with one of the women, who have great fun with the lovesick courtiers. Each lover tries to hide his feeling from the others until all are unmasked in a scene of sustained humor in Act IV. Humor of another sort than that provided by the wit combats of the gallants and ladies is furnished by Sir Nathaniel, an illiterate priest, and Holofernes, a pedant, and by a group of minor characters whose purpose in the play is to entertain the gallants.

The elaborate and artificial plot, as well as the wit combats already cited, owes much to the influence of John Lyly on Shakespeare at the time of its construction. The play abounds in puns and conceits. It contains more prose than verse, and of the latter, more rime than blank verse. The blank verse is in the earliest manner, with end-stopped lines and almost no light endings. The rimed lines appear as couplets, quatrains, and sonnets, and in a variety of meters, ranging from two to seven feet to a line.

Whether Shakespeare wrote his first plays in the order considered here can never be finally settled. But a close comparison of the plays assigned to the first period with those assigned to the second period will convince any reader that those who have labored on the problem of chronology are not far wrong. All the plays so far discussed bear evidence of being Shakespeare's early work. This evidence includes indebtedness to other playwrights, lack of ease in handling blank verse, and such experimentations with various forms as the one dominant character in *Richard III*, the adaptation of classical comedy in *The Comedy of Errors*, the revenge play in *Titus Andronicus*, the romantic comedy in *The Two Gentlemen of Verona*, and the social satire in *Love's Labour's Lost*. None of the plays of this period has intrinsic greatness, but the young playwright had to write them before he could advance to the next stage of his development.

SECOND PERIOD: HISTORIES AND JOYOUS COMEDIES

ROMEO AND JULIET

The first external evidence we have of *Romeo and Juliet* was the publication in 1597 of a bad quarto, in which was a statement that "it hath been often (with great applause) plaid publiquely, by the right Honourable the L. of Hunsdon his Seruants." Some scholars have held that it was written in 1591 because the Nurse mentions an earthquake as having occurred eleven years before, and there was an earthquake in London in 1580; but such a theory seems too tenuous to counterbalance obvious qualities of style and treatment that relate the play to the second period or at least to the latter part of the first period. Chambers[9] surmises that it preceded *A Midsummer-*

---
[9] Chambers, *op. cit.*, I, 345.

INTRODUCTIONS TO THE PLAYS 89

Night's Dream because the artisans' foolery about the wall in the latter play seems to parody the wall scenes in *Romeo and Juliet*, and he suggests 1595 as a date for the play. Adams[10] assigns it to 1596 because of the evidence of its great popularity about 1597, and he thinks it unlikely that such a stir would arise over any save a new play. Scholars date it variously from among the earliest of Shakespeare's plays—because of the earthquake reference—to as late as 1596. Because of certain affinities between it and the Sonnets and long poems, Adams conjectured that Shakespeare wrote part of the play when he was working on these poems and then completed it for the stage in 1596.

Meres lists the play among Shakespeare's dramas. No reputable scholar questions Shakespeare's hand in it, but some assume an older play by someone else, with Shakespeare's part in it being that of reviser. An old play on the subject was in existence as far back as 1562, when Arthur Brooke told the story in verse, but every evidence of style and treatment mark the play that has come down to us as Shakespeare's alone. Because the bad quarto of 1597 differs in so many respects from the good quarto of 1599 and from the Folio text, certain scholars have held that the former was an early version by other authors and that Shakespeare's contributions are confined to the changes in Q2, but the work of recent scholars makes it appear virtually certain that Q1 was a reported version and that Q2 is the correct text as written by Shakespeare.

The story of Romeo and Juliet is an old one. It was told successively by the Italian writers Masuccio of Salerno (1476), Luigi da Porto (1524), G. Bolderi (1553), and Matteo Bandello (1554). Pierre Boaistuau translated Bandello's version into French (1559), and William Painter in turn translated Boaistuau's version into English in *The Palace of Pleasure* (1565–1567). Arthur Brooke also used Boaistuau for his poem *The Tragicall Historye of Romeus and Juliet* (1562). Brooke mentions a play on the subject, but as this has not survived, it is impossible to tell whether Shakespeare used it as a source. The

---

[10] Adams, *op. cit.*, p. 219.

evidence is clear that Shakespeare knew at least Brooke's and Painter's versions, and that he used chiefly the former.

Although the ostensible concern of the story is the evil results of feuds and civil brawls, its chief interest is in the sympathetic presentation of young love. Romeo and Juliet, children of two important families of Verona who are carrying on a deadly feud, fall in love, and with youth's impetuosity surmount all obstacles and are secretly married. But the feud involves them in its tragic effects. Romeo is banished from Verona, and Juliet's father hastens her marriage to a highly eligible count. The hurry of events and the youthful impatience of the lovers so outpace the deliberate movements of their only helper, the aged Friar Laurence, that a tragic end is inescapable. Although a tragedy, the play lacks the terrible implications of the later tragedies. Save for the tragic death of the lovers, the play is more akin in spirit to the joyous comedies than to the tragedies of the third period. Even the death of the popular Mercutio contains elements of comedy, Mercutio dying with a jest on his tongue. The high wit of Mercutio and the low comedy of the Nurse and Peter, with able assistance from Old Capulet, keep the tone light even in tragic moments. And the exquisite poetry of the balcony scenes is surpassed rarely if ever even in Shakespeare.

RICHARD II

The first external evidence of *Richard II* is an entry in the Stationers' Register on August 29, 1597. It was issued in quarto the same year. In 1595 two editions of Samuel Daniel's *Civil Wars between Lancaster and York* were published, the second of which contained parallels to Shakespeare's play that were not in the first. Some slight evidence weighs in favor of Daniel's being the adapter. If this is true, the early part of 1595 may confidently be accepted as the date of the play's public appearance. Because style, versification, and treatment indicate a date close to 1595, this date is generally accepted as that of the play's composition.

Although a similarity between this play and Marlowe's *Edward II* has led some commentators to attribute it in whole or in part to Marlowe, the claim, considering the style and the poetry, seems more fantastic than similar claims about some of the early plays. It is very much in the manner of Shakespeare's other plays of the early part of the second period. Meres lists it as Shakespeare's in his *Palladis Tamia* (1598), Q2 (1598) names Shakespeare as the author, and it is included in the First Folio by Shakespeare's fellows, Heminges and Condell. Undoubtedly it owes something to Marlowe, but this can be explained as the influence of a strong and successful playwright who was in the field before Shakespeare. In *Richard II*, Shakespeare, in fact, is emerging from Marlowe's influence. The sort of rhetoric used in *Richard III*, which was derived from Marlowe, here gives place to a lyric style that is a hallmark of Shakespeare.

The main source of *Richard II* is the second edition (1587) of Holinshed's *Chronicles,* with some hints from other sources. It has been conjectured that Shakespeare may have made use also of an older play on the subject, but since the play is not extant, such conjectures are futile.

Though in form a chronicle play, dealing as did his earlier historical plays with the struggle between the houses of York and Lancaster, *Richard II* is primarily a drama of character. Richard, lovable and charming but weak, is contrasted throughout with Bolingbroke, later Henry IV, whose undeviating course and icy purpose set him off against Richard at every point. Richard vacillates; Bolingbroke pursues his aim with great singleness of purpose. Richard is sentimental; Bolingbroke is a hard realist. Richard is the more lovable, but Shakespeare obviously considered that his defects of character made him unfit for the responsibilities of kingship; and the play ends with Bolingbroke on the throne and Richard the victim of an assassin. The play gains in dramatic intensity by focusing in Bolingbroke the forces opposing Richard, but the tragedy results primarily from defects of character in Richard himself.

The play thus prefigures the great character studies of the third period.

In style *Richard II* marks an advance over the early plays. The verse is more flexible and lyrical, and it evidences a more assured mastery of touch. Puns and conceits are still plentiful, but many passages exemplify a new range of power. About three fourths of the play is written in blank verse, but a blank verse less rhetorical than that found in the earlier histories. Rime is freely employed; prose is not used at all.

A MIDSUMMER-NIGHT'S DREAM

The first reference we have to *A Midsummer-Night's Dream* is its listing by Meres in his *Palladis Tamia* (1598) as one of Shakespeare's comedies. It was entered in the Stationers' Register on October 8, 1600, and a quarto was published in that year. Such internal evidence as style, versification, and treatment of theme places it about 1594–1596. Most scholars believe that it was written for performance at the actual wedding festivities of some eminent person, and that it was afterward revised for public performance; but they cannot agree on the wedding for which it may have been written nor consequently on an exact date for the play.

The title page of Q1 reads: "A Midsommer nights dreame. As it hath beene sundry times publickely acted, by the Right honourable, the Lord Chamberlaine his seruants. Written by William Shakespeare." Its mention my Meres as Shakespeare's work, its ascription to Shakespeare in Q1, and its inclusion in the Folio seem sufficient grounds for nearly all authorities to accept Shakespeare as the sole author.

No specific source for the play as we know it has been discovered. Probably the main idea came from the story of "Cupid and Psyche" in *The Golden Ass* of Lucius Apuleius.[11] Hints for some of the characters and minor incidents probably came from

---

[11] See J. Dover Wilson's article, "Variations on the Theme of 'A Midsummer-Night's Dream,'" in *Tribute to Walter de la Mare on His 75th Birthday* (London: 1948), pp. 25–42.

Plutarch, from several of Chaucer's poems, and from plays by Greene and Lyly. Jorge de Montemayor's *Diana Enamorado*, which furnished the idea for *The Two Gentlemen of Verona*, perhaps suggested the use of the juice on Lysander's and Titania's eyes.[12] For Puck and his doings and other elements of the fairy plot, Shakespeare could doubtless rely on his own childhood memories.

The play is partly a fantasy and partly a comedy of incident. Theseus, Duke of Athens, is preparing to marry Hippolyta, Queen of the Amazons. While awaiting the wedding festivities, a group of artisans plan a play to be given before the Duke. The scenes in which they practice and then give the play contain some of Shakespeare's finest comedy. The fairies gather also to honor the Duke and his bride, and in their world matters become mixed up, for Oberon and Titania, king and queen of the fairies, are at odds. As a result of their quarrel and of a mistake by Oberon's servant, Puck, the action as it relates to two of the other groups becomes more involved, the results providing high comedy. To add to the complications, in the world of the ordinary citizens of Athens a situation arises, involving two sets of lovers, that for a while threatens the lovers with tragedy but provides much good fun for the onlookers. The tone is consistently gay, the mood light and jocund, and the various plots are perfectly blended and integrated. Some scenes are too close to farce and the entire play too full of fantasy to warrant our classing it among Shakespeare's greatest comedies, but the lilting poetry, the gay comedy, and the careful blending of the plots make it one of his most delightful plays to read or to see performed on the stage.

Shakespeare takes pains to create a proper style for each of his themes. For the Theseus-Hippolyta part he uses blank

---

[12] For other possible sources, see Chambers, *op. cit.*, I, 362–363.
Professor E. J. West—in *College English*, IX (February, 1948), 247–249—has noted the similarity of the acting groups in *Love's Labour's Lost* and *A Midsummer-Night's Dream*. He makes it appear plausible that the earlier play furnished the idea for the technique employed in the later play.

verse, for the lovers rimed couplets, for the artisans prose, and for the fairies a variety of verse forms—trochaic tetrameter, heroic couplets, and blank verse. The style is uneven in the various parts, the least satisfactory being the speeches of the lovers. The interest of the play depends on plot and incident rather than on analysis of character; for of the various characters only Bottom and perhaps Theseus are completely drawn. Nevertheless, the play, because of the carefully wrought plot, marks an advance in Shakespeare's development as a dramatist.

KING JOHN

The first external evidence we have of *King John* is its mention in the list of Shakespeare's plays by Francis Meres in his *Palladis Tamia* (1598). A two-part chronicle play, *The Troublesome Raigne of Iohn King of England* and *The Second part of the troublesome Raigne of King Iohn,* both of which together are only about three hundred lines longer than Shakespeare's *King John,* was published in 1591 and had already been on the stage for some time before that. This old two-part drama forms the basis of Shakespeare's play. On internal evidence, scholars generally agree in placing *King John* near *Richard II.* It has been conjectured that the lament of Constance over the death of her son Arthur may reflect Shakespeare's own feelings over the death of his son, Hamnet, in August, 1596, but of course this is mere theorizing. Yet considering the style, certain resemblances in phrasing to *The Merchant of Venice,* and other characteristics, we are probably not far wrong in assigning the play to 1596.

In the past, a few authorities have held that Shakespeare wrote the original two-part play on which the later play is based, but this view is now rarely accepted. The strongest case for the authorship of *The Troublesome Raigne* has been made for George Peele. That Shakespeare reworked the old play is not questioned. The source of *The Troublesome Raigne* was Holinshed's *Chronicles,* and in preparing his version Shakespeare also probably consulted Holinshed as well as Hall's *Chronicles.*

King John is a true chronicle play. It is episodical and lacks a strong central character to give it unity. It deals with political maneuverings at a critical point in English history, when John was bent on recovering his lost dominions on the Continent and was involved in a struggle with Rome. Because the England of Shakespeare's day was strongly Protestant and the play shows the Papacy in a bad light—even after Shakespeare toned down some of the anti-Catholic parts of *The Troublesome Raigne*—it was very popular in spite of its manifest faults. John is portrayed as a defender of England against France and the Pope; yet Shakespeare makes him no hero. Though technically not a murderer, John brings about the death of his nephew Arthur, whose crown he has usurped, and he is avaricious and cowardly. What to a modern audience would be one of the most dramatic episodes of John's reign, the signing of Magna Carta, is omitted entirely, doubtless out of deference to the Tudor policy of centralization of government. The strongest character in the play, and apparently Shakespeare's own favorite, is Falconbridge, an illegitimate son of Richard Coeur de Lion, who leads the army and epitomizes the patriotic spirit of England. At the end of the play, after the death of John by poison, it is Falconbridge who sustains the young Prince Henry, welcomes the news of peace, and speaks the words that stirred the hearts of Shakespeare's audiences:

> This England never did, nor ever shall,
> Lie at the proud foot of a conqueror
> But when it first did help to wound itself.
> Now these her princes are come home again,
> Come the three corners of the world in arms,
> And we shall shock them. Nought shall make us rue
> If England to itself do rest but true.

King John contains no prose, and only about 150 lines of rimed iambic pentameter. The rest of the play is in blank verse, which is less rhetorical than that employed in the earlier history plays but more formal than that used in *Richard II*. The play also lacks the lyrical qualities of *Richard II*. Several of the characters are well delineated: John, Cardinal Pandulph, Falconbridge, the young Prince Arthur, his mother Constance, and Hubert de Burgh, who was delegated by John to murder Arthur. In spite of the episodical nature of the play and its lack of a central unifying character, its high patriotism and its interesting dramatic situations endeared it to Englishmen of Shakespeare's day, and it has retained a hold on modern audiences beyond its intrinsic merits.

THE MERCHANT OF VENICE

The Merchant of Venice is one of the plays mentioned by Meres in his *Palladis Tamia* (1598). It was entered in the Stationers' Register on July 22, 1598, and again in 1600. The First Quarto was published in 1600 as "The most excellent Historie of the Merchant of Venice . . . . As it hath beene diuers times acted by the Lord Chamberlaine his Seruants. Written by William Shakespeare." This was a good quarto, and was used in setting up the Folio text. It has been held that in IV, i, 134,

> a wolf . . . hang'd for human slaughter,

Shakespeare had in mind the execution of a Jew, Dr. Roderigo Lopez, a physician to Queen Elizabeth, for an alleged attempt to poison Don Antonio, the pretender to the Portuguese crown, and the Queen herself; that in III, ii, 49 is an allusion to the coronation of Henry IV of France in February, 1594; and that the entire consideration of Shylock and his treatment of Antonio was designed to take advantage of a wave of anti-Semitism that was sweeping over England in 1594–1595. The style, the obvious advance in technical skill, and the ability shown in character portrayal indicate a date for the play well along in the second period; and scholars are in general agreement in dating it about 1595–1597. Perhaps we should not be far wrong in assigning it to late 1596.

INTRODUCTIONS TO THE PLAYS 97

Elements of the play come from various sources. Much of the story—the bond and pound of flesh, the lover and older friend, the wooing of a lady of Belmont, a woman lawyer, the request for a ring in payment for the lawyer's services, and others—comes from Giovanni Fiorentino's *Il Pecorone,* the first tale of the fourth day (collected about 1378, but printed in 1558). That Shakespeare also knew an old ballad, "The Crueltie of Gernutus," is indicated by the similarity of language between Shylock's speeches and parts of the ballad. He probably also knew Anthony Munday's *Zelauto* (1580), in which the story of the bond is connected with the winning of the usurer's daughter. The entire play, moreover, was doubtless influenced by Marlowe's *The Jew of Malta.* Various elements of the play appear in many tales from early literature, and Shakespeare of course may have been acquainted with some of these.

Romantic friendship, love, and racial hatred are the elements that Shakespeare blends to make his plot. Bassanio needs money in order to court a rich lady, Portia. His wealthy friend Antonio, who at the moment lacks ready money, borrows a sum from Shylock, a usurer, who requires Antonio's promise of a pound of flesh if he fails to make good the loan when it is due. A peculiar test, in which the suitor must choose the right one of three caskets to win Portia, confronts Bassanio, but the lover's intuition helps him make the right choice. Meanwhile the loan becomes due, and Antonio, having suffered many financial reverses, cannot repay it, whereupon Shylock demands his pound of flesh from over Antonio's heart. Portia, disguised as a young lawyer, turns the tables on Shylock, whose daughter Jessica has already eloped with a Christian, taking with her a part of Shylock's wealth. These are the main elements of the plot, and they are relatively unimportant in comparison with the masterly portrayal of Shylock and Portia as characters. Shakespeare's growing skill in delineating character, indeed, is readily apparent when we compare his achievement in this play with his best in early plays.

Apparent also is a considerable advance in technique and

versification. Approximately two thirds of the play is in blank verse. Not all of it reaches the level of Portia's famous speech, beginning, "The quality of mercy is not strain'd," but throughout the verse one feels a sense of new power and smoothness. Shakespeare's style is beginning to be adequate for the expression of each subtle turn of thought. With the verse he mixes prose in judicious proportions—prose that points forward to the speech of Falstaff rather than back to the sometimes labored prose of the early plays. Puns, quibbles, and conceits are still present, but they are emphasized less than formerly. In Launcelot Gobbo he creates a completely satisfactory clown.

HENRY IV, PART I and PART II

Henry IV, Part I, was entered in the Stationers' Register on February 25, 1598, and in the same year Q1 appeared without Shakespeare's name on the title page. In 1599, however, Q2 was published with the statement, "Newly corrected by W. Shakespeare." *Henry IV, Part II,* was entered in the Stationers' Register on August 23, 1600, with the notation, "Wrytten by master Shakespere," and in the same year a quarto edition of this part was issued. Meres in the *Palladis Tamia* list (1598) mentions *Henry IV* among Shakespeare's plays, but he does not distinguish between the parts. Most scholars agree in dating *Part I* about 1597 and *Part II* soon after *Part I*.

For the historical matter of *Henry IV,* Shakespeare relied on Holinshed's *Chronicles* (1587 edition), and he probably also consulted Hall's and Stowe's *Chronicles.* For the comic parts, his source was an old chronicle play, *The Famous Victories of Henry V,* which was on the boards by 1588.

Henry IV is a continuation of English history from where Shakespeare left off in *Richard II.* Henry IV is the Bolingbroke of *Richard II,* with the same realistic philosophy, the same lack of warm human qualities, and the same icy sureness of purpose. But the play is only incidentally about Henry IV. Henry's policies are responsible for the direction the action takes, but much more important in the action, and certainly more interesting, are the brave, lovable, rash, impetuous Hotspur; the Welshman Glendower, with his superstitions and love of song and poetry; and Prince Hal, companion of rogues, yet for all that a youth of princely qualities. The most important character of all, however, is Falstaff, who contributes nothing to the historical action with which the play deals. Taking a few hints from the old chronicle play, *The Famous Victories,* Shakespeare created in Falstaff one of the greatest comic figures in literature. So fat that he "larded the lean earth" where he walked,[13] so dextrous of wit that he could wriggle out of situations that would have shamed another forever, he is probably Shakespeare's best creation in the field of pure comedy. Shakespeare's growing skill as a dramatist is evident in the ability with which he fuses the serious and comic parts into one unified and integrated whole. He departs from history when it suits his purpose—as, for instance, when he makes Hotspur much younger than he actually was in order to pose him beside Prince Hal—but such liberties were held against him as little in his own day as they are in ours.

So far as history is concerned, the two parts of *Henry IV* cover a period of some eleven years—from about 1402 to the death of Henry IV in 1413. Henry is having trouble with Scotland, with Welsh rebels, and with the Percies, who had helped him attain the throne but are now plotting against him. An alliance is made by Henry's enemies, but dissensions among them and the disaffection of certain members of the alliance weaken them, so that when they meet the king's forces at Shrewsbury they are defeated and Hotspur is slain by Prince Hal. The struggle is continued for a time, however, but finally the leaders opposing Henry are induced to lay down their arms and are then treacherously executed. Soon after this, Henry dies, and Prince Hal becomes King Henry V.

Shakespeare wrote his two *Henry IV* plays in blank verse and prose in roughly equal proportions. The historical parts comprise most of the blank verse and the comedy scenes most of the

---

[13] That is, greased it with his sweat when he had to walk.

prose. In the latter he has attained full mastery of expression for the purposes of comedy. The blank verse, however, though greatly superior to that of his early plays, is still below the level he attained in the great tragedies of the third period. In characterization, he is completely successful among the serious characters only with Hotspur; but the probability may be that the creation of Falstaff so engaged his interest that he did not give careful attention to every minor character, as he did in later plays. He is moving toward the position of the consummate artist, but he still has ground to cover before he can write a *King Lear* and an *Antony and Cleopatra*.

HENRY V

Henry V is not listed among Shakespeare's dramas by Meres in his *Palladis Tamia* (1598), and although this is not conclusive evidence that it was not in existence then, since Meres took pains to balance his groups with six comedies and six "tragedies" in each, it is a safe inference that it had not been produced when Meres wrote his handbook. The play was entered in the Stationers' Register on August 4, 1600, and a quarto edition was issued that year. This was a bad quarto, as were two other quartos that followed in 1602 and 1619. The First Folio presents the first good version of the play. If we can assume that the Chorus of Act V was written at the same time as the rest of the play, we have an accurate date for the composition, for the Chorus refers to the Earl of Essex as absent in Ireland, and he was there between late March and late September, 1599. The play undoubtedly was written soon after the two parts of *Henry IV,* and on the basis of internal evidence, 1599 is a satisfactory date for it.

For his source, Shakespeare again went to Holinshed's *Chronicles* (second edition, 1587), but he also referred to Hall's and Stowe's *Chronicles* and the old chronicle play, *The Famous Victories of Henry V.*

Basically *Henry V* is itself a chronicle play, dealing with a great period in English history—from shortly after the coronation of Henry V until the time of his marriage to Katharine of France. It has to do principally with Henry's victories in France, especially the famous victory of Agincourt, when Henry with a small force destroyed a vastly superior French army.

Henry V appears to have been Shakespeare's ideal king. He was a man of action, was witty, magnanimous, patriotic, charming as a lover, and democratic, although he could be austere and peremptory when it suited his purpose. Some commentators have deplored his attitude toward Falstaff, now old, broken, and dying; but this is to misunderstand the higher implications of kingship as Shakespeare saw them. Falstaff, lovable as he is on the stage, was a questionable influence on the young prince. When Hal became king, he could not continue his relationship with Falstaff's band on the old terms without doing injustice to his high office. Those who believe he might at least have turned Falstaff away more gently are better acquainted with later romanticism than with the attitude toward the Crown of the average Englishman of Shakespeare's day. The failure of Richard II and other leaders in Shakespeare's plays resulted from the defect of too much sentimentality. Shakespeare's ideal leader is just, has no favorites, and is able to act without hesitation even when his personal feelings would direct him otherwise; but he is not superhuman. He has merely learned to submerge his personal feelings and to act for the common good. In all these ways, Henry V is an excellent ruler.

The comedy in *Henry V* is subordinated to the history. Henry's courting of Katharine, in which he can speak no French and she no English, is good comedy; and the characters of Bardolph, Fluellen, and Pistol are put in as a sop to the groundlings; but nowhere does the comedy approach the Falstaff scenes of the two previous plays. This is doubtless deliberate, for here Shakespeare deals with historical matters that interested him more than those he used to make up the historical episodes of *Henry IV,* and he needed his chief attention for them.

In *Henry V* Shakespeare has come into his full powers as a writer. He has thrown off the last shreds of Marlowe's influence. The blank verse, which comprises slightly more than half the lines of the play, is flexible, contains a fair proportion of light endings and run-on lines, and departs often from the decasyllabic lines of his earlier blank verse. The prose, especially in the parts dealing with the death of Falstaff, has the quality of actual speech. If the fun with Fluellen misses its point with us, it is well to remember that in Shakespeare's day the Welshman was often the butt of stage jokes and that the audiences of the time apparently relished this type of humor.

MUCH ADO ABOUT NOTHING

The first reference that has been found to *Much Ado about Nothing* is an entry in the Stationers' Register on August 4, 1600. In that year a good quarto was published. Meres does not mention the play; hence it is a fair inference that he did not know it when he made his list of Shakespeare's plays for his *Palladis Tamia* in 1598. In the quarto, the name of one of the actors, William Kempe, is preserved; but Kempe left the Lord Chamberlain's company early in 1599. These data apparently fix the time of the production of the play as the dramatic season of 1598–1599; and evidences of style, versification, and treatment of theme substantiate this date.

The main plot is a very old one, dating from about the fourth century; but Shakespeare found it in either Bandello's *Novelle* (1554) or Belleforest's *Histoires tragiques* (1569), which was translated from Bandello. Some of the finest parts of the play, the comic scenes in which Benedick and Beatrice and Dogberry and Verges appear, are apparently of Shakespeare's own invention.

The basic plot has implications of tragedy almost as dire as *Othello's*. Because of the villainy of one person, Don John, a sour, saturnine character who is embittered by his illegitimacy, the reputation of an innocent young woman, Hero, is destroyed in the eyes of nearly everyone, including her father. The theme is similar, therefore, to that used later, and much better, in *Othello;* and the machinations of the villain are almost as bad as those of Iago, and are based on as little reason. The treatment in the two plays, however, is very different, the activities of the villain in *Much Ado* being a subordinate part of the action. Here in the end matters turn out happily, or at least with a vindication of Hero's reputation and the patching up of a marriage between her and the young gallant who was courting her. By modern standards, influenced as they are by sentiment and romantic literature, Shakespeare seems to deal hardly with Hero, for she has little to say about who her lover is, she has to suffer the denunciations of everyone except her cousin Beatrice and one or two whom Beatrice's loyalty converts, and in the final resolution of the action she appears to be little more than a pawn. In considering these points, however, we must remember that Hero's part was taken at the time by a boy who as an apprentice would not loom very large among the actors, that Shakespeare was using an old plot about which he probably took little thought except to use it as a peg on which to hang the comic parts of the action, and that rapid stage performance tends to reduce the tragic implications of the plot. Shakespeare's real interest in *Much Ado* is shown in his characterizations of Beatrice and Benedick and of Dogberry and Verges. These are among his finest comic creations, the former two in the field of high comedy and the latter two in low comedy. The neat trick by which Benedick is caught and made to propose to Beatrice, and by which the wise Beatrice is caught and made to accept him, is one of Shakespeare's happiest bits of plotting. The whole play, in spite of the undertone of tragedy, is a "joyous" comedy. For the full enjoyment of the play the reader should not take the Hero-Claudio-Don John plot with too great seriousness, as some commentators have done. Shakespeare wrote the play for the stage, and on the stage interest centers on the comic characters. And in the end Hero gets her Claudio—and perhaps neither is much cheated.

About three fourths of *Much Ado* is prose, in the writing of which Shakespeare by this time has complete mastery. The play contains only 643 lines of blank verse and very few riming lines. Of these about one fifth have double, or feminine, endings, and there are many run-on lines.

JULIUS CAESAR

Our first unmistakable reference to *Julius Caesar* is in John Weever's *Mirror of Martyrs*, which was printed in 1601, but which Weever says in his book was ready for the printer "some two yeares agoe":

> The many-headed multitude were drawne
> By *Brutus* speach, that *Caesar* was ambitious;
> When eloquent *Mark Antonie* had showne
> His vertues, who but *Brutus* then was vicious?

Since Weever would hardly refer to the play unless it were reasonably new, this would indicate for it a date near 1599. Meres does not mention it in his *Palladis Tamia* list in 1598, a point which indicates that it appeared after Meres made his list. A possible reference to the play is in Thomas Platter's account of his travels where he reports crossing the Thames on September 21, 1599, to see a "Tragedy vom ersten Keyser Julio Caesare." Other plays about Julius Caesar were apparently in existence then, but certain details that Platter gives of the play he attended make us believe that it was Shakespeare's drama. Internal evidence, moreover, supports the date of 1599 as an acceptable one for the play.

Julius Caesar was first published in the Folio. A criticism of Shakespeare by Ben Jonson for a line in the play that ran originally:

> Caesar did never wrong, but with just cause,

indicates that Jonson did not question Shakespeare's authorship of the drama; and in his memorial poems to Shakespeare in the First and Second Folios, Leonard Digges singles out the play for special mention. Yet some scholars have professed to find in it the work of other writers, ranging from Marlowe and Kyd to Jonson himself and Drayton. Such conjectures arise from the difference in style between this and other plays of the period. It has, for instance, a greater simplicity of diction and a more marked restraint in the use of language than have other plays of this date, from which facts some scholars infer an early version; but the difference in style may just as easily be attributable to the theme and to what Chambers calls Shakespeare's deliberate experimentation "in a classical manner, with an extreme simplicity both of vocabulary and of phrasing." [14] On the whole this seems the correct explanation, especially in the light of Jonson's and Digges's comment and with no other reasons for attributing the authorship to anyone else.

Shakespeare's principal, and perhaps sole, source was Plutarch's *Lives of the Noble Grecians and Romans* in the translation of Sir Thomas North (1579), a work usually referred to simply as North's *Plutarch*. References have been found to older plays about Julius Caesar, but as none of these is extant, we have no way of knowing whether Shakespeare was indebted to any of them. He often uses the very words of North's *Plutarch;* hence even if he had other sources, we know that the North translation was a basic source.

Perhaps in his drama Shakespeare was doing no more than trying to catch and portray the action involving a great figure at a crucial point in history; but if so, by the time he came to write the play he had become so deeply interested in studying the characters and the motives of men that he placed his emphasis on these matters. As the plot develops, the most important character is Brutus, a noble idealist, whose motives Shakespeare scrutinizes with attentive care. The drama unfolds the story of Caesar's temptation to become emperor, and the decision of a band who considered themselves patriots to thwart this move. In the conflict, both Caesar and his leading

---

[14] Chambers, *op cit.*, I, 399.

opponents die, and we have no final answer to the question of what is right and what is wrong, or of how far men should go in trying to supplant Fate in the direction of history. An important minor theme of the play—one to which Shakespeare recurs in other dramas—is the fickleness of the mob and the ease with which it can be swayed.

AS YOU LIKE IT

As You Like It was entered in the Stationers' Register on August 4, 1600, where it was marked "to be staid" (that is, not to be printed at this time); and, so far as we know, it was never printed until its inclusion in the Folio. It is not listed by Meres. In Act III, v, 81–82, is a reference—

> Dead shepherd, now I know thy saw of might,
> "Who ever lov'd that lov'd not at first sight?"—

to Marlowe's *Hero and Leander,* which was first printed in 1598. These limits help to fix the date at about 1599, and the style, versification, and treatment of theme substantiate this date.

Shakespeare's source for the play was a romance by Thomas Lodge entitled *Rosalynde, or Euphues' Golden Legacy* (1590), and Lodge in turn took the story from an anonymous *Tale of Gamelyn,* which dates from the fourteenth century.

Shakespeare crowds his play with romantic elements. A duke whose place is usurped withdraws with his loyal followers to the greenwood. The duke's daughter, Rosalind, left behind with the usurping duke, her uncle, falls in love with a youth whom she sees win a wrestling match, and who, to escape a plot against him by a wicked brother, flees to the greenwood where Rosalind's father has taken refuge. Later, when Rosalind's uncle grows jealous of the people's pity and love for Rosalind and banishes her from the court, she too goes to the greenwood, accompanied by her loyal cousin, his daughter. In the forest, Rosalind disguises herself as a boy, and on meeting the youth

INTRODUCTIONS TO THE PLAYS 107

with whom she has fallen in love, and who is going about the forest pinning up verses to her, she persuades him to pretend that she is Rosalind and to make love to her. Among the followers of the banished duke is the melancholy Jaques, who represents one of the "humorous" types[15] made popular by Ben Jonson in his *Every Man in His Humour* (first acted about September, 1598, by Shakespeare's own company). The play also includes a number of minor themes in which Phebe, a shepherdess; Touchstone, one of Shakespeare's merriest clowns; and Aubrey, a county wench, play parts.

The elements that make up the play are too many and too diverse for perfect unity, but the play gave Elizabethan audiences just what they wanted. The title is probably taken from a line in Lodge's *Rosalynde,* in the address to the reader: "If you like it, so"—that is, "If you like it, well and good"—but it may possibly carry the additional meaning, "Here is a play with all the elements in it that you in the audience seem to expect in a drama." At least it had many of the elements most popular at the time with London audiences: a greenwood setting, the melancholy man, intrigue, a romantic love affair, a wrestling match, and many others—and a happy ending for all the good characters. The plot is involved and loosely constructed, but the delightful poetry and songs, the merry dialogue, and the philosophizings of Jaques make this one of the pleasantest of the "joyous" comedies.

Slightly more than half of *As You Like It* is prose. About a third is blank verse; the rest is rime. The verse has a great many run-on lines and double endings. Shakespeare's style is now completly adequate for what he wants to express. He has a masterly control over his language. If he still used occasional

---

[15] The Elizabethans distinguished four types of "humors": melancholia, phlegm, blood, and choler. These were four elements that when perfectly mixed made a sound, whole man; but if a man had a preponderance of any one element, he acted "in his humor." The humors, in other words, caused various types of indiosyncrasies.

puns, quibbles, and conceits, that too was as his audiences liked it.

TWELFTH NIGHT

John Manningham of the Middle Temple recorded in his *Diary* that on February 2, 1602, "wee had a play called Twelue Night, or What You Will," the play then apparently being new to him. A reference (III, ii, 85) to "The new map with the augmentation of the Indies" is probably to a map by Emerie Molyneux (*c*. 1599); and the "pension of thousands to be paid from the Sophy" (II, v, 197) is supposed to allude to the return from Persia of Sir Robert Shirley in 1599 with rich gifts from the Shah. Evidences of style, versification, and treatment identify the play with the joyous comedies of about 1599–1600. If, as some suppose, the title refers to the time when the play was first acted—that is, Epiphany, or Twelfth Night, the last day of the Christmas festivities—it must have been performed on Twelfth Night in 1600 or one of the following two years. Authorities incline toward the earlier date because of the treatment of the theme and the gay humor of the play. As indicated in the next paragraph, however, the title may have had nothing to do with the time of its first performance.

Shakespeare apparently knew a version of the story that forms the main plot of *Twelfth Night* as told by Barnabe Riche in his *Riche his Farewell to the Militarie Profession* (1581). Riche in turn got the story from Bandello's *Novelle* or from Belleforest's *Histoires tragiques,* a translation of Bandello, either or both of which Shakespeare probably knew also. The story goes back ultimately to a comedy, *Gl' Ingannati,* written about 1531 by an anonymous member of the academy of Intronati; and there seems a likelihood that Shakespeare knew this source, for in the induction to that play are the names Fabio and Malevolti, close approximations of Fabian and Malvolio, names that appear in Shakespeare's comedy but that are not in the other sources; and there also is mention of "la notte di Beffana," or Epiphany (Twelfth Night), which may possibly have suggested Shakespeare's title. The comic scenes relating to Sir Toby, Andrew Aguecheek, and Malvolio are apparently Shakespeare's own invention.

The main plot deals with the effort of Duke Orsino of Illyria to win the hand of a rich and noble lady, Olivia, who, claiming to be in seclusion because of the death of a brother, refuses to receive him. Viola, a young woman of good family, is shipwrecked on the coast of Illyria, and disguising herself as a page, enters the employ of Orsino, with whom she presently falls in love. Orsino sends Viola as his envoy to court Olivia, and Olivia falls in love with her. Meanwhile, Viola's twin brother, Sebastian, from whom she was separated in the shipwreck, arrives in the same neighborhood, and considerable confusion results over one's being mistaken for the other, before matters are cleared up. All of this leads to "much good foolery" before the action is resolved with Olivia's getting Sebastian for husband, and Orsino's deciding to be content with Viola. But as in other plays in which Shakespeare uses an old tale for his main plot, the best parts of the play are those he creates himself. In the subplot, in which Sir Toby, Andrew, Maria, and the clown use the vain and pedantic Malvolio, Olivia's steward, as the butt of an elaborate joke, Shakespeare gives us some of his best comic scenes.

The play has less wit than *Much Ado* and less exquisite poetry than *As You Like It,* but the plot is worked out with more art than in either of these. In *Twelfth Night,* indeed, the romantic main plot and the realistic details of the subplot are blended with more care and with a greater perfection than in any play Shakespeare had written up to then.

THE MERRY WIVES OF WINDSOR

The first external evidence that we have of *The Merry Wives of Windsor* is an entry in the Stationers' Register on January 18, 1602. In the same year a quarto was issued, with the title page running, in part, as follows: "A Most pleasaunt and excellent conceited Comedie, of Syr Iohn Falstaffe, and the merrie Wiues of Windsor Entermixed with sundrie variable and pleasing humours, of Syr Hugh the Welch Knight, Iustice Shallow, and his wise Cousin M. Slender. With the swaggering vaine of Auncient Pistoll, and Corporall Nym. By William Shakespeare. As it hath bene diuers times Acted by the right Honorable my Lord Chamberlaines seruants. Both before her Maiestie, and else-where." This was a bad quarto, apparently made by a reporter who played the part of the Host in the play.

Authorities differ considerably over the date of the play. According to an old legend, Shakespeare wrote it in response to a command of Queen Elizabeth to write a play showing Falstaff in love. In *Henry V* he had shown Falstaff dying, but if *The Merry Wives* was written in response to a royal command, it is not necessary to suppose that it antedates *Henry V*. Even in the Folio text the play shows evidence of haste in composition, and there may be truth in the old tradition that Shakespeare wrote it in fourteen days in response to the Queen's request. Some elements of the play have been shown to satirize events connected with a visit to England of Frederick, Count of Mömpelgart, and subsequent matters connected with the visit. This visit took place in 1592, but as echoes of it lasted throughout Elizabeth's reign, about all that can be asserted from this information is that the play was not written before about 1593. Some scholars, however, assign the play to that year, and conjecture a later revision. But all the internal evidence points to a later date; and on the basis of all the evidence that can be gathered, it seems best to assume that the play as we have it is not a revision and that the date of composition was about 1598–1600.

In spite of the title page of the quarto, the inclusion of the play in the Folio, and the legend about Shakespeare's writing it in response to the Queen's command, some scholars profess to find in it the hands of other authors, but their conjectures rest on the most flimsy evidence, or none, and are not accepted by most reputable scholars.

The plot was possibly Shakespeare's own invention, though he may have based it on an old play, now lost. He perhaps received suggestions from a number of sources: "The Two Lovers of Pisa" in Tarleton's *Newes out of Purgatorie* (1590), which in turn was based on Giovanni Straparola's *Le Tredeci piacevoli notte; The Jealous Comedy* (1593); Plautus's *Casina*, and others. But the indebtedness to any of these would have been slight.

This is Shakespeare's sole play dealing with bourgeois characters and manners. The treatment is farcical. Falstaff—and an utterly different Falstaff from the one of *Henry IV*—makes love to two matrons, one of whom has an excessively jealous husband. The matrons lead Falstaff on and involve him in a number of humiliating incidents. A minor subplot concerns the efforts of the daughter of one of the matrons to marry a man of her own choice instead of either of the two men selected for her by her parents. The characters for the most part are mere types—a rare occurrence in Shakespeare's plays. Among them Slender is best individualized. Sir Hugh Evans and Dr. Caius are types of the "humorous" character made popular by Ben Jonson in his *Every Man in His Humour* (1598).

The play, except for some three hundred lines, is written in prose. Because of the subject matter of the play, the prose is undistinguished, but it reflects well the characters who make up the comedy.

The plays of the second period evidence a marked advance in style and technical skill and characterization. In prose Shakespeare had achieved full mastery. In poetry he had developed a flowing, flexible style that lent itself excellently to the stage and gave the illusion of actual speech. He had learned to deal with plots in such a way that he was not bound by them, yet was able to use them well for his purposes. Also, he had gone far deeper in his probings of human nature and his understanding of character. He was now ready for his greatest works.

THIRD PERIOD: TRAGEDIES AND "BITTER" COMEDIES

HAMLET

A play concerning Hamlet was apparently well known by 1589. In that year Thomas Nashe, in an address "To the Gentlemen Students of both Vniuersities" in Robert Greene's *Menaphon* wrote, ". . . if you intreate him [Seneca] faire in a frostie morning, he will affoord you whole *Hamlets,* I should say handfulls of tragical speaches." On June 11, 1594, Philip Henslowe recorded in his diary a performance of *Hamlet* by the Admiral's or Chamberlain's Men, and he did not mark the play as "new," as he was accustomed to do for first performances. Thomas Lodge in *Wit's Miserie* (1596) speaks of "the Visard of ye ghost which cried so miserably at ye Theator, like an oister wife, Hamlet, revenge." Several clues point to Thomas Kyd as the author of this play. The theme, so far as this can be ascertained from a study of Shakespeare's version, bore a close resemblance to the theme of Kyd's *Spanish Tragedy*. Before Kyd had turned translator and dramatist, he had followed his father's occupation of scrivener or "noverint"—a copier of writs, wills, and other law documents. In his "address" at the point where Nashe makes his reference to "whole *Hamlets,*" he is attacking those who "leave the trade of *Noverint* whereto they were born, and busy themselves with the endeavors of Art" and who base their work on Seneca. Then he goes on, "Seneca let blood line by line and page by page at length must needs die to our stage: which makes his famisht followers to imitate the Kidde in Aesop, who enamored with the Fox's new fangles, forsook all hopes of life to leap into a new occupation." This is thought to be a direct allusion to Kyd. From these allusions and references, scholars generally accept the theory of an early version of *Hamlet* and of Kyd's authorship of it.

A further assumption which is generally agreed on is that the old play came into possession of the Chamberlain's Men as a result of the changes which took place after the plague years of 1592–1594, and that as the old play continued popular, it was turned over to Shakespeare for revision. If we accept this theory, we must also assume that Shakespeare became interested in the theme or saw possibilities in it that the early version lacked, for he reworked it completely. Exactly when this revision took place is not known, but all clues point to its being near 1600–1602.

The play was entered in the Stationers' Register on July 26, 1602, and in 1603 a bad quarto was issued. A second quarto was published in 1604 with a title page that read, "The Tragicall Historie of Hamlet, Prince of Denmarke. By William Shakespeare. Newly imprinted and enlarged to almost as much againe as it was, according to the true and perfect Coppie." Not only is Q2 nearly twice as long as Q1, but it contains more than two hundred lines not in the Folio. The Folio version, in turn, has about eighty-five lines not in Q2. An exceptionally poor piece of work, Q1 was obviously a stolen copy, and it was probably to replace so corrupt a version that Q2 was issued.

The old play already discussed was doubtless Shakespeare's main source for *Hamlet*. It in turn probably was based on a story in the *Historiae Danicae* of Saxo Grammaticus. Belleforest also went to Saxo Grammaticus for his version in the *Histoires tragiques*, which apparently Shakespeare also knew.

On the surface, *Hamlet* is a "revenge" play, a type made popular by Kyd and his followers; but in Shakespeare's hands it becomes a study of a sensitive young man, brought up to believe in abstract justice and the rightness of men's motives, who is thrown into a state of maladjustment and mental confusion when he discovers that all his preconceived notions are wrong. This confusion results from his having to face a series of evils, one coming so quickly on another that he has no time to become adjusted to one set of circumstances before another confronts him. These are (1) the remarriage of his mother so shortly after her husband's death that she has not completed even a decent period of mourning; (2) the thwarting of justice by the connivance of the nobles with Claudius to secure for the latter the crown that Hamlet considers rightfully his; (3) the terrible knowledge that the new king has murdered his own brother, the former king and Hamlet's father, and has seduced Hamlet's mother; (4) the jilting of Hamlet, as he took it, by Ophelia, with whom he is in love; and (5) the betrayal of friendship by his supposed former friends Rosencrantz and Guildenstern. While faced with all these matters, Hamlet is given an assignment that might well dash the spirit even of a man of action— to avenge his father's death by destroying the new king. Hamlet, unfortunately for him as matters turn out, is less a man of action than a poet and philosopher. His sudden awareness of all the evil in the world about him, in contrast to his previous concepts, and his failure for a time to find anything in which he can believe, plunge him into such despondency that rather than accept the responsibility laid on him he longs for death and is restrained from killing himself only by his religious training. He reaches his nadir in the scenes in which he expresses doubt as to the honesty of the ghost and, shortly afterward, speaks the famous soliloquy beginning, "To be or not to be." From this point begins his slow recovery. First, he finds in Horatio a friend he can trust. Through the "mouse-trap" play he learns that the ghost is really that of his father and not an evil spirit sent to entrap him. After a terrible scene with his mother, he comes to a better understanding with her. Even his accidental killing of Polonius, since it involved action, aids in his adjustment. And after the death of Ophelia he apparently comes to a better opinion of her than he had when he so cuttingly advised her to enter a nunnery.

The problem of *Hamlet* as Shakespeare developed the play was really a double one: how the hero could become adjusted to the world as it really existed and how he could carry out the injunction of the ghost to rid Denmark of a king who was a murderer and adulterer. In both these respects the problem is worked out successfully. The play, nevertheless, is a tragedy, and a tragedy that results from a defect in Hamlet's character, his slowness to act. In the early part of the play, while he delays the task imposed on him, the evil forces become stronger. He is able in the end to destroy them, but they have gathered strength enough to carry him with them in the general destruction.

Shakespeare's *Hamlet* is doubtless conditioned by the old drama on which it was based, and the end is in accordance with the earlier version. The play, nevertheless, has a unity that is obvious if we keep in mind Shakespeare's main intention. We must bear in mind that Hamlet rightfully should have been king. Then if we consider Henry V, who was Shakespeare's ideal king, we can see how far short of kingly attributes Hamlet was in the early part of the play. Because Hamlet at first lacked an essential quality of kingship, that of action, the initiative was taken from him, and in the latter part of the play, things are done to him instead of by him. The contrast is between a man of action, Claudius, and a man of inaction; and the final events occur because a man of action plans them—or plans the main situation out of which the final action evolves. The tragedy is that Hamlet dies just when he has learned the lessons anyone must know who would rule well. If we understand these matters rightly, *Hamlet* will be seen to have a consistency throughout.

Almost two thirds of *Hamlet* is written in blank verse and a little less than a third in prose. Shakespeare's mastery of each medium is clearly evident. Because Hamlet attracts our notice so constantly, we tend sometimes to neglect the many minor excellencies of the play: the portrayal of the court butterfly Osric, with his outmoded euphuism; the inspired picture of the mad Ophelia; the beautifully drawn character of the loyal and devoted Horatio; and the fine lecture—the only one on this particular subject in Shakespeare—on drama and acting, by the greatest of all dramatists.

TROILUS AND CRESSIDA

Troilus and Cressida was entered in the Stationers' Register on February 7, 1603, but no edition was issued then. It was entered again on January 28, 1609, and a quarto edition was published that year. The first issue of Q1 bore on the title page the notation "As it was acted by the Kings Maiesties seruants at the Globe. Written by William Shakespeare." Shortly after, a second issue appeared omitting the statement about the play's having been acted, and with an epistle stating that it was "neuer stal'd with the Stage." We have no way of knowing which statement is true or why the divergent statements were made or who caused the change. The first quarto is now considered a good quarto; hence if the statement of the play's being acted is an error, it was probably made through an oversight, which the second issue corrected.

It is probable that the speech of the Prologue, "And hither am I come/A prologue arm'd . . . ," carries a reference to the Prologue of Jonson's *Poetaster* (1601). This of course may not have been written at the time of the play itself, but other references in the body of the play to writings that can be dated indicate that it was written about 1601–1602. The links with the bitter comedies and early tragedies of the period, the style, and the general treatment point to a date close to 1602.

In spite of the ascription of the play to Shakespeare in Q1 and its inclusion in the Folio, certain scholars have thought that they detected in it the hand of some other dramatist or dramatists, but there is no valid evidence for such conjectures, and only the flimsiest of reasons for them. The matter has perhaps been confused somewhat because of the existence of other plays on the theme. Also the theme itself and the treatment have led some authorities to try to father the play on someone else. Shakespeare, however, no more than any other author, could be permanently on the mountain top. There appears no valid reason to doubt that the play is wholly Shakespeare's, nor any scholarly evidence on which to base a different assumption.

Shakespeare's chief source was Chaucer's *Troilus and Criseyde,* but he apparently also used Caxton's *Recuyell of the*

Historyes of Troye, Chapman's translation of Homer's *Iliad,* Robert Henryson's *Testament of Cresseid,* and perhaps Lydgate's *Hystorye, Sege and dystruccyon of Troye.* Although the background is that of the latter years of the Trojan war, told from the Trojan point of view, the play is a study of several unlovable characters. The main plot is about Troilus, youngest son of Priam, King of Troy, and Cressida, a beautiful Trojan maiden with whom Troilus is madly in love. She is attracted to him, but feigns indifference. With the help of her uncle, Pandarus, Troilus becomes her lover, but after one night with her he is told that her father, a Trojan priest who is serving with the Greeks, has arranged to have her brought to him in exchange for a captured Trojan, and that she must go to the Greek camp. The lovers vow eternal constancy and exchange tokens, but afterward, when Troilus spies on her in the Greek camp, he finds her flirting with the Greek Diomedes and arranging an assignation with him. Disillusioned, Troilus returns to Troy, and in the next day's fighting he seeks out Diomedes but does not slay him. As he leaves the field, Troilus meets Pandarus, whom he denounces. There the story ends, with nothing resolved. Troilus is merely a little wiser concerning women, or at least one kind of woman. A minor plot has to do with the sullenness of Achilles, his being aroused finally to fight, and his killing of Hector, which, according to this version, he does by taking Hector when the latter is unarmed. The play contains only two admirable characters: the brave Hector and the wise Ulysses. Cressida is a heartless coquette or worse, Troilus a weak but romantic lover, Pandarus a sensual realist, Achilles lacking in chivalry, and Thersites, though but a minor character, the most foulmouthed of all Shakespeare's creations. Many explanations have been offered for Shakespeare's manner of treating his theme in this play. Of these, perhaps the most satisfactory is that he was trying his hand at a type of play then popular, in which love and heroism are treated satirically.

ALL'S WELL THAT ENDS WELL

There is no external evidence by which to date *All's Well*. It was first published in the Folio. Some scholars have sought to identify it with *Love's Labour's Won*, a title appearing in Francis Meres' list in his *Palladis Tamia* (1598), because no play of this title has come down to us, and the title fits the theme of *All's Well That Ends Well*. This identification, however, is mere conjecture; the title would fit several other comedies as well as this play. A line in the play, "*Lustig*, as the Dutchman says," apparently refers to the frequent use of "lustick" by a Dutchman in *The Weakest Goeth to the Wall* (*c.* 1600). If this is true, such a reference would be made only when the term was in everyone's mind, and this evidence, though extremely slight, may indicate an early limit for the play. Some elements of style, however, link it with the third period, and the theme and the way the theme is treated link it with the bitter comedies. Because of the many classical allusions, the use of rime in letters and other passages where prose would be used normally, and the marked differences in style between passages, most authorities believe that the play as we have it is a revision of an earlier draft, and on this theory to identify it with the *Love's Labour's Won* mentioned by Meres. If so, the early version was of course written before 1598. Chambers,[16] however, explains the use of rime as having, in general, a dramatic purpose, and he rejects the theory of an early version. Whatever may be the truth about an early version, scholars are in general agreement in dating the Folio version between 1600 and 1603.

Because of the unpleasantness of the main plot, the unsavoriness of some of the characters, and the unevenness of the style, some scholars have been reluctant to attribute the play wholly to Shakespeare. But no grounds other than the belief that it is inferior to the joyous comedies and the great tragedies of the third period exist for such an assumption. Most scholars, there-

---

[16] Chambers, *op. cit.*, I, 451.

fore, accept it as the sole work of Shakespeare, whether written early and revised or belonging wholly to the third period.

The main plot is taken from Boccaccio's *Decameron* (the ninth story of the third day) as retold by William Painter in his *Palace of Pleasure* (1566). The play relates how Helena, a woman of comparatively low birth, by constancy and intrigue wins as her husband a man of noble birth. As the daughter of a physician, Helena has a remedy with which she saves the life of the king of France. He promises her as reward whatever she asks, and she requests that she be given her choice of husband from the men at Court. Bertram, the man she loves, is there, but when she chooses him, he rejects her, and only the command of the king forces him to marry her. Immediately after the ceremony he leaves her, saying that he will never receive her as his wife until she possesses the ring on his finger and is with child by him. Through complicated intrigue Helena fulfills these requirements and is accepted by Bertram as his wife.

Various estimates of Helena have been made by scholars, ranging from those who consider her wholly admirable to those who regard her as a forward and designing woman. Bertram is no ideal hero, and several of the minor characters are far from estimable, the worst being Bertram's follower, Parolles. One who helps redeem the list of unpleasant characters is Bertram's mother, the Countess of Rousillon, who is both gracious and charming.

The style of *All's Well* is very uneven, a circumstance that favors scholars who believe Shakespeare revised an early version of the play. A considerable part is written in rimed couplets, with puns and conceits. Another part is in blank verse of his later period—with run-on lines, double endings, and compact expression.

MEASURE FOR MEASURE

The first mention of *Measure for Measure* is a record in the *Revels Account* of a performance at Court on December 26,

1604. A severe epidemic of the plague had led to the closing of the theaters from May, 1603, to April, 1604, and it is probable that *Measure for Measure* was one of the new plays performed after the reopening of the theaters. In theme, method of treatment, and style it can be grouped with *Troilus and Cressida* and *All's Well That Ends Well*. The play was first published in the Folio. There the text is so corrupt that it suggests either attempts at revision or a garbled copy.

Shakespeare's main source for *Measure for Measure* was a play by George Whetstone, *Promos and Cassandra* (1578), and a prose version of the story by the same author in his *Heptameron of Civil Discourses* (1582); but he also consulted Whetstone's source, Geraldi Cinthio's *Hecatommithi* (1565). He seems to have used Cinthio's play, *Epitia*, too, on the same theme. Cinthio's story is said to have been based on an actual happening near Milan in 1547.

The rather complicated plot provides a drama of romantic intrigue. Vincentio, Duke of Vienna, pretending to be called away on urgent business, leaves affairs in the hands of Angelo, one of whose first acts is to condemn to death a young gentleman, Claudio, for seducing his fiancee, Juliet. Vincentio, however, disguised as a friar, remains in Vienna to observe Angelo's rule and the actions of his people. Claudio enlists the aid of his sister, Isabella, a novice in a convent, to appeal to Angelo, who falls in love with her and offers to spare her brother if she will become his mistress. In a highly dramatic scene, Isabella informs Claudio of the condition on which he may be saved, declaring that she will not sacrifice her honor for his life and expecting him to agree with her. Claudio at first accepts her decision, but the thought of death makes him change his mind and plead with her to make the sacrifice. Finally, through the aid of Vincentio, who has kept up with the affair, Claudio is saved and marries Juliet, Angelo is condemned but later is spared at the request of Mariana, who has taken Isabella's place by a device similar to that employed in *All's Well That Ends Well*. Vincentio marries Isabella.

A little more than half of *Measure for Measure* is written in blank verse, and a little more than a third is in prose. The poetry is uneven. The blank verse is in Shakespeare's later style, with run-on lines, double endings, pauses in the middle of lines, and substitute feet; but some of the riming lines are poor, as if they were written hurriedly. The prose is that of his later periods: it still contains quibbles, puns, and innuendoes, but it is more compact, yet more like natural speech, than was much of his early prose. Some of the scenes are in his best vein, but the play is lacking in the high comedy that turned such a commonplace plot as that of *Much Ado about Nothing* into a superlative drama. Some authorities believe that Shakespeare at first designed the play as a tragedy and later devised a "happy" ending, and that this may account for the quality of the humor. In general, the characterizations are weak, yet Isabella is one of his greatest feminine creations, and Angelo and Vincentio are well drawn.

OTHELLO

In the *Revels Account* is an entry of *Othello's* being played at Court, "in the banqueting house at Whitehall," on November 1, 1604. Scholars usually assign its composition to that year, because the internal evidence indicates that it was written at about that period. It was first published in 1622, a quarto edition being issued shortly before the publication of the Folio. The quarto and Folio versions are slightly different: the quarto has about 160 lines not in the Folio, the spelling of some names is different, and a few other minor differences occur. Both, however, are based on good texts.

Shakespeare took his plot for *Othello* from Cinthio's *Hecatommithi*, but he changed in many ways the story as told by Cinthio: he added all of Act I, introduced new elements, created the Othello and Iago of the play, and changed the ending.

The plot relates how a noble Moor who marries a young Venetian girl is aroused to such jealousy by the machinations of a villain, Iago, that he murders his completely innocent wife. But the psychological problem of the play is why Iago turns to such villainy. Iago has been called the greatest villain in literature, but actually he is no worse than Claudius in *Hamlet* and not so bad as Aaron in *Titus Andronicus*. What makes him appear so villainous is the exquisite care with which Shakespeare delineates his character, the small compass of the action, and the extent to which our interest in Othello and Desdemona is aroused, so that we are made to feel the utmost reach of the tragedy. Iago's moves are actuated by a philosophy of egoism that leads him to wish to dominate others. Like other egoists, he misjudges his abilities, supposing that he has such qualities as will enable him to involve others without involving himself. At first, apparently, he has no aim except to stir up trouble between Othello and his wife to see what may happen, as a child with an unawakened conscience might torture a cat to watch its actions. But Othello is a stronger, more powerful, and more complex character than Iago has suspected. In arousing Othello's jealousy, Iago arouses a force beyond his power to control; and at last, to save his own life, he is compelled to extend his plans to include the deaths of Desdemona and Cassio, whom he makes Othello believe to be Desdemona's lover. But this extension of his plan does not save him, for his villainy is brought to light from a quarter wholly unexpected by him, when his wife, Emilia, whom he had supposed completely under his domination, defies his orders and exposes him. The evil forces set in motion by Iago move to an inevitable conclusion, in which Othello, one of Shakespeare's noblest creations, realizing that he has been duped by a villain into murdering his wholly innocent wife, commits suicide out of a sense of justice, honor, and love.

Othello is the most realistic of Shakespeare's tragedies. The poetry rises to the height of the tragic situation, the humor is made part of the action, and every step of the action is carefully motivated. The technique is flawless, and the portrayal of character, at least in Iago and Othello, matches the technique. Many consider this Shakespeare's greatest play.

KING LEAR

King Lear was entered in the Stationers' Register on November 26, 1607; and the entry included a notation that "yt was played before the Kinges maiestie at Whitehall vppon Sainct Stephens night at Christmas Last" (December 26, 1606). The names of devils mentioned by Edgar in IV, i, 60–65, were apparently taken from Samuel Harsnett's *Declaration of Popish Impostures,* which was published in 1603. The mention of "these late eclipses" by Gloucester is thought to be a reference to a partial eclipse of the moon and a total eclipse of the sun in September and October, 1605. Some editors also conjecture that Gloucester's speech about "machinations, hollowness, treachery" glanced at the Gunpowder Plot of November 5, 1605; and Kent's assertion that he ate no fish as testimony of his loyalty[17] possibly supports this conjecture. On the basis of these conjectural allusions, the external evidence, and all internal evidence, scholars are in general agreement in dating the play as late 1605 or early 1606.

An old play, *The moste famous Chronicle historye of Leire kinge of England and His Three Daughters,* probably suggested Shakespeare's tragedy, but if it did, he received little from it beyond the suggestion. He obviously knew the story in Holinshed's *Chronicles,* his chief source, and he apparently also knew the versions of the Lear story in John Higgins' *Mirror for Magistrates* and in Spenser's *Faerie Queene.* But he dealt freely with his sources, adding a subplot, creating the fool, and providing a tragic ending instead of the traditional one in which Cordelia wins the war, restores Lear to the throne, and on his

---

[17] The Gunpowder Plot was engineered by Catholic conspirators who planned to blow up the Parliament and King James. For a time after the discovery of the plot, feeling against Catholics was bitter. As the eating of fish on certain days was a Catholic observance, anyone hearing Kent's statement in this period of excitement would catch its significance. Some authorities do not accept this explanation, but it seems unlikely that Kent's speech would have any importance except at a time of such high tension.

death succeeds to the crown. For the subplot dealing with Gloucester and his two sons he went to Sidney's *Arcadia,* where he found a story entitled "The pitifull state, and story of the Paphlagonian unkinde kinge, and his kinde sonne," which, like the Lear story, dealt with the different attitudes of children in the same family toward a parent.

King Lear was published in a quarto edition in 1608; and a second quarto, set up from Q1, was issued in 1619. The first quarto and the Folio versions were set from different manuscripts, with a resultant difference in the texts. In Q1 there are about three hundred lines not in the Folio, and in the Folio about a hundred lines not in the quarto.[18]

King Lear is a tragedy of old age, the specific problem being one of the relation of parents to children and children to parents, and especially the differing attitudes of children in the same family toward a parent. In both the main plot and the subplot one child loves the parent but loses his favor, whereas another child—or two in the main plot—hates him but wins his favor. In the main plot, Lear, having no son, decides to divide his kingdom and to give an equal portion to each of his three daughters, of whom two are married and one is being courted by two suitors. As the play opens, the suitors for the hand of the youngest daughter, Cordelia, are about to receive their answer, and while waiting for them to be brought in, Lear tells the others of his decision to divide the kingdom. Because he is in his dotage and loves flattery, he invites his daughters to tell him how much they love him, promising to give most to the one who in this rivalry merits most. The fulsome flattery of the two elder daughters—and perhaps an attachment to one of the suitors that occupies part of her attention—leads Cordelia, who actually loves her father dearly, to refuse to engage in the rivalry. Lear, misapprehending the cause of her refusal, thereupon disinherits her and divides the kingdom

---

[18] For a discussion of the reasons for these differences, see Chambers, *op. cit.,* I, 464-467.

between the other daughters, Goneril and Regan, who actually hate him. In his anger, moreover, he makes other decisions that were not a part of the original plan, the chief one being to give away his actual power as king and to become, in effect, a dependent of the two daughters. The latter shortly combine to take away even the semblance of authority that he still retains. Their actions drive him from their shelter and finally to madness, whereupon Cordelia reappears, gives him succor, restores him to sanity, and wages war against the wicked sisters to regain his throne for him. In this last effort, however, she is unsuccessful. Through the villainy of Edmund (who, in the subplot, bears the same relation to his father as that of Goneril and Regan in the main plot to their father) Cordelia is hanged, and shortly afterward Lear follows her in death. Throughout the play the elder sisters rival each other in wickedness, and the deaths of Lear and Cordelia are made bearable for us only because Goneril and Regan and their wicked followers meet their just deserts. As in *Hamlet* and *Othello,* the good characters have strength enough to destroy the evil against which they struggle, but not enough to save themselves in the process.

In the subplot, Gloucester's illegitimate son plots to gain his father's title and estates. His motives for villainy are more obvious than those of Lear's two daughters, for as an illegitimate child he has no prospect of inheriting either property or rank. He joins forces with Lear's wicked daughters and for a time is successful, but in the end he loses, and Gloucester's loyal son is left to succeed his father and support the State.

King Lear lacks the closely knit structure of *Othello,* but the play is greater than *Othello* in the scope of its theme. The superb characterization of Lear himself is unsurpassed, and the other characters are scarcely less well portrayed. The poetry, in sweep and majesty, reaches a height that even Shakespeare rarely attains elsewhere. The fusion of comedy and tragedy through the use of the fool, whose foolery contributes to Lear's madness, led the poet Shelley to call *Lear* the greatest play ever written.

MACBETH

Macbeth was first published in the Folio. The earliest reference to it was a notation in the diary of Simon Forman on April 20, 1610, of his having seen it at the Globe.[19] Since it deals with the history of Scotland and has many elements that would have interested King James, scholars are in virtually unanimous agreement in the assumption that it was written after James's accession to the English throne. The meter and style are such as Shakespeare employed in the latter part of the third period. Adams[20] conjectures that it was one of the plays acted before the king at Whitehall during the Christmas season of 1606–1607, and scholars in general agree in assigning it to 1606.

Shakespeare's source was Holinshed's *Chronicles,* to which he went for all his English historical plays. In William Kempe's *Nine Days' Wonder* (1600) is a reference to an old play on the subject, but as this play has not survived, we are not certain that Shakespeare even knew it. All the elements he needed for his drama are in Holinshed.

The tragedy is a study of what happens to a noble, brave, loyal man, full of the milk of human kindness, with high imagination and poetical sensitivity, who yields to his own and his wife's ambition to embark on a career of crime in order to attain his ends. A comparison of the description of Macbeth

---

[19] Simon Forman was an astrological quack doctor who left notes on several of Shakespeare's plays. These notes are preserved in some manuscripts now in the Bodleian Library, Oxford. They were brought to light by J. P. Collier, a notorious forger of Shakespearean documents, and for this reason some scholars have been reluctant to accept them as genuine. See J. Q. Adams, *Macbeth* (Boston: 1931), pp. 293–298. It is now generally conceded, however, that they were not a Collier forgery. Yet if they were not a forgery, there was some error about the date, and Chambers believes the date to have been 1611, and that Forman wrote 1610 through an error. See Chambers, *op. cit.,* II, 337–338, where the notes are reproduced.

[20] Adams, *Life,* p. 377.

as the play opens with his own expressions of the futility of life in the last act serves to indicate the tragedy that results from this mistaken course. The use made by Shakespeare of the witches is a device only—and perhaps a gesture to the beliefs of James I—and hardly deserves the attention that it usually receives in high school studies of the play. The emphasis throughout is on the changes that take place in Macbeth's mind as he proceeds from crime to crime, and the effects on his inner being as he tries to stifle his conscience and dull his sensibilities by engaging in tyrannical acts that are more and more revolting.

In *Macbeth,* as in his other tragedies of this period, Shakespeare's style is consummate and incomparable: it has an economy of words, a weightiness of meaning, soaring poetry in which he uses every device—pauses, substitute feet, alternating strong and weak endings, run-on lines—to express each nuance and shade of meaning, and a use of metaphor and other figures of speech much less for ornamentation than for exact expression.

The Folio text indicates that the copy used was that of an acting version. It is the shortest of Shakespeare's plays except *The Comedy of Errors.* Adams conjectures that it was written in haste at the special request of James I. Most authorities believe that it underwent revision at other hands before its publication in the Folio. An analysis of the play discloses inconsistencies that make such a theory plausible; and it is possible that some scenes from the original version were lost by the time the copy was being gathered for the Folio. In one way, however, the brevity of the play is an advantage, for it makes the structure more clearly obvious: the first act portrays Macbeth as he was before he began his career of crime, and shows his temptation; the second act deals with his first crime and its immediate effects on him; the third act deals with the second crime and the growing effects on his mind and character; the fourth act deals with the third crime and prepares for the retribution, which comes in the fifth act.

ANTONY AND CLEOPATRA

Antony and Cleopatra was entered in the Stationers' Register on May 20, 1608. This fact, of course, fixes a final limit for the date, but a still earlier one can probably be established. In 1607, Samuel Daniel published a revised edition of his tragedy *Cleopatra,* in which he made changes that brought his portrayal of Cleopatra into conformity with that of Shakespeare's play. If Daniel instead of Shakespeare was the copyist, as what evidence we have indicates, the final date for *Antony and Cleopatra* can be fixed as 1607. Because all the internal evidence clearly places it late among Shakespeare's tragedies, authorities usually assign it to 1607 or at the earliest to 1606. Shakespeare's main source was Plutarch's *Lives*. In the historical events, he follows Plutarch closely, but his Cleopatra differs somewhat from Plutarch's version of her. As the Antony and Cleopatra story was popular in Renaissance literature, and it was Shakespeare's method to consult all available sources when he was treating a theme, it is plausible to suppose that he derived ideas for the character of Cleopatra from some source other than Plutarch. In spite of the entry in the Stationers' Register, no edition was issued. It first appeared in the Folio of 1623.

Antony and Cleopatra is a story of mature passion, as *Romeo and Juliet* is of youthful passion. Dryden's title for his adaptation of the story, *All for Love,* best suggests the theme, for it treats of Antony's loss of his kingdom and finally his life through his love for Cleopatra. The play deals with historical events over a number of years and is thus in form a chronicle, but it bears little resemblance to the chronicle plays that were popular when Shakespeare began his public career. In his treatment, Antony and Cleopatra become great tragic characters. The play has the color and sweep of a pageant, yet we are never allowed to lose sight of the two main characters and the struggle in which they are involved. Despite the lapse of years between the early and final episodes of the play, the tragedy has a unity more actual than any mere surface unity of time and place. Students of dramatic technique have criticized the play as lacking a middle, in the Aristotelian sense of the term, for Shakespeare used a technique often seen in moving pictures, that of developing fully the events at the beginning and end of the play, and summarizing those of the intervening years in a succession of brief scenes, or flashes. From the point of view of dramatic technique, such criticism is valid. But Shakespeare had to make a choice if he was to deal adequately with his material and yet develop his characters fully: he had to write a two-part chronicle in which there would be space for all these matters, or develop the first and last parts of the play—in which circumstance he needed to establish the relationships of his main characters and show how the seeds of tragedy were sown and how the final harvest grew from these seeds—at the expense of the middle. When we consider the great scenes of the first and last parts of the play, we cannot doubt the wisdom of his choice.

In *Antony and Cleopatra* Shakespeare's mastery of language and poetry is abundantly evident. The style is compressed, just a word or phrase often conveying what another playwright would require a scene to express. The words are freighted with meaning; yet they have a liquid quality unsurpassed even in his sonnets and early poetry. The characterizations are superb. Even minor characters are individualized, sometimes in a single speech. The two chief characters are drawn with the utmost fidelity. We feel that we know everything about Antony that can be known; of Cleopatra, however, we are not so certain. She is Shakespeare's most subtle character. Antony called her his serpent of old Nile—and we must remember that the Bible says the serpent is "more subtle than any beast of the field." Antony and Caesar are a complete contrast: Antony is warm, impetuous, quick to become angry and to be placated; Caesar is cool, deliberate, angry only when such a display can gain some end for him, but implacable in carrying out his policies. Even in small things they are different: Antony loves good food and good drink, Caesar is abstemious; Antony treats even servants with kindness, Caesar sneers at those who "smell of sweat." The tragedy results from the opposition of these two characters, though Antony's faults bring about the conflict and are therefore the underlying cause of the tragedy. Antony, Cleopatra, and Caesar being what they are, the result is inevitable—and inevitable action resulting from the character of the actors is the essence of great drama. Yet, however important Caesar's role, he is important only as he directs the action. The tragedy is about Antony and Cleopatra; and that Shakespeare recognized their equality as dramatic figures is shown by his giving the fourth act to Antony, who dies at the end of it, and the fifth to Cleopatra.

CORIOLANUS

Coriolanus was first published in the Folio, and there is no external evidence by which to date it. Style, versification, and treatment of theme, however, serve to place it very late in the third period. Most authorities believe it was written immediately after *Antony and Cleopatra,* because both plays are derived from the same source and the themes of both are treated similarly. In each, a strong man is brought to a tragic end by a woman—Antony because of his love for Cleopatra, Coriolanus because of the influence of his mother. Although the internal-external evidence is less reliable, several bits seem to point to a date near 1608. Of this evidence perhaps the most plausible is a reference to "the coal of fire upon the ice" (I, i, 179), which is thought to be an allusion to the burning of coals on the ice in the Thames River during the exceptionally cold winter of 1607–1608. Ben Jonson's *Silent Woman* (1609) has a line, "you have lurch'd your friends of the better half of the garland," which some scholars believe an echo of *Coriolanus* II, ii, 106: "he lurch'd all swords of the garland." If these surmises are correct, the limiting initial and terminal dates would be late 1607 and 1609. Most authorities assign the play to 1608.

Shakespeare took the story of Coriolanus from North's translation of Plutarch's *Lives,* the source he had used for *Antony*

INTRODUCTIONS TO THE PLAYS 131

and Cleopatra. A fable related in the first scene of Act I probably came from William Camden's *Remaines of a Greater Worke, Concerning Britain* (1605).

The play tells the story of Caius Marcius, later called Coriolanus, an exceptionally brave and able military leader, who is too proud and haughty to seek the favor of the people. This attitude so angers the mob that in spite of his past heroic deeds in defense of Rome they banish him, whereupon he joins the enemies of Rome, the Volscians. Because it is apparent to the Romans that he and Aufidius, the Volscian leader, are strong enough through their alliance to destroy Rome, his friends plead with him to spare the city. Finally, when members of his own family appeal to him, he relents, but Aufidius considers this an act of treachery and has him killed. The conflict in Coriolanus is between his great pride and his love for his wife and mother. His nobility, his greatness, and his generalship rival these qualities in Antony, but he lacks Antony's warmth and lovableness. As Antony's tragedy results from his great love for Cleopatra, so Coriolanus's tragedy results from his great affection for his family. The play, however, is usually considered a study of pride and of the destruction of a noble patrician by a Roman mob, for whom Shakespeare shows great distaste.

A little less than a fourth of *Coriolanus* is written in prose; nearly all the rest is blank verse. It belongs to the period when Shakespeare's style was most condensed and the words most heavily freighted with meaning. He employs ellipsis, substitute feet, run-on lines, and extra syllables freely. His writing in this period seems to indicate his impatience over the barrier of language between his idea and his audience.

TIMON OF ATHENS

No external evidence exists whereby we can date *Timon of Athens.* It was first published in the Folio, where it was inserted in the place of *Troilus and Cressida,* when the latter was temporarily withdrawn. Some authorities believe that Shakespeare left it in an incomplete state, that it was never staged, and that it was inserted by the editors in the Folio only to fill space left by the removal of *Troilus and Cressida*. These are only surmises, however, as we have no means of knowing whether it was ever played in Shakespeare's lifetime. The verse, style, theme, and general treatment suggest a late date in the third period, and most scholars agree in dating it about 1607–1608.

Shakespeare found a brief account of the story of Timon in Plutarch's life of Antony, but he apparently knew also a longer version of the story in William Painter's *Palace of Pleasure* (1566–1567). It is probable that he knew the *Timon* of the Greek satirist Lucian, for his play contains details that are in Lucian but are not in the other versions.

Timon of Athens is a tragedy of one who squanders his wealth on fawning sycophants until he has nothing left, and then learns too late how little he can trust the friendship of such persons. It is a study in disillusionment. Timon, in spite of the warning of his faithful steward, Flavius, and the ridicule of the churlish Apemantus, lavishes his wealth on those he believes to be his friends. On finding his wealth gone and on being pressed by creditors, he tries to borrow from those on whom he had showered gifts, but he is refused by them all. Thereupon he becomes a misanthrope and retires to a cave, where, while digging for roots on which to live, he finds buried treasure. Meanwhile, another Athenian, Alcibiades, who like Timon had suffered from the ingratitude of his fellows, raises an army and prepares to attack Athens. On his march to Athens, Alcibiades passes the cave of Timon, who on hearing of his mission furnishes him with funds. Word of Timon's wealth gets abroad, and he is visited by treasure-seekers and two thieves. To the latter Timon gives gold and such bitter praise of thievery that the thieves are almost converted. He is visited also by his faithful steward Flavius, whom he recognizes as the one honest man. To him Timon gives a huge sum on condition that Flavius will avoid men and show charity to none. Alcibiades meanwhile prepares to attack Athens but is appeased by the Senators, who agree that he may bring to judgment his and Timon's personal enemies. As the agreement is reached, word comes that Timon has died in his cave.

Timon's experience somewhat resembles that of Lear, and in a few passages the poetry of *Timon* rises to the level of that in *Lear*. For the most part, however, the dialogue is dull and lacking in beauty, the comedy is poor, and the structure incoherent. These flaws have led to a vast amount of speculation among scholars, some of whom conjecture that Shakespeare wrote a draft which someone else revised, and others that Shakespeare revised in a few places the work of another writer. E. K. Chambers believes that Shakespeare started work on the play but for some reason laid it by, and that as it stands it represents a half-finished product.[21]

FOURTH PERIOD: TRAGICOMEDIES

PERICLES, PRINCE OF TYRE

Pericles was entered in the Stationers' Register on May 20, 1608, and in 1609 a bad quarto was published by Henry Gosson. From the testimony of one Odoardo Guatz at a trial in Venice in 1617, we learn that the Venetian ambassador Giustinian when in London had accompanied the French ambassador and his wife to see *Pericles*. As Giustinian was in London from January 5, 1606, to November 23, 1608, *Pericles* must have been playing between these dates. A prose version of the story was written by George Wilkins and was published in 1608; it almost certainly followed the play. Because the theme and treatment have much in common with the tragicomedies of the fourth period, scholars generally agree in placing it early in the period. On the whole, the dramatic season of 1607–1608 seems a plausible date for it.

The work of at least two authors can be detected in the play. Because George Wilkins wrote a prose version of the story and because he is known to have been writing for the King's

---
[21] Chambers, *op. cit.*, I, 482.

Men in 1607, most authorities believe that he was one of the collaborators. Conjectures differ, however, as to the relationship of the authors. The problem is whether Wilkins, or another, started the play and Shakespeare completed it or whether Shakespeare discontinued the play after writing part of it and Wilkins was employed to finish it. As the last three acts are those now generally thought to be Shakespeare's, the fair inference is that he completed what someone else had begun. *Pericles* was omitted from the First Folio by the editors and was not included among Shakespeare's works until the second issue of the Third Folio (1664). The inference is that Heminges and Condell, Shakespeare's fellows, did not consider the play his; but on evidences of style and manner of writing, modern scholars generally agree that all or most of the last three acts are by him. Chambers thinks that the prologues and epilogue, spoken by Gower, as well as the first two acts, are by Shakespeare's collaborator.[22]

The immediate source of *Pericles* was Gower's *Confessio Amantis* (1390) and Lawrence Twine's *Patterne of Paineful Adventures* (1576). The story also appears in the *Gesta Romanorum*, a work known to Shakespeare. It goes back ultimately to *Apollonius of Tyre,* a tale that was old probably in the sixth century, whence dates the earliest extant reference to it.

The plot of *Pericles* is both intricate and episodical. To win the beautiful daughter of the king of Antioch, suitors must guess a riddle and must agree to forfeit their lives if they guess wrongly. Pericles guesses the riddle, which exposes the incestuous relationship of the girl and her father; but knowing that the father will kill him for possessing the secret, he escapes and returns home. The vengeance of Antiochus follows him, however, and keeps him a fugitive until he is shipwrecked and cast on the shores of Pentapolis. Here he so distinguishes himself in a tournament that he wins the love of Thaisa, daughter of King Simonides, and marries her. After some time, news

---
[22] *Ibid.*, p. 521.

INTRODUCTIONS TO THE PLAYS 135

reaches Pericles that his enemy, Antiochus, is dead, and that his own people, also supposing him dead, are about to choose another king. He starts home with his wife, who on the way apparently dies in giving birth to a daughter. To satisfy the superstitious sailors, Pericles allows her body to be placed in a chest and cast overboard. The chest, however, is washed ashore on the coast of Ephesus, and Thaisa is restored by a physician and becomes a priestess of Diana. Pericles leaves his infant daughter, Marina, to be reared by Cleon, governor of Tarsus, and goes home to Tyre. After fourteen years, Marina has become so beautiful that Cleon's wife plots her murder in order to remove Marina as a rival of her own daughter. Marina is saved, however, by a group of pirates, who take her to Mytilene and sell her to the keeper of a brothel; there she manages to preserve her innocence and even to convert some who visit the brothel, among whom is the governor of Mytilene. The brothel keeper, glad to be rid of her, allows her to become a singer and dancer. At last, Pericles goes to Tarsus for her, hears of her supposed death, and is so stricken with grief that for months he does not speak. On the way home, he is blown off his course and lands in Mytilene, where to cheer him the lovely singing girl Marina is produced. With joy, he recognizes her as his daughter. Then a vision directs him to the shrine of Diana at Ephesus, where he finds Thaisa. Thus in Pericles, his queen, and his daughter the audience has seen

> Virtue preserv'd from fell destruction's blast,
> Led on by heaven, and crown'd with joy at last.

Much of this story is related by Gower, who acts as a chorus and thus bridges the action between the scenes. Yet in spite of this device, the play lacks unity. Some of the poetry in the scenes attributed to Shakespeare, as well as a few passages in the first two acts, is of exceptionally high quality. The text is very corrupt, however, in both Q1 and the Folio, so that an appraisal of the style is hardly fair to the author or authors.

CYMBELINE

Cymbeline was first published in the Folio of 1623. The earliest reference to it is in the diary of Simon Forman. The date of Forman's entry is not clear, but Chambers makes a good case for April 20-30, 1611.[23] Internal evidence has led most scholars to assign it to 1609-1610.

Shakespeare derived the story from two sources, and this material he blended with great skill. The historical background came from Holinshed's *Chronicles,* and the main plot from Boccaccio's *Decameron.* He may have taken some details from other sources, for the wager theme was common in Renaissance literature. The plot resembles somewhat that of Beaumont and Fletcher's *Philaster,* which was written by October, 1610; but proof is lacking to show whether Shakespeare was indebted to these playwrights or they to him.

The plot of *Cymbeline* is less complicated than that of *Pericles,* but it lacks the tightly knit qualities of his best plays. The theme concerns the trials and sufferings of a chaste woman in her effort to preserve her reputation and honor. Imogen, daughter of Cymbeline, king of Britain, has secretly married Posthumus, a poor but worthy gentleman; and for this act Cymbeline banishes the husband. He goes to Rome, where a villain, Iachimo, induces him to wager that his wife is incorruptible. To win the wager, Iachimo goes to Britain, where he uses a stratagem to get into Imogen's bedchamber while she is asleep and thus gain information that persuades Posthumus of his wife's infidelity. In despair, Posthumus sends word to a servant to kill Imogen, but the servant, knowing her innocence, helps her to flee. Disguised as a page, she takes up residence in a cave with Belarius, a banished nobleman, who, unknown to Cymbeline, is bringing up the king's two sons, whom he had stolen in revenge for what he considered the king's injustice in banishing him. Cloten, son of Cymbeline's queen by a former marriage, whom Cymbeline selects for Imogen's husband, pur-

---

[23] *Ibid.,* p. 485. The entry itself is given on pages 338-339.

sues her and is slain by one of the princes. Meanwhile, Imogen takes a sleeping potion which the Queen, thinking it poison, had given to Pisanio, Posthumus's servant, hoping to be rid of him. She had told Pisanio that it had miraculous powers, and he had therefore given it to Imogen. The princes, thinking Imogen dead, place her beside Cloten, cover her with leaves, and chant the beautiful lyric, "Fear no more the heat o' the sun." Cymbeline, to escape paying tribute, prepares for war against Rome; and in the ensuing battle, Belarius and the two princes rescue Cymbeline. Posthumus, who has returned and fought on the side of the Britons, courts death because he thinks Imogen dead. But all ends well. Cymbeline's queen dies after confessing her treachery, Imogen is restored to Posthumus, the king recovers his lost sons, a truce is arranged with Rome, and even Iachimo is pardoned.

In *Cymbeline* Shakespeare uses a number of devices he had found effective in earlier plays. The complicated and melodramatic plot is typical of the tragicomedies that were highly popular for a time on the Jacobean stage. In them, spectacle, surprise, and involved action tend to replace the probing character studies of Shakespeare's greatest plays. In the tragicomedies, his style is less compressed and elliptical than in the great tragedies, but the poetry is often exquisitely beautiful. He employs substitute feet, weak endings, and irregular rhythms freely. Perhaps the nature of the plots makes emphasis on character less important than in such plays as *Othello* and *Macbeth*; yet in Imogen he creates one of his excellent women characters.

THE WINTER'S TALE

Simon Forman in his diary noted a performance of *Winter's Tale* at the Globe on May 15, 1611, and we have a record of its being given at Court on November 5, 1611. If, as some believe, the dance of the satyrs in IV, iv, was suggested by Ben Jonson's *Oberon,* which was performed January 1, 1611, the play can be assigned with some confidence to early 1611. On the basis of meter, theme, and treatment, authorities generally place it between *Cymbeline* and *The Tempest,* an arrangement that makes 1611 a satisfactory date.

The play was first printed in the Folio of 1623. Evidence gathered from a study of the make-up of the Folio suggests that the compositors were delayed in setting it up because of lack of copy, so that some of the histories, which in the Folio followed the comedies, were set up before it. This possibility has led some authorities to surmise that the Folio text was assembled from actors' parts.

The story comes from Robert Greene's *Pandosto,* a prose romance; but Shakespeare changed the plot considerably. In Greene's tale, for instance, Leontes commits suicide; and Greene has no character resembling Shakespeare's delightful rogue Autolycus, nor a suggestion of the statue scene.

The main theme of *The Winter's Tale* is jealousy, but a number of minor themes create the chief appeal of the play. Leontes, king of Sicilia, is host to one of his oldest friends, Polixenes, king of Bohemia. Suddenly and without reason, Leontes becomes violently jealous of Polixenes and seeks to kill him, but Polixenes is warned and escapes. When Hermione, Leontes' queen, gives birth soon after to a daughter, Leontes declares Polixenes the father of the child and places Hermione on trial for adultery. At the trial he directs the prosecution and, in spite of a message from the Oracle of Delphi that affirms Hermione's innocence, he declares her guilty. But the death of his little son, a brother of the infant whose paternity is in question, sudden news of the death of Hermione, and the staunch belief in the queen's innocence by some of his courtiers convince Leontes of his error. Meanwhile, his infant daughter, whom he had ordered to be killed, is left exposed in a desert place in Bohemia and is found by an old shepherd and brought up as his daughter. Years later, this child, Perdita, meets the son of Polixenes, Prince Florizel, who falls in love and wishes to marry her. Polixenes, learning of Florizel's infatuation, disguises himself and attends a sheepshearing in order to spy on the lovers. He then orders an end to the affair, but Camillo, a counselor who had warned him of Leontes' plot and has since served him, advises the lovers to flee to Sicilia, where he promises to find them aid. Polixenes pursues them, is reconciled to Leontes, the identity of Perdita is established, and she and Florizel are allowed to marry. Hermione, whom Leontes has long supposed dead, poses as a statue of herself, seems to come to life, and is joyfully reunited with her husband.

Like the other tragicomedies, the play contains improbable, if not impossible, situations and romantic episodes. But the improbabilities of plot and the loosely knit structure of the play are more than compensated for by the exquisite poetry—especially that of the fourth act—and by the comic character Autolycus, one of the merriest and most delightful rogues in literature. The blank verse, which comprises nearly two thirds of the play, is less compressed than that of his third period, but it has a fluidity and lyric quality that mark it as the work of a supreme master.

THE TEMPEST

The first record of *The Tempest* thus far discovered is an account by the Revels' Office of its performance at Court on November 1, 1611. Since it is based on stories of the shipwreck of Sir George Somers in the Bermudas and of his discoveries on the voyage, word of which did not reach England till September, 1610, the play can with some confidence be dated as early in 1611. Its style and treatment have led scholars to place it last among the tragicomedies. Although this can be only a surmise, some scholars have seen in Prospero's breaking his wand, and his famous speech about the actors in the masque in Act IV, Shakespeare's own valedictory on closing his career as a playwright.

Except for details gathered from the stories of Sir George Somers' voyage, Shakespeare appears to have created the plot of *The Tempest*.

The plot, unlike those of *Cymbeline* and *The Winter's Tale*, is extremely simple. Prospero, once Duke of Milan, whose place was usurped by his brother, has become a mighty magician. Finding all his former enemies on one ship near his island, he uses his magic to get them into his power, recover his dukedom, and find a suitable husband for his daughter. The play is rare among Shakespeare's dramas in adhering closely to the classic unities. The comic scenes about the drunken Stephano and Trinculo and their dealings with Caliban are in Shakespeare's best vein. Ariel and Caliban, the former symbolizing the higher elements and the latter the lower, are creations of a mind still at the zenith of its powers. The structure of the play is perfect. The poetry is graceful, yet vigorous, and is admirably designed to give the effect of actual speech and yet convey a heightened emotional sense. The tone of the play is light, in spite of an undertone of tragedy, which Prospero's magical power keeps from materializing. The play, without being obviously didactic, seems to say that though evil exists and is abundantly in evidence, it can be controlled and even directed by wisdom wedded to power. *The Tempest* is one of Shakespeare's best and happiest plays, and fittingly comes at the end of his consummate career.

HENRY VIII

Our first reference to *Henry VIII* is in a letter by Sir Henry Wotton to Sir Edmund Bacon, dated June 29, 1613, giving intelligence of the burning of the Globe Theater during the acting of *Henry VIII*, which Wotton described as a new play. Style and treatment place it very late among Shakespeare's works, and scholars are in general agreement in assigning it to 1611–1613, with the latter year having the most adherents. The play was first published in the 1623 Folio.

Two hands are clearly evident in the play, and on the basis of many careful analyses of the style, Shakespeare's collaborator is generally accepted as having been John Fletcher. The parts usually attributed to Shakespeare are I, i and ii; II, iii and iv; III, ii, 1–203; and V, i.

The main source was Holinshed's *Chronicles*, but the authors made use also of Hall's *Chronicles* and George Cavendish's *Life of Cardinal Wolsey*. Foxe's *Actes and Monuments* furnished material for V, i–iv.

The play deals especially with the part of Henry VIII's life that involves his effort to divorce Katherine of Aragon and marry Anne Boleyn. It ends with the announcement of the birth of Princess Elizabeth. Deeply involved in the action is Cardinal Wolsey, and he and Queen Katherine are tragic figures in the play. Katherine is treated sympathetically. Wolsey is portrayed at first as proud, dominant, and overbearing, but later as pathetic and tragic. Because of these different characteristics, his part calls for a versatile actor, and it has therefore been considered a desirable role by many actors.

As a whole, *Henry VIII* is epic and episodical rather than essentially dramatic; yet expertly played, it is successful on the stage.

THE TWO NOBLE KINSMEN

All the evidence points to 1613 as being an approximately correct date for *The Two Noble Kinsmen*. In the morris dance in III, v, for instance, the authors clearly had in mind Beaumont's *Inner Temple and Gray's Inn Mask,* which was performed on February 20, 1613; and an allusion in Ben Jonson's *Bartholomew Fair* (1614), IV, iii, to a play about Palamon is thought to refer to *The Two Noble Kinsmen*.

The play was not included in the First Folio and is usually not included among Shakespeare's works. A quarto was issued in 1634, with the inscription on the title page reading, "The Two Noble Kinsmen: Presented at the Blackfriers by the Kings Majesties servants, with great applause: Written by the memorable Worthies of their time; Mr. John Fletcher, and Mr. William Shakespeare. Gent." Scholars generally agree in attributing to Shakespeare most of Act I; III, i; and the invocations in Act V.

The source was Chaucer's *Knight's Tale,* and except for some changes to make their play conform to the tragicomedies then highly popular, the authors followed their source closely.

The plot deals with what happens when friends fall in love with the same woman and become rivals. Palamon and Arcite, cousins and inseparable friends, having fallen in love with the same woman, arrange a tournament to see which shall have her. Arcite wins the tournament, but dies, and Palamon marries her. The tragedy is that of broken friendship.

The play is uneven, probably the result of the collaboration, but it contains passages of exceptionally beautiful poetry. The parts attributed to Shakespeare are in the best style of his fourth period.

VIII

SHAKESPEAREAN CRITICISM AND SCHOLARSHIP

No writer without essential qualities of greatness achieves a pre-eminent position in literature; nevertheless, an author is to some extent what good scholars and critics help to make him. Shakespeare by general suffrage is considered the first of English authors and among the chief men of letters of all time. This position, however, he did not attain at one step. Although his popularity was high in his own time, it is a question—in spite of Dryden's statement, quoted later—whether the most discriminating among his contemporaries considered him superior to Ben Jonson and even lesser writers.[1] Critics, scholars, and actors have all added to his luster by their interpretations and explanations of his work. This they have done in several ways: by providing an accurate text so that he can be read with understanding; by illuminating the text with their explanations of difficult terms and passages; by interpreting his characters on the stage; and by interpreting his philosophy and basic designs as a poet and dramatist. Only a small part of even the most significant contributions to Shakespearean scholarship and criticism can be noted in a brief chapter, but a summary of the main directions this work has taken, with mention of some of the more important contributors, may be useful in indicating how the present evaluation of Shakespeare has been reached.

Little if any of what can pass as formal criticism of Shakespeare has come down to us from his own time, mainly because formal criticism is of later development in English literature.

---

[1] See, for example, G. E. Bentley, *Shakespeare and Jonson: Their Reputations in the Seventeenth Century Compared* (Chicago: 1945).

The nearest approach to it are the brief comments by Meres in his *Palladis Tamia* and by Ben Jonson in his *Timber;*[2] for though such poems as those by Jonson and Digges in the First Folio and other such contemporary estimates may be in a sense formal criticism, as representing the considered opinions of their authors, the place and function of these estimates prevent them from escaping the taint of bias. Yet that Shakespeare's plays and poems were popular in his own day is easily demonstrable, and this interest continued, in spite of changing tastes at Court and in the public theaters, until the fall of the theaters in 1642.

On the revival of drama at the time of the Restoration (1660), however, a change in the tastes of theatergoers for a while diminished Shakespeare's popularity. The analysis of deep human emotions gave way on the stage to a consideration of the frivolities of society, with the result that he seemed out of fashion. To a lesser degree, physical changes in the stage probably contributed to his loss of popularity: the large Elizabethan stage, extending into the center of the theater, gave way to the modern type of stage, on which soliloquies and asides lost some of their effectiveness. Also at this time women replaced boys in women's parts, and as the greater number of Shakespeare's plays lack leading roles for women, actresses could not display their abilities in many of the plays so well as could the actors. Samuel Pepys, a discerning theatergoer, thought *Othello* "a mean thing" in comparison with Sir Samuel Tuke's mediocre comedy, *The Five Hours' Adventure;* and though he liked *Hamlet,* he thought *A Midsummer-Night's Dream* "the most insipid, ridiculous play that ever I saw in my life." And Thomas Rymer, a leading critic of the Restoration period, in his *Tragedies of the Last Age Consider'd* (1678) and his *Short View of Tragedy* (1693) attacked Shakespeare for not adhering to the principles of Aristotle, and referred to *Othello* as "a bloody farce without salt or savor."

Yet even then Shakespeare had powerful defenders. Dryden

---

[2] For their statements, see Appendix A.

called him "the man who of all modern, and perhaps ancient, poets had the largest and most comprehensive soul." And he added, "All the images of Nature were still present to him . . . ; when he describes anything, you more than see it, you feel it too. Those who accuse him to have wanted learning, give him the greater commendation: he was naturally learned; he needed not the spectacles of books to read Nature; he looked inwards and found her there. I cannot say he is everywhere alike. . . . But he is always great when some great occasion is presented to him. . . . The consideration of this made Mr. Hales of Eaton say that there was no subject of which any poet ever writ but he would produce it much better done in Shakespeare; and however others are now generally preferred before him, yet the age wherein he lived, which had contemporaries with him Fletcher and Jonson, never equalled them to him in their esteem: and in the last king's court [that of Charles I], when Ben's reputation was at highest, Sir John Suckling, and with him the greater part of the courtiers, set our Shakespeare far above him. . . . Shakespeare was the Homer, or father, of our dramatic poets; Jonson was the Virgil, the pattern of elaborate writing; I admire him, but I love Shakespeare." [3]

Even amid the comedies of manners of the Restoration stage, Shakespeare continued to be played; and he also continued to be read. The Third Folio was published in 1663 and was reissued the next year, and the Fourth Folio was published in 1685.

With the lapse of time, however, the need became greater for a text that could be understood better by the general reader. The First Folio contained many errors, and each subsequent Folio added to the number. Changes in language rendered some words obsolete and made obscure passages harder to unravel. Early in the eighteenth century, therefore, Tonson, a leading publisher of the time, made the first move toward providing a more accurate text of Shakespeare's works. As editor he procured the services of Nicholas Rowe, a poet, playwright, and

---

[3] John Dryden, *An Essay of Dramatic Poesy* (London: 1668).

later Poet Laureate; and Rowe's edition—the first to be edited as we use the term—was published in 1709. For his text, Rowe used the Fourth Folio and made some use of a few of the quartos, but he did little collating with the earlier Folios. He corrected many of the obvious errors made by printers and transcribers, made a number of emendations, and contributed considerably to the external appearance of the plays. Of the plays in the First Folio, only seven had lists of dramatis personae; Rowe added the lists for the others. Many of the plays lacked act divisions, and in still more the scenes were not indicated; Rowe divided the plays into acts and scenes in accordance with the stage customs of his day. He arranged as poetry many passages that the Folio printers had set up as prose. And he added entrances and exits where these were lacking, and made the spelling and punctuation conform to current usage. As a pioneer, he holds an important place in Shakespearean scholarship; yet he made only a bare start in providing an accurate text.

With the growing recognition of Shakespeare's greatness as a poet and dramatist, interest in the works increased. Before the end of the eighteenth century, seven editors in England followed Rowe in bringing out editions, some of which went through several revisions; and editions were brought out also in the United States and in Germany. A second edition of Rowe's work was published in 1714. Next, Tonson published an edition edited by Alexander Pope, the leading literary figure of his day. To this edition (1725) Pope contributed a laudatory and able article on Shakespeare, but as editor he was disappointing. Although professing "a religious abhorrence of all innovation" and claiming to have performed his task "without any indulgence to my private sense or conjecture," he exercised his judgment freely in relegating what he considered spurious passages to footnotes or in omitting them without comment, and in attempting to regularize Shakespeare's meter according to the standards of his own day. Yet his explanation of obsolete terms and some of his conjectures concerning obscure passages were valuable. Perhaps the chief value of his work, however, was that it incited Lewis Theobald to join the list of Shakespearean editors. Theobald was trained in the methods of strict scholarship, and he was in addition a brilliant student of Shakespeare. In 1726, he published his *Shakespeare Restored: or, a Specimen of the many Errors, as well committed, as unamended, by Mr. Pope in his late edition of this poet. Designed not only to correct the said edition, but to restore the True Reading of Shakespeare in all the Editions ever yet publish'd;* and this he followed in 1734 with his own edition of Shakespeare's works. Of all Shakespearean editors, he was the most brilliant emendator; more than three hundred of his conjectural readings are now generally accepted.

Sir Thomas Hanmer (1744) and Bishop William Warburton (1747) added a few plausible emendations in their editions, but otherwise their importance as editors was negligible. An important contribution to both criticism and scholarship, however, was made by Samuel Johnson, literary arbiter of his age, in an edition brought out in 1765. He did not make a close collation of the texts, but his explanations of difficult passages helped to clarify the reading; and his introductory essay, in spite of some evidence of poor judgment—such as that "in [Shakespeare's] tragic scenes there is always something wanting"—did much to enhance Shakespeare's position at the time. Johnson's became for many years the standard edition. He revised it in 1773 with the help of George Steevens; and after Johnson's death the editorial work was carried on by Isaac Reed, who designated the fifth (1803) and sixth (1813) editions as the First and Second Variorum editions. Edward Capell was the first editor to make a careful collation of the folios and quartos, and in this lay the chief value of his edition (1768). The final noteworthy edition of the eighteenth century was that by Edward Malone (1790), who in his "Essay on the Chronology of Shakespeare's Plays," which he contributed to Johnson's second edition, had already laid the foundation for all the subsequent work in this department of Shakespearean research. Malone, who was both learned and conscientious, did his work with scrupulous honesty, and his edition was probably the best up to that time. Later notes by Malone were included in a second edition (called the Third Variorum), which was published in 1821 by James Boswell, son of Johnson's biographer.

Although nearly all modern editions of Shakespeare are better than any of these early editions, the basic work of collating and editing the text was done when Johnson, Capell, and Malone completed their tasks.

The chief contributions of the Romantic Period were in aesthetic criticism. Critics of that age were not concerned, as were those of the eighteenth century, in weighing Shakespeare's virtues and faults. Indeed, they could find no faults, and such a matter as his lack of adherence to classical standards, which some eighteenth-century critics deplored, they considered an actual advantage. They were intent rather in pointing out what seemed to them the almost superhuman qualities of greatness in his style and in his treatment of character. They looked on him as a supreme guide in the interpretation of life, the study of the deeper emotions, and the analysis of complex individuals. Bringing to their interpretations highly endowed imaginations and an enkindled enthusiasm, they sometimes found in his work more of themselves than of Shakespeare; yet to a greater degree than is true of critics of any previous period they understood his greatness as a poet. Chief among these interpreters were Lamb, Coleridge, and Hazlitt in England, and Goethe and Schlegel in Germany; but many others joined in their chorus of praise.

Lamb's chief contribution was his essay "On the Tragedies of Shakespeare" (1810), the main intention of which was to show that Shakespeare's tragedies contain such depth and complexity of matter that no stage representation can do them justice. Such a view implies, of course, that Lamb, regarding Shakespeare primarily as a poet, believed his genius beyond the reach of even the best actors. Coleridge, in two series of lectures given in 1811–1812 and 1818, sought to explain Shakespeare's basic philosophy and to show how each play fitted into a philosophical pattern. As a poet of great sensitivity himself, he was able to indicate beauties in the poetry that no one before him had noted. William Hazlitt in his *Characters in Shakespeare's Plays* (1817) wrote a commentary on each play, in which he sought to show the truth of Pope's statement that Shakespeare's "characters are so much more nature herself that it is a sort of injury to call them by so distant a name as copies of her." His commentaries were not profound, but his sensitivity to the beauty of many passages and his warm enthusiasm did much to increase the appreciation of Shakespeare. In Germany, the Romanticists adopted Shakespeare as their own, and by their appreciative interpretations of his work, they insured his reception there as one of the world's greatest writers. As early as 1759, Gotthold Lessing had proclaimed the superiority of Shakespeare over the leading French dramatists, and in his *Hamburgische Dramaturgie* (1767-1768) he commended Shakespeare to the favorable attention of German dramatists. Christoph Wieland began a prose translation of Shakespeare's plays (1762-1766), which Johann Eschenburg revised and completed (1775-1782); and other German scholars gave increasing attention to his works; but it was the young Goethe, in his *Wilhelm Meisters Lehrjahre,* who did most to bring Shakespeare to the notice of the younger Romanticists. Then August W. Schlegel, in a series of lectures which he gave in Vienna in 1808 and that he revised and published as *Über dramatische Kunst und Literatur* (1811), laid the foundation for the lasting appreciation of Shakespeare in Germany.[4]

---

[4] In contributing to the appreciation of Shakespeare in Germany, perhaps even more important than Schlegel's lectures was his edition of the plays (1797-1810). Schlegel himself translated fourteen plays, and the work was carried on later by others. The edition has been called one of the most successful efforts at translation in literary history. Concerning Shakespeare's influence outside English-speaking countries, only Germany is touched on here because the chief contribution to Shakespearean studies outside Great Britain and America was made there. For his reception and treatment elsewhere, see the *Cambridge History of English Literature* (London: 1910), V, 315-343.

During the nineteenth century, both textual and aesthetic criticism increased prodigiously in quantity and to some degree in quality. The tendency of the aesthetic critics, however, was to treat the characters in the plays as real people and to attribute to Shakespeare a consistent system of philosophy throughout his works and to find in all he wrote a high moral purpose. The best products of the nineteenth-century school of criticism were Edward Dowden's *Shakespeare: His Mind and Art* (1874) and A. C. Bradley's *Shakespearean Tragedy* (1904). Textual criticism, meanwhile, developed markedly during the century. J. O. Halliwell-Phillips published an edition (1853–1865) in which he reprinted all of some quartos and parts of others and parts of the Folio, noted all variant readings, and reprinted the sources that Shakespeare used, thus for the first time including in one edition all the materials necessary for a study of Shakespeare's text.[5] In 1857, Alexander Dyce, a scholarly antiquary, edited what was perhaps the best edition of the works published up to that time. His wide knowledge of Elizabethan literature, his sane study of the texts, and his intelligent emendations give him a high place among editors of Shakespeare in any period. The most important nineteenth-century edition, however, was the *Cambridge Shakespeare* (1863–1866), with W. G. Clark, J. Glover, and W. A. Wright as editors. With its collation of texts, full notes, and scholarly introductions, it came nearer to acceptance as a standard text than any previous edition, and is still a basic text for reference by scholars. In the United States, Richard Grant White (1857–1865) and Henry Norman Hudson (1880–1881) published good editions. An American, H. H. Furness, began in 1871 the publication of the most ambitious of all editions, the *New Variorum,* a monumental work that he did not live to complete. This edition was continued by his son, H. H. Furness, Jr., but it was still far from complete at his death in 1930; it is now being completed under

---

[5] In his *Life of William Shakespeare* (London: 1848; revised editions, with slight changes of title, 1874, 1881), Halliwell-Phillips also made the chief contribution to Shakespearean biography up to that time.

the direction of a group of American scholars.[6] In Germany, Nikolaus Delius, one of Germany's best Shakespearean scholars, published an edition (1854–1861) in which he incorporated the best of what had been done in Germany up to that time, including his own valuable contributions to the study of the text. These were the most noteworthy editions of the nineteenth century, though many others, of varying merit, were published. For the scholar, F. J. Furnivall's publication of the *Shakespeare Quarto Facsimiles* (43 volumes, 1880–1889), making these rare works generally accessible, and the publication of several facsimiles of the First Folio, especially that by Sidney Lee in 1902, were of the utmost value.

For the general reader, the most important development in the publication of Shakespeare's works in the twentieth century has been the appearance of well-edited single-volume editions at moderate prices: the Oxford edition (1904), by W. J. Craig; the Cambridge (United States) edition (1906), by W. A. Neilson; the Globe edition (1864, revised in 1911), by W. G. Clark and W. A. Wright; and the edition by G. L. Kittredge (1936). Many good editions of the plays, published separately, priced moderately, and including such aids as notes, glossary, and a discussion of textual matters and sources are available. Representative examples are the English Arden edition (1899–1924), under the general editorship of W. J. Craig and R. H. Case, and the American Tudor edition (1913), under the general editorship of W. A. Neilson and A. H. Thorndike. The most ambitious undertaking in editing the works in recent years, other than the completion of the *New Variorum,* is that of the *New Cambridge Shakespeare* (1921, and still in progress), by the late Sir Arthur Quiller-Couch and J. Dover Wilson.

The major part of the work of providing a text free of corrup-

---

[6] The *New Variorum,* especially the earlier volumes, because of the inclusion indiscriminately of valuable and worthless or silly comments is a tool for the mature scholar who can make his way intelligently through the mass of material. But for the plays so far published—twenty-one, with eight more in preparation by 1950—a student probably can find a summary of the pertinent comments on any question he is likely to have.

tions and reasonably close to Shakespeare's manuscripts is probably now finished. Yet work still remains to be done. It is, therefore, reasonable to expect more perfect editions in the future. The chief contributions of the present century, however, have been in other directions. Patient and painstaking research has added greatly to our knowledge of Shakespeare's works by making available to us new information about the theater, dramatic organizations, and the way plays were written, produced, and published in Elizabethan times. Such scholars as V. E. Albright, J. Q. Adams, Lily B. Campbell, W. W. Greg, and especially E. K. Chambers[7] have added greatly to our understanding of the physical characteristics of the Elizabethan theater and stage. T. W. Baldwin, Chambers, and J. T. Murray have thrown light on the organization and working of Elizabethan dramatic companies. Lily B. Campbell, W. J. Lawrence, and A. C. Sprague have traced the influence of theatrical conventions on drama in Shakespeare's time, or the nature of the audience and its effect on drama. G. E. Bentley, F. S. Boas, and F. E. Schelling have considered Shakespeare's predecessors and contemporaries and their effect on Shakespeare's plays. Evelyn M. Albright, W. W. Greg, R. B. McKerrow, and A. W. Pollard have done exceptionally valuable work in explaining how manuscripts were prepared, revised, and used in the theater, and how plays were written and published. All these lines of investigation have helped to a better understanding of Shakespeare's plays.

Literary critics also have made new contributions to the understanding of Shakespeare and of his plays. On the theory that the style is the man, they have sought to explain the workings of Shakespeare's mind by making studies of his poetic techniques and his use of imagery.[8] Further contributions have

---

[7] Only a few of the scholars who have done important work are listed here. For some of their major publications and for the names of other scholars, see the bibliography at the end of this volume.

[8] As examples, see works by Lily B. Campbell, G. Wilson Knight, Caroline F. E. Spurgeon, and E. M. W. Tillyard listed in the bibliography.

been made by dramatic producers. By reversing the trend toward more elaborate stage settings and by returning to something of the simplicity of the Shakespearean stage, they have shown how effective the plays can be simply as plays.

As a result of these new approaches to the study of Shakespeare, we have a better understanding of both the man and his works than men have had at any period since his own time. To the twentieth-century student, Shakespeare appears not as a demigod, as he did to some of the Romanticists, but as the first man of letters of one of the richly flowering periods of literary history—as a man who was both of his time and above it. And as intelligent scholarly and literary criticism and interpretation continue, students of the next century will doubtless know him even better than we do today.

IX

A NOTE ON READING SHAKESPEARE

The study of a play by Shakespeare must of course begin with the play itself. For a full understanding of a play it may be necessary ultimately to know about the age in which Shakespeare lived, the conditions of dramatic production, and the author's sources and how he used them, and to be informed on biographical and bibliographical matters of every sort; but all these things can wait until after the reading of the play itself. Fortunately rare is the student with such faith in scholarly apparatus as that displayed by a young woman who put rubber bands around a play so that she could refer to the introduction and notes without having to bother with the play itself.

Since Shakespeare's chief preoccupation was with characters —the ways in which they act and why they act as they do—the student should likewise focus his attention primarily on the characters and try to understand them and their motives and what tends to aid or thwart them in accomplishing their purposes. Because high school teachers sometimes place emphasis on the time element and the place where the action occurs— even to the extent of having pupils make elaborate time analyses and draw maps of the scene of action for the plays studied—it is worth remarking here that such activities rarely have much value in helping a reader understand a play and may even have the disadvantage of diverting the emphasis to matters of secondary importance. When the time element has a profound influence on the plot—as it has in *Romeo and Juliet,* for instance—Shakespeare is meticulous in noting it. In plays where the plot is not affected by the times when the actions occur, his method is to obscure the time element in order to give his audience a better idea of the wholeness of the action.

The time encompassed by the action of *Antony and Cleopatra*, for example, can be worked out from historical sources—and it may be interesting to have this information in order to note Shakespeare's methods of composition—but having this information does not help us in the slightest way to understand better the causes of the tragedy.

The scene of the action, likewise, is rarely of great importance in the plays. Because the Elizabethans were losing their insularity and were becoming acquainted with foreign literatures and places, they liked the sound of unfamiliar names. It was therefore almost a stage convention, especially in romantic drama, to lay the scene of action in some distant place. Often, too, Shakespeare's sources were Continental, and he simply followed his source in locating the action. The scene of *A Midsummer-Night's Dream,* for instance, might just as well have been Stratford-on-Avon as Athens—except that a Stratford man would hardly bring home a captive Amazon nor would Stratford maidens be threatened with capital punishment if they disobeyed their fathers. If the time and place of the action have no important bearing on the plot, to emphasize them is to misdirect our interest as we study a play. It is well in *King Lear* to know that the action is pre-Christian, or in *Othello* that the place in the last four acts is an island too far from Venice for easy communication with this city; but more than such general knowledge is rarely necessary.

If a knowledge of the motives and actions of the characters, then, is of primary importance for an understanding of the plays, it seems obvious that a student's main aim should be to acquire this knowledge—and the only way to do so is to study thoroughly what the characters say. We have a slang expression to the effect that a man "does not talk our language" when he uses terminology or a frame of reference unfamiliar to us or when he is looking at something from a point of view wholly different from ours. To communicate, men must use the same terminology and frame of reference and must look at things from the same general point of view. For Shakespeare to communicate with us, the same requirements must be met. But here the task is ours. Shakespeare cannot come to us except through the words he wrote three and a half centuries ago; however, by using dictionaries, glossaries, and explanatory notes, we can go to him. The first step in the comprehension of Shakespeare, therefore, is to learn the meaning of his words in the context he gave them; and the more accurate our knowledge of his words, the better we shall understand his plays.

Essential also for the comprehension of a play is a correct visualization of the characters and their actions. It is not necessary that everyone visualize alike—that, for instance, we see every action of a character as a specific actor sees it. But some visual image of a scene is necessary if we are to follow the action intelligently. In the theater, a dramatist is successful in proportion to his ability to create in the mind of his audience the illusion that it is witnessing actual life. Aiding him in the creation of this illusion are authentic costumes and properties and well trained actors. A student reading a play must identify himself with the director and actors who help bring the play to life on the stage rather than with a passive member of the audience who watches it from a seat in the pit or balcony.

Once we know the meaning of the words and have a clear visual image of the scene—what characters are present, how they are disposed on the stage, what actions they employ—the next step is to practice saying each speech until we can suggest exactly the tone in which Shakespeare intended it to be spoken. To do this, we must know what lies behind the speech—the emotions and state of mind of the speaker, what effect he hopes to produce by the speech, what sort of person he really is, and whether as he speaks he is being entirely himself or is pretending to be what he is not. When we have reached a conclusion on these matters, we should try, while reading aloud, to give the exact emphasis to each word and to reproduce the exact tone of the speaker. Not only will such reading aloud help us to avoid such mistakes as assuming that the artificial language of Romeo in his speeches about Rosaline are the words of one deeply and seriously in love, or that the warmed-over saws with which Polonius takes leave of Laertes are evidence of a deeply philosophical mind, but it will also bring to our notice the beauty and melody of Shakespeare's lines and help us to understand the quality of the poetry and the matchless style of the greatest of English writers.

Another matter to which a student must give attention is the poet's imagery, especially his figures of speech. Although poets sometimes employ figures of speech merely as decorations of their style, they often employ them to illuminate the text; and when the student does not understand the figurative language, it is like the flames in Milton's hell in that it gives darkness rather than light to the passage where it is employed. An author's imagery, furthermore, is a key that opens the door to his inner mind and allows us to become acquainted with his ways of thinking, his methods of composition, and what he wants to suggest as well as say directly. Noting the imagery, therefore, and arriving at an understanding of it will go far toward helping us understand the play and the poet as well.

To know the meaning of every word in its context, to be aware of the tone a character employs in speaking, to have a clear visual image of the actions of the characters, and to take note of the poet's imagery, then, are first requirements for reading Shakespeare intelligently. It should be obvious that even a mature student will need to read a scene many times before he can begin to understand it as the author conceived it. But to read with full, or even partial, comprehension is to become in some measure a creative artist oneself, and to approach in some sense the mind that first created the scene. When this is the mind of Shakespeare, such reading does more than illuminate a scene: it gives us a better understanding of all types of men of every age, and it helps us finally to understand better our own selves.

Beyond such primary essentials for the intelligent reading of a play, there is no end to what a student can do to acquire a greater understanding of Shakespeare and his works. The entire realm of scholarship and criticism awaits his explorations. Where to begin his excursions depends, of course, on his own interests. The bibliography at the end of this book will give some suggestions. Such brief general treatments as Logan Pearsall Smith's *On Reading Shakespeare* and J. Dover Wilson's *The Essential Shakespeare* are good to begin with; and they might lead to such works as A. C. Bradley's *Shakespearean Tragedy*, G. P. Baker's *The Development of Shakespeare as a Dramatist*, Hardin Craig's *An Interpretation of Shakespeare*, Harley Granville-Barker's *Prefaces to Shakespeare*, and G. Wilson Knight's *The Wheel of Fire* or his other books. A good biography for the beginner is J. Q. Adams's *A Life of William Shakespeare*, and for the student with a little more background, Hazelton Spencer's *The Art and Life of William Shakespeare*. Good background books are W. S. Davis's *Life in Elizabethan Days* and G. B. Harrison's *The Elizabethan Journals*. Later, the student might like to become acquainted with such works as W. W. Lawrence's *Shakespeare's Problem Comedies* and E. E. Stoll's *Shakespeare Studies* and *Art and Artifice in Shakespeare;* and he should know E. K. Chambers's *William Shakespeare: A Study of Facts and Problems,* which is one of the best reference books for all general matters. Each book he reads will lead him to others, and each will tell him something about Shakespeare that will increase his interest and perhaps his understanding. But no matter how many books of interpretation and criticism he reads, he should return again and again to the plays themselves. They, after all, are his mine, and all the books, literary and scholarly, about them are merely tools that help him dig the better for this richest of all literary ore.

APPENDIXES

A
CONTEMPORARY COMMENT
AND PRAISE

The comments in this appendix are selected from literature and records of Shakespeare's own age as examples of what his contemporaries thought of him. No attempt is made to record every allusion to him. For all allusions so far discovered, see *The Shakespeare Allusion Book* (1909) and other collections. All the really important references are in E. K. Chambers's *William Shakespeare* (II, 186–237).

1594

The following allusion to Shakespeare's *Lucrece* is from Michael Drayton's historical poem, *Matilda*, which was published in the same year as *Lucrece*. Drayton is using the appearance of a poem about Lucrece as a reason for his telling the story of "the fair and chaste daughter of the Lord Robert Fitzwater."

> Lucrece, of whom proud Rome hath boasted long,
> Lately revived to live another age,
> And here arrived to tell of Tarquin's wrong,
> Her chaste denial, and the tyrant's rage,
> Acting her passions on our stately stage:
>   She is remembered, all forgetting me,
>   Yet I as fair and chaste as ere was she.

1598

The following lines are from "A Remembrance of Some English Poets," in Richard Barnfield's *Poems in Divers Humours*, 1598. Barnfield (1574–1627) was a minor English poet.

And Shakespeare, thou, whose honey-flowing vein,
Pleasing the world, thy praises doth obtain;
Whose Venus, and whose Lucrece, sweet and chaste,
Thy name in fame's immortal book have placed:
Live ever you, at least in fame live ever;
Well may the body die, but fame dies never.

1598

The following excerpts are from *Palladis Tamia: Wits Treasury*, by Francis Meres (1565–1647), who after attending Cambridge lived for some time in London. His work was designed as a handbook for the general reader and for use in schools. In it he surveys English literature from the time of Chaucer, treating in all about 125 writers, whom he contrasts with classical writers. The quotations given here are from a section entitled "A comparative discourse of our English Poets with the Greek, Latin, and Italian Poets."

As the Greek tongue is made famous and eloquent by Homer, Hesiod, Euripides, Aeschylus, Sophocles, Pindar, Phocylides, and Aristophanes; and the Latin tongue by Virgil, Ovid, Horace, Silius Italicus, Lucanus, Lucretius, Ausonius, and Claudianus: so the English tongue is mightily enriched and gorgeously invested in rare ornaments and resplendent habiliments by Sir Philip Sidney, Spenser, Daniel, Drayton, Warner, Shakespeare, Marlowe, and Chapman. . . .

As the soul of Euphorbus was thought to live in Pythagoras, so the sweet witty soul of Ovid lives in mellifluous and honey-tongued Shakespeare: witness his *Venus and Adonis*, his *Lucrece*, his sugared sonnets among his private friends, &c.

As Plautus and Seneca are accounted the best for comedy and tragedy among the Latins, so Shakespeare among the English is the most excellent in both kinds for the stage; for comedy, witness his *Gentlemen of Verona*, his *Errors*, his *Love's Labour's Lost*, his *Love's Labour's Won*, his *Midsummer Night's Dream*, and his *Merchant of Venice*: for tragedy his *Richard II*, *Richard III*, *Henry IV*, *King John*, *Titus Andronicus*, and his *Romeo and Juliet*.

As Epius Stolo said, that the muses would speak with Plautus' tongue if they would speak Latin, so I say that the muses would speak with Shakespeare's fine filed phrase if they would speak English. . . .

As Pindarus, Anacreon, and Callimachus among the Greeks, and Horace and Catullus among the Latins, are the best lyric poets, so in this faculty the best among our poets are Spenser (who excelleth in all kinds), Daniel, Drayton, Shakespeare, Bretton. . . .

These are our best for tragedy: . . . Marlowe, Peele, Watson, Kid, Shakespeare, Drayton, Chapman, Dekker, and Benjamin Jonson. . . .

The best for comedy amongst us be . . . eloquent and witty John Lyly, Lodge, Gascoigne, Greene, Shakespeare, Thomas Nashe, Thomas Heywood, Anthony Munday (our best plotter), Chapman, Porter, Wilson, Hathaway, and Henry Chettle. . . .

These are the most passionate among us to bewail and bemoan the perplexities of love: Henry Howard, Earl of Surrey, Sir Thomas Wyatt the Elder, Sir Francis Brian, Sir Philip Sidney, Sir Walter Raleigh, Sir Edward Dyer, Spenser, Daniel, Drayton, Shakespeare, Whetstone, Gascoigne, Samuel Page, sometimes fellow of Corpus Christi College in Oxford, Churchyard, Bretton.

1600 (?)

Gabriel Harvey (c. 1545–1630), Cambridge scholar, minor author, and friend of Edmund Spenser, in 1598 acquired a copy of Speght's *Chaucer;* and sometime between then and February 25, 1601, he wrote a lengthy comment on the back of folio 394 in his copy. The following excerpt is from Harvey's comment.

The younger sort takes much delight in Shakespeare's *Venus and Adonis,* but his *Lucrece* and his tragedy of *Hamlet, Prince of Denmark,* have it in them to please the wiser sort. . . . [Dyer's] *Amaryllis* and Sir Walter Raleigh's *Cynthia,* how fine and sweet inventions? Excellent matter for emulation for Spenser, Constable, France, Watson, Daniel, Warner, Chapman, Silvester, Shakespeare, and the rest of our flowering metricians.

1605

The following comment is by William Camden (1551–1623), famous historian and antiquarian, in his *Remains of a Greater Work concerning Britain.*

These may suffice for some poetical descriptions of our ancient poets. If I would come to our time, what a world could I present to you out of Sir Philip Sidney, Ed. Spenser, Samuel Daniel, Hugh Holland, Ben Jonson, Thomas Campion, John Marston, William Shakespeare, and other most pregnant wits of these our times, whom succeeding ages may justly admire.

1610

The following poem by John Davies of Hereford (*c.* 1565–1618) is from his *Scourge of Folly*. It was entitled "To Our English Terence, Mr. Will. Shakespeare." Davies was a prolific minor poet, whose profession was that of writing master.

> Some say, good Will, (which I in sport do sing)
>   Hadst thou not played some kingly parts in sport,
> Thou hadst been a companion for a king,
> And been a king among the meaner sort.
> Some others rail; but, rail as they think fit,
> Thou hast no railing, but a reigning, wit;
>   And honesty thou sow'st, which they do reap,
>   So to increase their stock—which they do keep.

1614

The following poem is Epigram 92, "To Master W. Shakespeare," in *Runne and a Great Cast,* by Thomas Freeman, an Oxford man.

> Shakespeare, that nimble Mercury thy brain
> Lulls many hundred Argus-eyes asleep,
> So fit, for all thou fashionest thy vein,
> At th' horse-foot fountain thou hast drunk full deep,
> Virtues or vices theme to thee all one is:
> Who loves chaste life, there's *Lucrece* for a teacher;
> Who list read lust, there's *Venus and Adonis,*
> True model of a most lascivious letcher.
> Besides in plays thy wit winds like Meander:
> Whence needy new-composers borrow more
> Than Terence doth from Plautus and Menander.
> But to praise thee aright I want thy store:

Then let thine own works thine own worth upraise,
And help to adorn thee with deserved bays.

1616 (?)

The following poem is from the *Lansdowne Ms.* 777, in the British Museum. It was first printed in John Donne's *Poems* (1633) but was omitted in later editions. It appears to have been circulated widely after Shakespeare's death, for several manuscript versions are extant and a number of references were made to it by other poets, among whom was Ben Jonson in his memorial poem to Shakespeare in the First Folio. In several manuscripts it is attributed to William Basse (*c.* 1583–*c.* 1653), an Oxford man who spent most of his life in the service of Sir Richard, later Lord, Wenman, of Thama Park. In the *Lansdowne Ms.* it is entitled "On Mr. Wm. Shakespeare / he died in April 1616."

>Renowned Spenser, lie a thought more nigh
>To learned Chaucer; and rare Beaumont lie
>A little nearer Spenser to make room
>For Shakespeare in your threefold, fourfold tomb.
>To lodge all four in one bed make a shift
>Until doomsday, for hardly will a fifth
>Betwixt this day and that by Fate be slain,
>For whom your curtains may be drawn again.
>If your precedency in death doth bar
>A fourth place in your sacred sepulcher,
>Under this carved marble of thine own
>Sleep, rare tragedian, Shakespeare, sleep alone;
>Thy unmolested peace, unshared cave,
>Possess as lord, not tenant, of thy grave,
>>That unto us and others it may be
>>Honor hereafter to be laid by thee.

1623

In the First Folio were included a number of comments of high interest to students of Shakespeare. Chief among them was this memorial poem by Ben Jonson. Another, of less interest, was a poem by Leonard Digges (1588–1635), a translator and Oxford man. Heminges and Condell wrote for the First Folio a dedicatory epistle to the Earls of Pembroke and Montgomery and "To the Great Variety of Readers."

To the Memory of My Beloved the Author, Mr. William Shakespeare, and What He Hath Left Us

Ben Jonson

To draw no envy, Shakespeare, on thy name,
   Am I thus ample to thy book and fame,
While I confess thy writings to be such
   As neither man nor Muse can praise too much;
'Tis true, and all men's suffrage. But these ways
   Were not the paths I meant unto thy praise,
For seeliest ignorance on these may light,
   Which when it sounds at best but echoes right;
Or blind affection which doth ne'er advance
   The truth, but gropes and urgeth all by chance;
Or crafty malice might pretend this praise,
   And think to ruin where it seemed to raise.
These are as some infamous bawd or whore
   Should praise a matron; what could hurt her more?
But thou art proof against them, and indeed
   Above th' ill fortune of them, or the need.
I, therefore, will begin. Soul of the age!
   The applause, delight, the wonder of our stage!
My Shakespeare, rise; I will not lodge thee by
   Chaucer, or Spenser, or bid Beaumont lie
A little further to make thee a room;
   Thou art a monument, without a tomb,
And art alive still, while thy book doth live
   And we have wits to read and praise to give.
That I not mix thee so, my brain excuses—
   I mean with great but disproportioned muses,—
For if I thought my judgment were of years
   I should commit thee surely with thy peers,
And tell how far thou didst our Lyly outshine,
   Or sporting Kyd, or Marlowe's mighty line.

APPENDIX

And though thou hadst small Latin and less Greek,
  From thence to honor thee I would not seek
For names, but call forth thund'ring Aeschylus,
  Euripides, and Sophocles to us,
Pacuvius, Accius, him of Cordova dead,
  To life again, to hear thy buskin tread
And shake a stage; or, when thy socks were on,
  Leave thee alone for the comparison
Of all that insolent Greece or haughty Rome
  Sent forth, or since did from their ashes come.
Triumph, my Britain, thou hast one to show
  To whom all scenes of Europe homage owe.
He was not of an age, but for all time!
  And all the Muses still were in their prime,
When like Apollo he came forth to warm
  Our ears, or like a Mercury to charm!
Nature herself was proud of his designs,
  And joyed to wear the dressing of his lines
Which were so richly spun, and woven so fit,
  As since, she will vouchsafe no other wit;
The merry Greek, tart Aristophanes,
  Neat Terence, witty Plautus, now not please,
But antiquated and deserted lie
  As they were not of nature's family.
Yet must I not give nature all; thy art,
  My gentle Shakespeare, must enjoy a part;
For though the poet's matter nature be,
  His art doth give the fashion; and that he
Who casts to write a living line, must sweat,
  Such as thine are, and strike the second heat
Upon the Muses' anvil, turn the same,
  And himself with it, that he thinks to frame;
Or for the laurel he may gain a scorn,
  For a good poet's made, as well as born;
And such wert thou. Look how the father's face
  Lives in his issue; even so the race
Of Shakespeare's mind and manners brightly shines
  In his well-turned and true-filed lines,
In each of which he seems to shake a lance,

As brandished at the eyes of ignorance.
Sweet swan of Avon! what a sight it were
  To see thee in our waters yet appear,
And make those flights upon the banks of Thames
  That so did take Eliza, and our James!
But stay, I see thee in the hemisphere
  Advanced, and made a constellation there!
Shine forth, thou star of poets, and with rage
  Or influence chide or cheer the drooping stage;
Which since thy flight from hence, hath mourned like night,
  And despairs day, but for thy volume's light.

To the Memory of the Deceased Author Master W. Shakespeare

Leonard Digges

Shakespeare, at length thy pious fellows give
The world thy works: thy works, by which outlive
Thy tomb, thy name must. When that stone is rent,
And time dissolves thy Stratford monument,
Here we alive shall view thee still. This book,
When brass and marble fade, shall make thee look
Fresh to all ages; when posterity
Shall loath what's new, think all is prodigy
That is not Shakespeare's; every line, each verse,
Here shall revive, redeem thee from thy herse.
Nor fire nor cankering age, as Naso said
Of his, thy wit-fraught book shall once invade.
Nor shall I e'er believe, or think, thee dead,
Though missed, until our bankrout stage be sped
(Impossible) with some new strain t' outdo
Passions of Juliet and her Romeo;
Or till I hear a scene more nobly take,
Than when thy half-sword parlying Romans spake.
Till these, till any of thy volumes rest
Shall with more fire, more feeling, be expressed,
Be sure, our Shakespeare, thou can'st never die,
But crown'd with laurel, live eternally.

Dedicatory Epistle to the Earls of
Pembroke and Montgomery

Right Honorable, Whilst we study to be thankful in our particular for the many favors we have received from your Lordships, we are fallen upon the ill fortune to mingle two the most diverse things that can be, fear and rashness—rashness in the enterprise and fear of the success. For when we value the places your Highnesses sustain, we cannot but know their dignity greater than to descend to the reading of these trifles: and, while we name them trifles, we have deprived ourselves of the defence of our dedication. But since your Lordships have been pleased to think these trifles something heretofore, and have prosecuted both them and their author living with so much favor, we hope that (they outliving him, and he not having the fate, common with some, to be executor to his own writings) you will use the like indulgence toward them, you have done unto their parent. There is a great difference whether any book choose his patrons or find them: this hath done both. For, so much were your Lordships' likings of the several parts when they were acted, as before they were published, the volume asked to be yours. We have but collected them, and done an office to the dead to procure his orphans guardians, without ambition either of self-profit or fame: only to keep the memory of so worthy a friend and fellow alive as was our Shakespeare, by humble offer of his plays to your most noble patronage. Wherein, as we have justly observed, no man to come near your Lordships but with a kind of religious address, it hath been the height of our care, who are the presenters, to make the present worthy of your Highnesses by the perfection. But there we must also crave our abilities to be considered, my Lords. We cannot go beyond our own powers. Country hands reach forth milk, cream, fruits, or what they have; and many nations, we have heard, that had not gums and incense, obtained their requests with a leavened cake. It was no fault to approach their gods by what means they could. And the most, though meanest, of things are made more precious when they are dedicated to temples. In that name, therefore, we most humbly consecrate to your Highnesses these remains of your servant Shakespeare; that what delight is in them may be ever your Lordships, the reputation his, and the faults ours, if any be committed by a

pair so careful to show their gratitude both to the living and the dead, as is
>Your Lordships' most bounden
>John Heminge
>Henry Condell

To the Great Variety of Readers

From the most able to him that can but spell: there you are numbered. We had rather you were weighed. Especially when the fate of all books depends upon your capacities, and not of your heads alone but of your purses. Well! it is now public and you will stand for your privileges, we know, to read and censure. Do so, but buy it first. That doth best commend a book, the stationer says. Then, how odd soever your brains be, or your wisdoms, make your license the same, and spare not. Judge your six-pen'orth, your shilling's worth, your five shillings' worth at a time, or higher, so you rise to the just rates and welcome; but whatever you do, buy. Censure will not drive a trade or make the jack go. And though you be a magistrate of wit and sit on the stage at Blackfriars or the Cock-pit to arraign plays daily, know, these plays have had their trial already and stood out all appeals, and do now come forth quitted rather by a decree of court than any purchased letters of commendation.

It had been a thing, we confess, worthy to have been wished that the author himself had lived to have set forth and overseen his own writings; but since it hath been ordained otherwise, and he by death departed from that right, we pray you do not envy his friends the office of their care and pain to have collected and published them; and so to have published them, as where before you were abused with diverse stolen and surreptitious copies, maimed and deformed by the frauds and stealths of injurious imposters that exposed them; even those are now offered to your view cured and perfect of their limbs, and all the rest, absolute in their numbers, as he conceived them. Who, as he was a happy imitator of nature, was a most gentle expresser of it. His mind and hand went together, and what he thought, he uttered with that easiness that we have scarce received from him a blot in his papers. But it is not our province, who only gather his works and give them you, to praise him. It is yours that read him. And there we hope, to your divers capacities, you will find enough both to draw and hold you, for his wit can no more

APPENDIX   171

lie hid than it could be lost. Read him, therefore, and again and
again; and if then you do not like him, surely you are in some manifest danger not to understand him. And so we leave you to other
of his friends whom if you need can be your guides; if you need them
not, you can lead yourselves and others. And such readers we wish
him.

John Heminge
Henry Condell

1630

John Milton contributed a memorial to the Second Folio
(1632). The poem, dated 1630 by Milton in his own *Poems*
(1645), was entitled "An Epitaph on the Admirable Dramatic
Poet, W. Shakespeare."

> What needs my Shakespeare for his honored bones
> The labor of an age in piled stones?
> Or that his hallowed reliques should be hid
> Under a star-ypointing pyramid?
> Dear son of memory, great heir of fame,
> What need'st thou such weak witness of thy name?
> Thou in our wonder and astonishment
> Hast built thyself a livelong monument.
> For whilst, to the shame of slow-endeavoring art,
> Thy easy numbers flow, and that each heart
> Hath from the leaves of thy unvalued book
> Those Delphic lines with deep impression took,
> Then thou, our fancy of itself bereaving,
> Dost make us marble with too much conceiving,
> And so sepulchred in such pomp dost lie
> That kings for such a tomb would wish to die.

1623–1637

Among the notes left at his death in 1637 by Ben Jonson, and
published in *Timber: or, Discoveries; Made upon Men and
Matter* (1641), was the following comment. He wrote it sometime between 1623, when his earlier notebooks were burned,
and his death.

De Shakespeare Nostrati
Ben Jonson

I remember the players have often mentioned it as an honor to Shakespeare that in his writing (whatsoever he penned) he never blotted out a line. My answer hath been, "Would he had blotted a thousand," which they thought a malevolent speech. I had not told posterity this but for their ignorance who choose that circumstance to commend their friend by wherein he most faulted; and to justify mine own candor, for I loved the man, and do honor his memory, on this side idolatry, as much as any. He was, indeed, honest, and of an open and free nature; had an excellent fancy, brave notions, and gentle expressions, wherein he flowed with that facility that sometimes it was necessary he should be stopped. *Sufflaminandus erat,* as Augustus said of Haterius. His wit was in his own power; would the rule of it had been so too. Many times he fell into those things could not escape laughter, as when he said in the person of Caesar, one speaking to him, "Caesar, thou dost me wrong," he replied, "Caesar did never wrong but with just cause"; and such like, which were ridiculous. But he redeemed his vices with his virtues. There was ever more in him to be praised than to be pardoned.

B

EARLY BIOGRAPHICAL REFERENCES

Biographical information concerning Shakespeare was meager at first and grew slowly in the first century after his death. A few anecdotes about him were written down during his lifetime or shortly after his death, but they are of almost no importance. The more important notations up to the time of Rowe and including part of the sketch appended to his edition are given here. For other references, see E. K. Chambers, *William Shakespeare: A Study of Facts and Problems* (II, 241–302).

THOMAS FULLER (after 1643)

Thomas Fuller (1608–1661), an Anglican divine, gathered notes for his work, *The History of the Worthies of England,* which was published in 1662, the year after his death. His comments on Shakespeare appear in a section on the worthies of Warwickshire.

William Shakespeare was born at Stratford-on-Avon in this county; in whom three eminent poets may seem in some sort to be compounded.
1. Martial, in the warlike sound of his surname (whence some may conjecture him of a military extraction) *Hasti-vibrans,* or Shakespeare.
2. Ovid, the most natural and witty of all poets; and hence it was that Queen Elizabeth, coming into a grammar school, made this extempory verse:

> "Persius a crab-staff, bawdy Martial,
> Ovid a fine wag."

3. Plautus, who was an exact comedian, yet never any scholar, as our Shakespeare (if alive) would confess himself. Add to all these that though his genius generally was jocular and inclining him to festivity, yet he could (when so disposed) be solemn and serious, as appears by his tragedies; so that Heraclitus himself (I mean if secret and unseen) might afford to smile at his comedies, they were so merry; and Democritus scarce forbear to sigh at his tragedies, they were so mournful.

He was an eminent instance of the truth of that rule, *Poeta non fit, sed nascitur* (one is not made, but born a poet). Indeed his learning was very little; so that, as Cornish diamonds are not polished by any lapidary, but are pointed and smoothed even as they are taken out of the earth, so nature itself was all the art which was used upon him.

Many were the wit-combats betwixt him and Ben Jonson; which two I behold like a Spanish great galleon and an English man-of-war; Master Jonson (like the former) was built far higher in learning; solid, but slow, in his performances. Shakespeare, with the English man-of-war, lesser in bulk, but lighter in sailing, could turn with all tides, tack about, and take advantage of all winds, by the quickness of his wit and invention. He died *anno Domini* 1616, and was buried at Stratford-on-Avon, the town of his nativity.

JOHN WARD (1661–1663)

John Ward, who was vicar of Stratford from 1662 to 1681, kept a diary from 1629 until his death. In the years 1661–1663 are the following references to Shakespeare.

Shakespeare had two daughters, one whereof Master Hall, the physician, married, and by her had one daughter, to wit, the Lady Barnard of Abbingdon. . . .

I have heard that Master Shakespeare was a natural wit, without any art at all. He frequented the plays all his younger time, but in his elder days lived at Stratford: and supplied the stage with two plays every year, and for that had an allowance so large that he spent at the rate of a thousand pounds a year, as I have heard.

Shakespeare, Drayton, and Ben Jonson had a merry meeting, and it seems drank too hard, for Shakespeare died of a fever there contracted.

APPENDIX 175

JOHN AUBREY (c. 1681)

John Aubrey (1626–1697), an antiquary and minor author, aided Anthony Wood in gathering material for his *Athenae Oxonienses*. Among Aubrey's notes, now in manuscripts in the Bodleian Library, Oxford, some jottings that he made for a sketch, and a finished sketch for his *Brief Lives*, contain information that he picked up about Shakespeare. Since a good deal that Aubrey gathered was gossip, it cannot be relied on always, but as evidence gathered early, while some persons still living could remember men who had known Shakespeare, it is interesting. Item 1 below consists of Aubrey's notes. Item 2 is his completed sketch. Evidently Aubrey applied for information about Shakespeare to John Lacy, an actor, who referred him to William Beeston, another actor, whose father, Christopher Beeston, was a member of Shakespeare's company.

1. the more to be admired q[uia] he was not a company keeper lived in Shoreditch, wouldn't be debauched, & if invited to, writ: he was in paine.

W. Shakespeare
q[uaere] Mr Beeston who knows most of him fr[om] Mr Lacy

2. Master William Shakespeare was born at Stratford-upon-Avon, in the county of Warwick. His father was a butcher, and I have been told heretofore by some of the neighbors that when he was a boy he exercised his father's trade, but when he killed a calf, he would do it in a high style and make a speech. There was at that time another butcher's son in this town, that was held not at all inferior to him for a natural wit, his acquaintance and coetanean, but died young. This William, being inclined naturally to poetry and acting, came to London I guess about 18, and was an actor at one of the playhouses and did act exceedingly well. Now Ben Jonson was never a good actor, but an excellent instructor. He began early to make essays at dramatic poetry, which at that time was very low; and his plays took well. He was a handsome, well-shaped man, very good company, and of a very ready and pleasant smooth wit. The humor of ―――― the constable in *A Midsummer-Night's Dream*, he happened to take at Grendon [in margin: "I think it was Midsummer-night that he

happened to lie there"] in Bucks, which is the road from London to Stratford, and there was living that constable about 1642 when I first came to Oxford. Master Joseph Howe is of that parish and knew him. Ben Jonson and he did gather humors of men daily wherever they came. One time as he was at the Tavern at Stratford-upon-Avon, one Combes, an old rich usurer, was to be buried, he makes there this extempory epitaph:

> Ten in the hundred the devil allows,
> But Combes will have twelve, he swears and vows:
> If anyone asks who lies in this tomb:
> Ho! quoth the devil, 'tis my John o' Combe.

He was wont to go to his native country once a year. I think I have been told that he left two or three hundred pounds per annum there and thereabout: to a sister. I have heard Sir William Davenant and Master Thomas Shadwell (who is counted the best comedian we have now) say that he had a most prodigious wit, and did admire his natural parts beyond all other dramatical writers. He was wont to say that he never blotted out a line in his life. Said Ben Jonson, "I wish he had blotted out a thousand." His comedies will remain wit as long as the English tongue is understood, for that he handles *mores hominum*. Now our present writers reflect so much upon particular persons and coxcombries that twenty years hence they will not be understood. Though as Ben Jonson says of him that he had but little Latin and less Greek, he understood Latin pretty well, for he had been in his younger years a schoolmaster in the country.

Opposite the latter sentence, Aubrey wrote in the margin, "from Mʳ —— Beeston."

RICHARD DAVIES (1688–1708)

The following notes are given because they are the source of all the reports, first and last, about Shakespeare and his stealing of Sir Thomas Lucy's deer. The notes are preserved in a manuscript in one of the college libraries at Oxford. Their history seems to be as follows: The papers of William Fulman (*d.* 1688), a clergyman of Gloucestershire, came into the possession of

Richard Davies (*d.* 1708), Archdeacon of Coventry, after whose death they were presented to the college library. Someone—doubtless Fulman—had made two or three notations about Shakespeare: "William Shakespeare was born at Stratford-upon-Avon in Warwickshire about 1563–4. From an actor of plays he became a composer. *Aetat* 53. He died April 23, 1616, probably at Stratford, for there he is buried and hath a monument." After the first sentence Davies added, without giving the source of his information, item 1 below, and at the end, after "monument," item 2.

1. much given to all unluckiness in stealing venison and rabbits, particularly from Sr. Lucy, who had him oft whipped and sometimes imprisoned, and at last made him fly his native country to his great advancement; but his revenge was so great that he is his Justice Clodpate and calls him a great man and that in allusion to his name bore three louses rampant for his arms.

2. on which he lays a heavy curse upon anyone who shall remove his bones. He died a papist.

MR. DOWDALL (*1693*)

The following extract is from a letter, found among the family papers of Lord de Clifford, which was written to a Mr. Southwell by a Mr. Dowdall on April 10, 1693. The Mr. Dowdall, whoever he was, had visited Stratford, and in his letter he described Shakespeare's monument and epitaph, and then added the following paragraph.

The clerk that showed me this church is about eighty years old. He says that this Shakespeare was formerly in this town bound apprentice to a butcher, but that he run (*sic*) from his master to London, and there was received into the playhouse as a serviture, and by this means had an opportunity to be what he afterwards proved. He was the best of his family, but the male line is extinguished. Not one for fear of the curse abovesaid dare touch his gravestone, though his wife and daughters did earnestly desire to be laid in the same grave with him.

WILLIAM HALL (1694)

William Hall, a rector of Acton, Middlesex, in about 1694 wrote a letter to Edward Thwaites, a professor at Oxford, in which he described a visit he had made to Stratford-on-Avon. After quoting Shakespeare's epitaph, Hall added the following paragraph.

The little learning these verses contain would be a very strong argument of the want of it in the author, did not they carry something in them which stands in need of a comment. There is in this Church a place which they call the bone-house, a repository for all bones they dig up, which are so many that they would load a great number of wagons. The Poet, being willing to preserve his bones unmoved, lays a curse upon him that moves them; and having to do with clerks and sextons, for the most part a very ignorant sort of people, he descends to the meanest of their capacities, and disrobes himself of that art which none of his contemporaries wore in greater perfection. Nor has the design missed of its effect, for lest they should not only draw this curse upon themselves, but also entail it upon their posterity, they have laid him full seventeen foot deep, deep enough to secure him.

NICHOLAS ROWE (1709)

The first extended biographical note on Shakespeare was written by Nicholas Rowe for his edition of Shakespeare's *Works* (1709). The following excerpts are from Rowe's sketch.

He was the son of Mr. John Shakespeare, and was born at Stratford-upon-Avon, in Warwickshire, in April, 1564. His family, as appears by the Register and public writings relating to that town, were of good figure and fashion there, and are mentioned as gentlemen. His father, who was a considerable dealer in wool, had so large a family, ten children in all, that though he was his eldest son, he could give him no better education than his own employment. He had bred him, 'tis true, for some time at a Free-school, where 'tis probable he acquired that little Latin he was master of. But the narrowness of his circumstances, and the want of his assistance at home, forced his

APPENDIX 179

father to withdraw him from thence, and unhappily prevented his further proficiency in that language. . . .

Upon his leaving school, he seems to have given entirely into that way of living which his father proposed to him; and in order to settle in the world after a family manner, he thought fit to marry while he was yet very young. His wife was the daughter of one Hathaway, said to have been a substantial yeoman in the neighborhood of Stratford. In this kind of settlement he continued for some time, till an extravagance that he was guilty of forced him both out of his country and that way of living which he had taken up; and though it seemed at first to be a blemish upon his good manners, and a misfortune to him, yet it afterwards happily proved the occasion of exerting one of the greatest geniuses that ever was known in dramatic poetry. He had, by misfortune common enough to young fellows, fallen into ill company; and amongst them, some that made a frequent practice of deer-stealing engaged him with them more than once in robbing a park that belonged to Sir Thomas Lucy of Cherlecot, near Stratford. For this he was prosecuted by that gentleman, as he thought, somewhat too severely; and in order to revenge that ill usage, he made a ballad upon him. And though this, probably the first essay of his poetry, be lost, yet it is said to have been so very bitter that it redoubled the prosecution against him to that degree that he was obliged to leave his business and family in Warwickshire, for some time, and shelter himself in London.

It is at this time, and upon this accident, that he is said to have made his first acquaintance in the playhouse. He was received into the company then in being, at first in a very mean rank; but his admirable wit, and the natural turn of it to the stage, soon distinguished him, if not as an extraordinary actor, yet as an excellent writer. His name is printed, as the custom was in those times, amongst those of the other players, before some old plays, but without any particular account of what sort of parts he used to play; and though I have inquired, I could never meet with any further account of him this way than that the top of his performance was the Ghost in his own *Hamlet*. . . .

Besides the advantages of his wit, he was in himself a good-natured man, of great sweetness in his manners, and a most agreeable companion; so that it is no wonder if with so many good qualities he made himself acquainted with the best conversations of those times.

Queen Elizabeth had several of his plays acted before her, and without doubt gave him many gracious marks of her favor: It is that maiden Princess plainly, whom he intends by

—A fair Vestal, Throned by the West.
Midsummer-Night's Dream.

And that whole passage is a compliment very properly brought in, and very handsomely applied to her. She was so well pleased with that admirable character of Falstaff, in the two parts of *Henry the Fourth,* that she commanded him to continue it for one play more, and to show him in love. This is said to be the occasion of his writing *The Merry Wives of Windsor.* How well she was obeyed, the play itself is an admirable proof. . . .

He had the honor to meet with many great and uncommon marks of favor and friendship from the Earl of Southampton, famous in the histories of that time for his friendship to the unfortunate Earl of Essex. It was to that noble Lord that he dedicated his poem of *Venus and Adonis,* the only piece of his poetry which he ever published himself, though many of his plays were surreptitiously and lamely printed in his lifetime. There is one instance so singular in the magnificence of this patron of Shakespeare's, that if I had not been assured that the story was handed down by Sir William D'Avenant, who was probably very well acquainted with his affairs, I should not have ventured to have inserted, that my Lord Southampton at one time gave him a thousand pounds to enable him to go through with a purchase which he heard he had a mind to. . . .

His acquaintance with Ben Jonson began with a remarkable piece of humanity and good nature; Mr. Jonson, who was at that time altogether unknown to the world, had offered one of his plays to the players, in order to have it acted; and the persons into whose hands it was put, after having turned it carelessly and superciliously over, were just upon returning it to him with an ill-natured answer, that it would be of no service to their company, when Shakespeare luckily cast his eye upon it, and found something so well in it as to engage him first to read it through, and afterwards to recommend Mr. Jonson and his writings to the public. After this they were professed friends. . . .

Jonson was certainly a very good scholar, and in that had the advantage of Shakespeare; though at the same time I believe it must be allowed, that what Nature gave the latter, was more than a balance for what books had given the former. . . .

I cannot leave *Hamlet* without taking notice of the advantage with which we have seen this masterpiece of Shakespeare distinguish itself upon the stage by Mr. Betterton's fine performance of that part: A man who, though he had no other good qualities, as he has a great many, must have made his way into the esteem of all men of letters by this only excellency. . . .

I must own a particular obligation to him, for the most considerable part of the passages relating to this life, which I have here transmitted to the public; his veneration for the memory of Shakespeare having engaged him to make a journey into Warwickshire on purpose to gather up what remains he could of a name for which he had so great a value. . . .

The latter part of his life was spent, as all men of good sense will wish theirs may be, in ease, retirement, and the conversation of his friends. He had the good fortune to gather an estate equal to his occasion, and, in that, to his wish; and is said to have spent some years before his death at his native Stratford. His pleasurable wit, and good nature, engaged him in the acquaintance, and entitled him to the friendship of the gentlemen of the neighborhood. . . .

He died in the fifty-third year of his age, and was buried on the north side of the chancel, in the great church at Stratford, where a monument, as engraved in the plate, is placed in the wall. . . .

He had three daughters, of which two lived to be married: Judith, the elder, to one Mr. Thomas Quiney, by whom she had three sons, who all died without children; and Susannah, who was his favorite, to Dr. John Hall, a physician of good reputation in that country. She left one child only, a daughter, who was married first to Thomas Nash, Esq., and afterwards to Sir John Bernard of Abington, but died likewise without issue.

This is what I could learn of any note, either relating to himself or family. The character of the man is best seen in his writings. . . .

C

SHAKESPEAREAN ACTORS AND PRODUCERS

Although in this volume Shakespeare's plays have been considered chiefly as literature, because students usually become acquainted with them as literature before seeing them performed, we must remember that Shakespeare wrote them to be played, not read. Except for the years from 1642 to 1660, when under the Puritan regime all theaters were closed, his plays have been performed in every generation since his own day. Producers and players who staged and interpreted them have naturally influenced the attitude of the public toward them. And though critics and scholars have affected the interpretation of the plays on the stage, producers and actors in turn have added their contributions to our understanding of Shakespeare. In an introductory work of this sort, space is lacking for a detailed account of the history of Shakespeare on the stage, but a brief consideration of some of the leading actors and producers may help to show the trends in the staging of the plays.[1]

The popularity of Shakespeare's plays on the Elizabethan and Jacobean stages is attested by many references and by the number of times the plays were performed at Court for both Elizabeth and James. A list of the principal actors in the plays is included in the First Folio. Outstanding among them is Richard Burbage (*c.* 1567–1619), who was considered the best actor, or among the top two or three, of his time. From contemporary references we know that he performed the parts of Richard III, Romeo, Hamlet, Othello, and Lear, among others.

---

[1] For a detailed history, see G. C. D. Odell's *Shakespeare from Betterton to Irving* (New York: 1920) and the same author's *Annals of the New York Stage* (New York: 1927–   ). Other books on the subject are listed in the bibliography to this volume.

APPENDIX 183

The principal comic parts in the earlier plays were taken by William Kempe and later by Robert Armin.[2]

Shakespeare continued to be played until the closing of the theaters in 1642, and although Carolinian taste seems to have preferred Beaumont and Fletcher to him, his plays were still highly popular and he was preferred to Ben Jonson, if we can assume the lines of Leonard Digges in a 1640 edition of Shakespeare's *Poems* to be true:

> How could the Globe have prospered, since through want
> Of change, the plays and poems have grown scant. . . .
> So I have seen, when Caesar would appear,
> And on the stage at half-sword parley were
> Brutus and Cassius, oh, how the audience
> Was ravished! With what wonder they went thence,
> When some new day they would not brook a line
> Of tedious, though well-labored, *Cataline.*
> *Sejanus* too was irksome. They prized more
> Honest Iago or the jealous Moor.
> And though the *Fox* and subtle *Alchemist,*
> Long intermitted, could not quite be missed,
> Though these have shamed all th' ancients and might raise
> Their author's merit with a crown of bays,
> Yet these sometimes, even at a friend's desire
> Acted, have scarce defrayed the sea-coal fire
> And doorkeepers; when let but Falstaff come,
> Hal, Poins, the rest, you scarce shall have a room,
> All is so pestered; let but Beatrice
> And Benedick be seen, lo in a trice
> The Cockpit galleries, boxes, all are full
> To hear Malvolio, that cross-gartered gull.

Because the stage tradition was continuous up to 1642, the plays were given until then as they were acted while Shakespeare was still alive. We have no record, however, in late Jacobean and

---

[2] For a reconstruction of the probable parts taken in the plays by other members of the company, including Shakespeare himself, see T. W. Baldwin, *Organization and Personnel of the Shakespearean Company* (Princeton, N. J.: 1927).

Carolinian times of any actor's having won outstanding success in a Shakespearean role.

After the Restoration, changes in the theater occurred that naturally affected dramas written for Elizabethan playhouses. The open-air playhouses were replaced by inclosed theaters; the large Elizabethan stage gave way to the modern type of stage; and women began to perform female parts. These changes and the tastes of a new generation of playgoers led a succession of innovators to rework many of Shakespeare's plays in an attempt to adapt them to new conditions. To William Davenant and Thomas Killigrew, Charles II granted the sole right to form theatrical companies and produce plays. Each of these producers secured some of Shakespeare's plays, though Davenant's share was the larger, and each made changes in the plays. Davenant, for instance, introduced Benedick and Beatrice from *Much Ado* into a rewritten version of *Measure for Measure,* and added a girl singer and dancer. He added new scenes, including flying witches, to *Macbeth,* and with Dryden's help turned *The Tempest* into a musical show. Others who were busy reworking the plays were the dramatist Thomas Shadwell and the poet Nahum Tate. Tate went to the extreme of changing *Lear* into a comedy, making Cordelia and Edgar lovers, and having the play end with their marriage and Lear's restoration to the throne. It is easy today, of course, to impeach these innovators, but we must credit them with keeping Shakespeare alive before audiences that might not have accepted the plays in their original state. More blameworthy are the producers and actors who continued to play the "improved" versions of the plays until well into the nineteenth century.

The most famous actor of Shakespearean roles in Restoration days was Thomas Betterton (*c.* 1635–1710). Although performing in the reworked versions of Davenant, Dryden, Tate, and others, he won great acclaim for his interpretations of Brutus, Hamlet, Othello, Macbeth, and other characters. Critics as different as Samuel Pepys, Alexander Pope, and Richard Steele joined in praising his acting. His wife, Mary Saunderson,

APPENDIX 185

was the first actress to play a succession of the feminine roles.[3] Succeeding Betterton were several good, but less renowned, actors, of whom the best were Robert Wilks (1670–1732), Barton Booth (1681–1733), and Colley Cibber (1671–1757). More highly acclaimed in the period than these actors were the actresses Anne Bracegirdle and Elizabeth Barry, both of whom appeared in various Shakespearean roles.

By the beginning of the eighteenth century, Shakespeare's position as the greatest of the older dramatists was firmly established. His tragedies were the most frequently acted stock pieces at the two licensed theaters, and his comedies, in the Restoration versions, retained their popularity. During the first years of the century, the chief Shakespearean actor was Colley Cibber, who, though not one of the great interpreters of Shakespearean parts, was successful as Iago, Wolsey, Shallow, and Glendower, and made a notable success of the part of Richard III.

The greatest of eighteenth-century actors was David Garrick (1717–1779). Garrick made his debut as a Shakespearean actor in 1741 in the part of Richard III, and Pope greeted the performance with the statement that he "never had his equal as an actor, and he will never have a rival." Instead of the sonorous declamation and stately manner of previous actors, he assumed a natural expression, with rapid changes of voice and gesture to portray passion or humor. During his career he played seventeen Shakespearean roles, his most successful being those of Hamlet, Lear, Richard III, and Benedick. Later as manager of the Drury Lane theater he produced twenty-four of Shakespeare's plays. Although he retained most of the Restoration versions of the plays, he introduced costumes and properties that were historically correct. A contemporary of Garrick's was Charles Macklin (c. 1699–1797), an Irish actor and playwright. He appeared in many Shakespearean roles,

---

[3] From records so far discovered, it appears that the first woman to appear on a London stage was Margaret Hughes, who in 1660 acted the part of Desdemona.

but perhaps his greatest claim to our attention is his revival of *The Merchant of Venice* in its original form and his portrayal of Shylock as a tragic character. The best actresses of the time were Catherine Clive, who played Portia to Macklin's Shylock; Hannah Pritchard, who was Lady Macbeth in Garrick's production and who remained with his company for twenty years, during which time she appeared in many Shakespearean roles; Susanna Maria Cibber, whose best role was that of Constance in *King John;* and Peg Woffington, who played Rosalind, Portia, Constance, and several other parts.

Garrick's place as the leading producer and interpreter of Shakespeare was taken by John Philip Kemble (1757–1823), second of the twelve children of a strolling player and his actress wife. Kemble's first starring part was that of Hamlet, which he played in Dublin in 1781; and two years later he made his appearance in London at Drury Lane in the same role. In 1783, he and his sister, Sarah Kemble Siddons, probably the greatest of all Shakespearean actresses, appeared together as King John and Constance; and from the time of their appearance together as Macbeth and Lady Macbeth at Drury Lane in 1785, they were recognized as the leading interpreters of Shakespeare in their age. Kemble during his lifetime played twenty-seven Shakespearean roles, his most successful being Coriolanus and Macbeth. He was tall and imposing, with innate dignity and fine declamatory ability, gifts that fitted him especially well for parts in Shakespeare's Roman plays. After his appointment in 1788 as manager of Drury Lane, he produced a succession of Shakespeare's plays, some of which had not been performed for many years. Although he did not go so far as to return to the text of Shakespeare, he eliminated some of the Restoration changes, and he attempted to reproduce faithfully the costumes and setting of the time of the plays.

Kemble's sister, Mrs. Siddons, was brought to London by Garrick, but she failed in her initial appearance as Portia. After five more years of playing in the provinces, however, she returned to London and achieved the outstanding success already mentioned. Her tall, striking figure and her natural dignity did not fit her well for comedy parts, but in tragedy she has probably never been surpassed, or indeed rivaled, by more than one or two actresses. Her greatest parts were those of Lady Macbeth, Volumnia, Cordelia, Constance, Desdemona, and Ophelia. She was the first actress to discard eighteenth-century costumes for those representative of the time in which the action of the plays took place.

In the early nineteenth century, the chief rival of the Kembles in Shakespearean parts was Edmund Kean (1787–1833). He made his debut at Drury Lane in 1814 as Shylock, and later played the roles of Richard III, Hamlet, Othello, Lear, and Macbeth. He restored the original tragic ending of *Lear*—although after three performances he was forced to revert to Tate's version of the happy ending. His chief influence on Shakespearean stage history, however, was in his interpretation of tragic roles, which he played with such passion and fire that Coleridge, after seeing him perform, declared that witnessing his acting was like reading Shakespeare by flashes of lightning.

One of the main tendencies in Shakespearean production of the nineteenth century was to use more elaborate costumes and scenery, and to introduce spectacular elements. One of the producers who contributed to this tendency was William C. Macready (1793–1873), who for some years was manager of the Covent Garden theater, where he lent his influence as manager and actor to restoring the original Shakespeare, though he did not rid his productions of all the Restoration "improvements." The tendency toward the spectacular and toward elaborate productions was carried further by Charles Kean (1811–1868), son of the actor, Edmund Kean. He introduced great processions in some of the plays and gave close attention to a faithful reproduction of costumes and properties. Carrying on the tradition of elaborate and spectacular productions were Sir Henry Irving (1838–1905), one of the great Shakespearean actors and producers of the century, and Beerbohm Tree (1853–1917).

An opposite tendency, however, toward simple costumes and settings, with emphasis on a good, well-rounded company instead of one or two stars, began toward the middle of the century. In 1844, Samuel Phelps (1804–1878) began producing Shakespeare in London at a small suburban theater called Sadler's Wells. Because his theater was comparatively small and his top price for admission was a shilling, he used simple costumes and a minimum of scenery to keep down production costs; and because he could not afford famous names, he strove to develop a group of good players for all the parts. His innovations were acclaimed by critics, and since his time his principles have been used by Ben Greet, F. R. Benson, and successive producers at the Memorial Theater in Stratford-on-Avon.

Among other notable actors and actresses of the nineteenth century were Helen Faucit (1820–1898) and Charlotte Cushman (1816–1878), who were associated with Macready; Edwin Booth (1833–1893), who came from England to America and was for many years the greatest interpreter of Shakespeare in the United States;[4] Robert Mantell (1854–1928), an American, whose best roles were those of Lear, Macbeth, and Richard III; Helena Modjeska (1840–1909), a famous Polish actress, who appeared in many productions in the United States; Adelaide Neilson (1846–1880), a great favorite in this country; and Ellen Terry (1847–1928), who was associated for many years with Sir Henry Irving.

In the present century, the tendency has been to return somewhat to the manner of staging used in Shakespeare's time, with allowance for the difference between the Elizabethan and the modern stage, and to present plays with continuous action or with one short intermission, with a minimum of scenery, with as little cutting of scenes as possible, and with a close adherence to Shakespeare's text. Many experiments have been made with lighting, and such innovations as playing *Hamlet* in modern dress have been introduced.

---

[4] Booth was the first actor after the Restoration to adhere closely to Shakespeare's text in all his productions.

Until recently, motion-picture productions of the plays have been disappointing, but Laurence Olivier has shown with *Henry V* and *Hamlet* what excellent use can be made of this medium in reproducing Shakespeare and bringing him to the masses who attend motion-picture theaters.

Among even the best actors there is still a tendency, especially in the tragedies, to tear a passion to tatters; yet there seems to be a trend toward more restraint and naturalness in acting. Although this century has produced good actors and actresses —E. H. Sothern and Julia Marlowe, Walter Hampden, Sybil Thorndike, John Gielgud, John Barrymore, Maurice Evans, and Laurence Olivier, among others—no modern actor or actress has won such plaudits as met the acting of Garrick, Mrs. Siddons, and Kean. Perhaps this fact can be attributed, at least in some degree, to more discriminating audiences, with a greater understanding of Shakespeare, and therefore with higher standards for players. Whatever may be the truth of this conjecture, a number of actors—but, for some reason, fewer actresses— have nevertheless met with reasonable success in recent years in their interpretation of Shakespearean roles. And even now, as when Leonard Digges wrote his lines in 1640, when a play by Shakespeare is announced, the pit, boxes, and galleries are likely to be filled.

D

THE BACONIAN THEORY

~~

The comparatively late theory that the works ascribed to Shakespeare were written by someone else is so farfetched and is based on such specious reasoning that Shakespearean scholars for the most part either have ceased to bother with it or have treated it as a bit of humor injected into their serious business. Yet, because the question almost invariably comes up in introductory Shakespeare courses and because those who raise the question lack sufficient knowledge of the Elizabethan age to know how implausible the theory is, a brief discussion should be given here.

Shakespeare enthusiasts themselves were doubtless responsible for the heresy; for no hint that any person other than William Shakespeare of Stratford-on-Avon wrote the plays and poems ascribed to him (except for the suggestion that he may have had an occasional collaborator or have worked over an old play by someone else) was ever given until a century and a half after his death, and it was still another century before the idea had any vogue. By then the Romantic critics had succeeded in exalting Shakespeare to such eminence in every sphere of human understanding and knowledge that some readers, probably with an exaggerated concept of university training and a better acquaintance with critical works about Shakespeare than with his plays, found it hard to conceive of such extensive knowledge residing in any save the most highly trained mind of the age. And looking around for someone who presumably might have such knowledge, they found a likely candidate in Francis Bacon, eminent lawyer, statesman, essayist, and a leading thinker of his time.

The first suggestion that Bacon wrote the works ascribed to

APPENDIX 191

Shakespeare was made by Herbert Lawrence in *The Life and Adventures of Common Sense* (1769), but at the time no notice was taken of the idea. Nearly a century later, J. C. Hart, in *The Romance of Yachting* (1848), made a similar suggestion; but it was W. H. Smith, in *Was Bacon the Author of Shakespeare's Plays?* (1856) and *Bacon and Shakespeare* (1857), and D. Bacon, in *The Philosophy of the Plays of Shakespeare Unfolded* (1857), who gave impetus to the theory. Later, other writers, who added arguments of their own, considered the problem; but it is well to note that no advocate of the theory was a trained Shakespearean scholar, with a scholar's knowledge of all the problems involved and a scholar's detachment in dealing with them.

The anti-Shakespeareans began with the premise that it was impossible for a nearly illiterate "Stratford rustic" to write the great plays attributed to Shakespeare—a premise which would be more nearly valid if Shakespeare had actually been an uneducated village rustic. Ignoring the fact that we lack exact knowledge of Shakespeare's education, they expanded on Ben Jonson's statement that Shakespeare had small Latin and less Greek and arrived at the notion that he was virtually illiterate. On the other hand, they accepted, without analyzing his works, the exaggerated encomiums of some critics that whoever wrote the plays was thoroughly versed in the law, in marine lore, and in a score of other fields of knowledge. And putting together these two "facts," they decided that "the Stratford rustic" *could* not have written the plays. To arrive at such a conclusion they had to ignore dozens of contemporary references to Shakespeare's authorship of the poems and plays, and numerous records that point the same way; they had to assume a conspiracy among all those who participated in publishing the First Folio—and to accept the premise that so honest a person as Ben Jonson was either an out-and-out liar or as much a gull as a character in his own *Alchemist,* and could be imposed on beyond belief; and they had to account for the fact that a busy statesman had time amid all his other activities and a sufficient acquaintance with the stage to produce the entire body of work ascribed to Shakespeare.

An extension of the theory included the supposed finding in the plays or references to them of a cipher or cryptogram that "proved" Bacon's authorship of the plays; but this argument proved to be so palpably absurd that it was soon dropped even by the pro-Baconians.[1]

Meanwhile scholars with comprehensive knowledge of the Elizabethan age were able to demonstrate that the writer of the works ascribed to Shakespeare was no superman, and was not, as had been held, thoroughly trained in a number of professions or fields of knowledge. And they continued to bring forward substantial evidence, instead of implausible theories, that gave a good account of Shakespeare and his works. In this connection it is worth noting that every fact which has been turned up since the Baconian theory was advanced substantiates the basic assumption that "the man of Stratford" and the writer of the plays were identical and that not a single record or fact has been produced to substantiate the theories that someone else wrote the plays.

When the Baconian theory was first advanced, Shakespearean scholars gave serious attention to refuting it; and they succeeded so well that the anti-Shakespeareans began to shift their ground and to father the plays on someone else. In 1912, a Belgian professor, Celestin Demblon, in *Lord Rutland est Shakespeare,* advanced the case for Roger Manners, fifteenth earl of Rutland; in 1919, Professor Abel Lefranc, of the Collège de France, claimed that the author of the plays was William Stanley, sixth earl of Derby; and in 1920, J. T. Looney ascribed the plays to Edward de Vere, seventeenth earl of Oxford. These

---

[1] One advocate of the cipher theory, for instance, based his case on the occurrence of a very long Latin word in *Love's Labour's Lost.* Because he did not know that the word was in an elementary Latin textbook which every schoolboy of Shakespeare's day knew, he held that such a word would not have been used except to call attention to a cipher. Another cipher advocate developed an elaborate explanation that depended on Bacon's knowing Pope's translation of Homer a century after Bacon's time.

claims, of course, cancel out one another, though each claimant has his advocates.

The fact is that error, like truth, if crushed to earth will rise again. And the theory that someone else wrote the works ascribed to Shakespeare still gains an occasional recruit—even as, in a different stratum of society, does the cult which holds that the way to serve God is to handle poisonous snakes. The serious student who wonders why such matters claim attention if they are wholly unfounded should bear in mind that legends grow up around every great person and occasion; that the basic premise of the anti-Shakespeareans that a man without university training could not have written the works ascribed to Shakespeare, if extended, might apply as well to the theory that Abraham Lincoln could not have directed the destiny of the United States at a time of crisis, or that such inventors and industrialists as Thomas Edison and Henry Ford could never have done the things attributed to them; that of all persons who have accepted the theory, the few with sufficient intelligence to win consideration were laymen, so far as Elizabethan scholarship went, or were foreigners who lacked full understanding of many of the issues in controversy; and that not a single authority who is thoroughly grounded in Shakespearean scholarship has joined the ranks of the doubters.

E

SHAKESPEARE'S WILL

Shakespeare's will was doubtless written by a clerk in the employ of Francis Collins, a solicitor of Warwick. The spelling and punctuation, or lack of punctuation, were according to the usage of the time. In the copy that follows, I have modernized the spelling and added punctuation. The will was written on three sheets, the first of which was probably rewritten from an earlier draft. For an exact reproduction, with the original spelling and punctuation, see E. K. Chambers, *William Shakespeare* (II, 169–174); and for a discussion of the will and its provisions, see Chambers (pp. 174–180), and J. Q. Adams, *Life* (pp. 460–472). The will contained a few deletions and additions; I indicate these by a line through the deleted parts and italics for the additions.

> Vicesimo Quinto die ~~Januarii~~ *Martii* Anno Regni Domini nostri Jacobi nunc Regis Anglie &c decimo quarto & Scotie xlix⁰ Annoque domini 1616.

T[estamentum] W[illel]mi Shackspeare.

R[ecognoscatu]r. In the name of God, Amen! I, William Shackspeare, of Stratford upon Avon, in the county of Warwick, gentleman, in perfect health and memory, God be praised, do make and ordain this my last will and testament in manner and form following. That is to say, first, I commend my soul into the hands of God my Creator, hoping and assuredly believing, through the only merits of Jesus Christ my Saviour, to be made partaker of life everlasting, and my body to the earth whereof it is made. Item, I give and bequeath unto my ~~son in L~~ daughter Judith one hundred and fifty pounds of lawful English money, to be paid unto her in manner and form following, that is to say, one hundred pounds *in discharge of her marriage portion* within one year after my decease, with consideration after the rate of two shillings in the pound for so long time as the same shall be unpaid unto her after my decease, and the fifty pounds residue thereof upon her surrendering of, or giving of, such sufficient security as the overseers of this my will shall like of, to surrender or grant all her estate and right that shall descend or come unto her after my decease, or *that she* now hath, of, in, or to, one copyhold tenement, with the appurtenances, lying and being in Stratford upon Avon aforesaid, in the said county of Warr., being parcel or holden of the manor of Rowington, unto my daughter Susanna Hall and her heirs for ever. Item, I give and bequeath unto my said daughter Judith one hundred and fifty pounds more if she or any issue of her body be living at the end of three years next ensuing the day of the date of this my will, during which time my executors to pay her consideration from my decease according to the rate aforesaid; and if she die within the said term without issue of her body, then my will is, and I do give and bequeath one hundred pounds thereof to my niece Elizabeth Hall, and the fifty pounds to be set forth by my executors during the life of my sister Joan Hart, and the use and profit thereof coming shall be paid to my said sister Joan, and after her decease the said l^li shall remain amongst the children of my said sister, equally to be divided amongst them: but if my said daughter Judith be living at the end of the said three years, or any issue of her body, then my will is, and so I devise and bequeath, the said hundred and fifty pounds to be set out *by my executors and overseers* for the best benefit of her and her issue, and *the stock* not *to be* paid unto her so long as she shall be married and covert baron by my executors and overseers; but my will is that she shall have the consideration yearly paid unto her during her life, and after her decease the said stock and consideration to be paid to her children, if she have any, and if not, to her executors or assigns, she living the said term after my decease. Provided that if such husband as she shall at the end of the said three years be married unto, or at any after (*sic*), do sufficiently assure unto her and the issue of her body lands answerable to the portion by this my will given unto her, and to be adjudged so by my executors and overseers, then my will is that the said cl^li shall be paid to such husband as shall make such assurance, to his own use. Item, I give and bequeath unto my said sister Joan xx^li and all my wearing apparel, to be paid and delivered within one year after my decease; and I do will and devise unto her *the house* with the appurtenances in Stratford, wherein she dwelleth, for her natural life, under the yearly rent of xii^d. Item, I give and bequeath [SHEET 2] unto her three sons, William Hart,   Hart, (*sic*) and Michael Hart, five pounds a piece, to be paid within one year after my decease ~~to be set out for her within one year after my decease by my executors, with the advice and directions of my overseers, for her best profit, until her marriage, and then the same, with the increase thereof to be paid unto her~~. Item, I give and bequeath unto ~~her~~ *the said Elizabeth Hall* all my plate, *except my broad silver and gilt bowl,* that I now have at the date of this my will. Item, I give and bequeath unto the poor of Stratford aforesaid ten pounds; to Mr. Thomas Combe my sword; to Thomas Russell, Esquire, five pounds; and to Francis Collins, of the borough of Warwick in the county of Warwick, gentleman, thirteen pounds, six shillings, and eight pence, to be paid within one year after my decease. Item, I give and bequeath to ~~Mr. Richard Tyler the elder~~ *Hamlett Sadler* xxvi^s viii^d to buy him a ring; to *William Raynoldes, gent., xxvi^s viii^d to buy him a ring;* to my godson William Walker xx^s in gold; to Anthony Nashe, gent., xxvi^s viii^d; and to Mr. John Nashe xxvi^s viii^d ~~in gold~~; *and to my fellows John Hemynge, Richard Burbage, and Henry Cundell xxvi^s viii^d a piece to buy them rings.* Item, I give, will, bequeath, and devise unto my daughter Susanna Hall, *for better enabling of her to perform this my will, and towards the performance thereof,* all that capital messuage or tenement with the appurtenances, *in Stratford aforesaid,* called the New Place, wherein I now dwell, and two messuages or tenements with the appurtenances, situate, lying, and being in Henley Street, within the borough of Stratford aforesaid; and all my barns, stables, orchards, gardens, lands, tenements, and hereditaments whatsoever, situate, lying, and being, or to be had, received, perceived, or taken, within the towns, hamlets, villages, fields, and grounds of Stratford upon Avon, Oldstratford, Bushopton, and Welcombe, or in any of them in the said county of Warwick. And also all that messuage or tenement with the appurtenances wherein one John Robinson dwelleth, situate, lying, and being in the Blackfriers in London, near the Wardrobe; and all other my lands, tenements, and hereditaments whatsoever, to have and to hold all and singular the said premises with their appurtenances unto the said Susanna Hall for and during the term of her natural life, and after her decease to the first son of her body lawfully issuing, and to the heirs males of the body of the said first son lawfully issuing; and for default of such issue, to the second son of her body lawfully issuing, and ~~so~~ to the heirs males of the body of the said second son lawfully issuing; and for default of such heirs, to the third son of the body of the said Susanna lawfully issuing, and of the heirs males of the body of the said third son lawfully issuing; and for default of such issue, the same so to be and remain to the fourth ~~son~~, fifth, sixth, and seventh sons of her body lawfully issuing, one after another, and to the heirs [SHEET 3] males of the bodies of the said fourth, fifth, sixth, and seventh sons lawfully issuing, in such manner as it is before limited to be and remain to the first, second, and third sons of her body, and to their heirs males; and for default of such issue, the said premises to be and remain to my said niece Hall, and the heirs males of her body lawfully issuing; and for default of issue, to my daughter Judith, and the heirs males of her body lawfully issuing; and for default of such issue, to the right heirs of me the said William Shackspere for ever. *Item, I give unto my wife my second best bed with the furniture.* Item, I give and bequeath to my said daughter Judith my broad silver gilt bowl. All the rest of my goods, chattels, leases, plate, jewels, and household stuff whatsoever, after my debts and legacies paid and my funeral expenses discharged, I give, devise, and bequeath to my son-in-law, John Hall, Gent., and my daughter Susanna, his wife, whom I ordain and make executors of this my last will and testament. And I do entreat and appoint *the said* Thomas Russell, Esquire, and Francis Collins, Gent., to be overseers hereof, and do revoke all former wills, and publish this to be my last will and testament. In witness whereof I have hereunto put my ~~seal~~ hand, the day and year first above written.

By me William Shakspeare

Witness to the publishing
hereof, Fra. Collyns
   Julyus Shawe
   John Robinson
   Hamnet Sadler
   Robert Whattcott

[*Endorsed*] Probatum coram magistro Willielmo Byrde legum doctore Comissario &c xxii^{do} die mensis Junii Anno Domini 1616. Juramento Johannis Hall unius executoris &c cui &c de bene &c Jurato. Reservata potestate &c Susanne Hall alteri executori &c cum venerit &c petitura.

Inventorium exhibitum

APPENDIX

F. GENEALOGY OF THE HOUSES

Edward II (1284–1327) *m.* Isabella, sister of Louis X
  └ Edward III (1312–1377)

- Edward, the Black Prince (1st son, 1330–1376)
  - **Richard II** (1367–1400)
- Lionel, Duke of Clarence (3rd son, 1338–1368)
  - Philippa, *m.* Edmund Mortimer, Earl of March (1351–1381)
    - Elizabeth, *m.* Hotspur (*Henry IV*)
    - Roger, Earl of March (*d.* 1398)
      - Edmund, Earl of March (*d.* 1424)
      - Anne, *m.* Richard, Earl of Cambridge (beheaded, 1415)
        - Richard, Duke of York (1411–1460)
          - Edward IV (1442–1483)
            - Edward V (1470–1483)
            - Richard, Duke of York (1473–1483)
            - Elizabeth (1465–1503), *m.* Henry VII
              - **Henry VIII** (1491–1547)
                - Mary (1516–1558)
                - Edward VI (1537–1553)
                - Elizabeth (1533–1603)
          - Edmund, Earl of Rutland (slain at Wakefield, 1460)
          - George, Duke of Clarence (1449–1478), *m.* Isabelle Neville
            - Edward, Earl of Warwick (beheaded, 1499)
            - Margaret, Countess of Salisbury (beheaded, 1541), *m.* Sir Richard Pole
          - **Richard III** (1452–1485), *m.* Anne Neville
- Edmund, Duke of York (5th son, 1341–1402)
  - Edward, the Aumerle in *Richard II* and York in *Henry V* 1373–1415)
- Thomas, Duke of Gloucester (7th son, 1355–1397)
  - Anne (1380–1438), *m.* 2, Edmund, Earl of Stafford
    - Humphrey, Duke of Buckingham (1402–1460)
      - Humphrey, Earl of Devon 1439–1469)
      - Henry, Duke of Buckingham (1454–1483), in *Richard III*

OF LANCASTER AND YORK

of France (basis for English claim to France; see *Henry V*, I, ii)

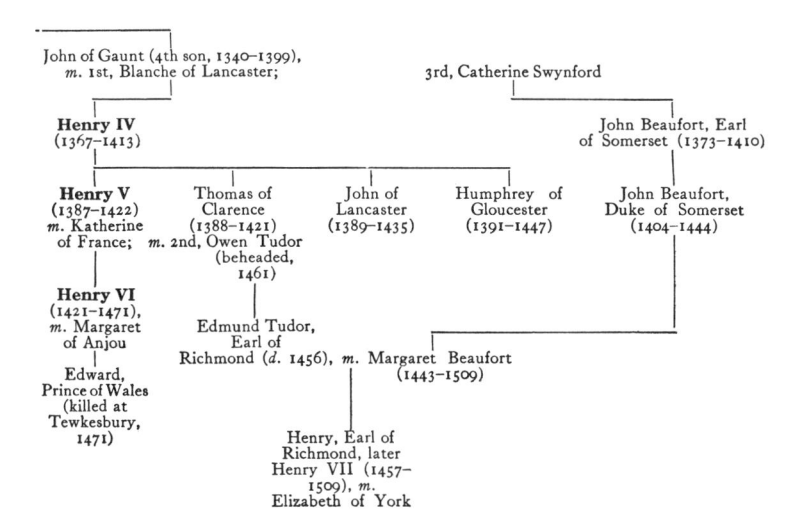

John of Gaunt (4th son, 1340–1399),
  m. 1st, Blanche of Lancaster;   3rd, Catherine Swynford

Henry IV (1367–1413)   John Beaufort, Earl of Somerset (1373–1410)

Henry V (1387–1422) *m.* Katherine of France;

Thomas of Clarence (1388–1421) *m.* 2nd, Owen Tudor (beheaded, 1461)

John of Lancaster (1389–1435)

Humphrey of Gloucester (1391–1447)

John Beaufort, Duke of Somerset (1404–1444)

Henry VI (1421–1471), *m.* Margaret of Anjou

Edward, Prince of Wales (killed at Tewkesbury, 1471)

Edmund Tudor, Earl of Richmond (*d.* 1456), *m.* Margaret Beaufort (1443–1509)

Henry, Earl of Richmond, later Henry VII (1457–1509), *m.* Elizabeth of York

BIBLIOGRAPHY

This bibliography lists only a few of the books on Shakespeare and his age. For a fuller list—yet one far from complete—see *The Cambridge Bibliography of English Literature* (1941, I, 539-608). The bibliographical notes that preface the various chapters in E. K. Chambers's *The Elizabethan Stage* and *William Shakespeare* are valuable. W. Jaggard's *Shakespeare Bibliography* (Stratford-on-Avon: 1911) lists "every known issue of the writings of our national poet and of recorded opinion thereon in the English language" to the date of its issue. The most important bibliography up to the present time is *A Shakespeare Bibliography*, by W. Ebisch and L. L. Schücking (London: 1931) and the *Supplement for the Years 1930-1935* (London: 1937). Students who wish to keep up with the latest work being done on Shakespeare will find it listed in *The Annual Bibliography of English Language and Literature*, published by the Modern Humanities Research Association; the *Bulletin* of the Shakespeare Association of America; and *The Year's Work in English Studies*, by the English Association. *The Review of English Studies* lists articles in periodicals; and a list of American contributions appears each year in "American Bibliography," in the *Publications of the Modern Language Association*.

LANGUAGE, VERSIFICATION, AND BOOKS OF REFERENCE

Abbott, E. A., *A Shakespearian Grammar* (3rd ed.). London: 1870.

> Still the best work on Shakespeare's language.

Bartlett, J., *A New Complete Concordance or Verbal Index to the Words, Phrases, and Passages in the Dramatic Works of Shakespeare, with a Supplementary Concordance to the Poems*. New York: 1894.

BIBLIOGRAPHY 201

Munro, John, *The Shakspere Allusion-Book: A Collection of Allusions to Shakspere from 1591 to 1700.* 2 vols. London: 1909; reissued, 1932.

Onions, C. T., *The Shakespeare Glossary* (2nd ed.). London: 1919.

A handy volume of Elizabethan words and meanings.

Schmidt, Alexander, *Shakespeare-Lexicon* (3rd ed.). 2 vols. Berlin: 1902.

"A complete Dictionary of all the English words, phrases, and constructions in the works of the poet."

Stevenson, Burton, *The Home Book of Shakespeare Quotations.* New York: 1937.

A ready source in which to locate any quotation from Shakespeare.

BIOGRAPHIES AND SPECIAL BIOGRAPHICAL STUDIES

Adams, J. Q., *A Life of William Shakespeare.* Boston: 1923.

The best general biography. Easy to read.

Baker, O., *In Shakespeare's Warwickshire and the Unknown Years.* London: 1937.

An attempt to answer questions about Shakespeare's ancestry and family. Interesting for the mature student.

Chambers, E. K., *William Shakespeare: A Study of Facts and Problems.* 2 vols. London: 1930.

Conservative and sane; invaluable for reference. Too scholarly for easy reading by the beginner.

Fripp, E. I., *Shakespeare, Man and Artist.* 2 vols. London: 1938.

Not trustworthy on all biographical matters, but a mine of antiquarian lore. Somewhat difficult reading for the beginner.

Gray, J. W., *Shakespeare's Marriage and Departure from Stratford.* London: 1905.

An important and scholarly work; conjectural but sensible.

Halliwell-Phillipps, J. O., *Outlines of the Life of Shakespeare* (7th ed.). London: 1887.

The first attempt at a complete biography; now outdated, but valuable for the scholar.

Lee, Sidney, *A Life of William Shakespeare* (14th ed.). New York: 1931.

A standard work, but now somewhat out of date.

Lewis, B. R., *The Shakespeare Documents.* Stanford, Calif.: 1940.

Reproduction of every contemporary document relating to Shakespeare and his works, with interpretive commentary. For reference.

Marcham, F., *William Shakespeare and His Daughter Susannah.* London: 1931.

On Shakespeare and his family.

Raleigh, Walter, *Shakespeare.* ("English Men of Letters Series.") New York: 1907.

A brief work, with penetrating and stimulating comments. Recommended for the college student.

Smart, J. S., *Shakespeare; Truth and Tradition.* New York: 1928.

Controversial, but containing valuable material.

Spencer, Hazelton, *The Art and Life of William Shakespeare.* New York: 1940.

A sane and scholarly work, with good short commentaries on the plays. Designed for the mature student.

Stopes, Charlotte C., *Shakespeare's Family.* New York: 1901.

An early study, but with valuable material, some conjectural.

TEXTUAL MATTERS

Albright, Evelyn M., *Dramatic Publication in England, 1580–1640: A Study of Conditions Affecting Content and Form of Drama.* ("Modern Language Association of America Monograph Series," II.) New York: 1927.

Information on publishing conditions, ownership of plays, and the like.

Bartlett, Henrietta C., Mr. *William Shakespeare: Original and Early Editions of His Quartos and Folios, His Source Books, and Those Containing Contemporary Notices.* New Haven, Conn.: 1922.

Chiefly useful to bibliographers and for reference.

—— and A. W. Pollard, *A Census of Shakespeare's Plays in Quarto, 1594–1709* (rev. ed.). New Haven, Conn.: 1939.

Bibliography, and list of places where extant quartos are to be found.

Duthie, G. I., *"Bad" Quarto of Hamlet.* London: 1941.

Designed for mature scholars.

Flatter, Richard, *Shakespeare's Producing Hand.* London: 1948.

A careful study of the punctuation of the Folio; interesting conclusions.

Greg, W. W., *Dramatic Documents from the Elizabethan Playhouses.* 2 vols. London: 1931.

Reproductions and enlightening commentary. Designed for mature scholars.

——, *The Editorial Problem in Shakespeare: A Survey of the Foundations of the Text.* London: 1942.

A good book for mature students interested in textual problems.

McKerrow, R. B., *An Introduction to Bibliography for Literary Students.* London: 1927.

Excellent for the undergraduate who wishes information about how Elizabethan books were made.

——, *Printers' and Publishers' Devices in England and Scotland, 1485–1640.* London: 1913.

A pioneer work; important for the scholar rather than the beginner.

Pollard, A. W., *The Foundations of Shakespeare's Text.* London: 1923.

A British Academy lecture; republished in *Aspects of Shakespeare.*

——, *Shakespeare Folios and Quartos: A Study in the Bibliography of Shakespeare's Plays, 1594–1685.* London: 1909.

A scholarly study that introduced ideas, now largely accepted, about 'good' and 'bad' quartos.

———, *Shakespeare's Fight with the Pirates and the Problems of the Transmission of His Text* (2nd ed.). London: 1920.

Some highly important conjectures and conclusions; for mature scholars.

Willoughby, E. E., *The Printing of the First Folio of Shakespeare*. London: 1932.

CRITICAL WORKS AND STUDIES OF SOURCES

Anders, H. R. D., *Shakespeare's Books: A Dissertation on Shakespeare's Reading and the Immediate Sources of His Works*. Berlin: 1904.

Aspects of Shakespeare. London: 1933.

A reprint of a number of British Academy Lectures on Shakespeare. Very good.

Bentley, G. E., *Shakespeare and Jonson: Their Reputations in the Seventeenth Century Compared*. Chicago: 1945.

Boswell-Stone, W. G., *Holinshed's Chronicle As Used in Shakespeare's Plays*. London: 1896.

The pertinent passages in Holinshed that Shakespeare used for his histories.

Bradby, Anne (ed.), *Shakespeare Criticism 1919–35*. ("World's Classics.") London: 1936.

Representative selections by recent commentators.

Bradley, A. C., *Oxford Lectures on Poetry*. New York: 1909, "The Rejection of Falstaff" and "Antony and Cleopatra."

———, *Shakespearean Tragedy*. New York: 1904.

The high-water mark of the critical approach exemplified by nineteenth-century interpreters; excellent for the beginner.

Brooke, C. F. Tucker, *Essays on Shakespeare and Other Elizabethans*. New Haven, Conn.: 1948.

A collection of pleasant yet scholarly essays on various subjects.

Campbell, Lily B., *Shakespeare's Histories*. San Marino, Calif.: 1947.

> Scholarly but rewarding for the earnest student.

———, *Shakespeare's Tragic Heroes: Slaves of Passion*. London: 1930.

> A consideration of the tragedies in relation to the Elizabethan philosophy concerning the nature of the emotions; scholarly.

Campbell, Oscar J., *Shakespeare's Satire*. New York: 1943.

> A scholarly discussion of an important element in Shakespeare's works.

Charlton, H. B., *Shakespearian Comedy*. New York: 1938.

———, *Shakespearian Tragedy*. London: 1948.

> Interesting commentaries by a careful scholar.

Craig, Hardin, *An Interpretation of Shakespeare*. New York: 1948.

> A sane, conservative volume, containing a brief comment on each play; a good book for the college student to read.

Fairchild, A. H. R., *Shakespeare and the Arts of Design*. ("University of Missouri Studies," Vol. XII, No. 1.) Columbia, Mo.: 1937.

> A sane study of a special topic; for the mature student.

Gollancz, Israel (ed.), *A Book of Homage to Shakespeare*. London: 1916.

> A collection of essays by various writers for the Shakespeare anniversary.

Gordon, G. S., *Shakespearian Comedy and Other Studies*. London: 1944.

> Pleasantly written; the early essays in the volume are the best.

Granville-Barker, Harley, *Prefaces to Shakespeare*. Princeton, N. J.: 1927–1930.

> Valuable interpretations by an authority on acting and the stage; meant as introductions to the separate plays, but reworked and expanded for the Princeton edition.

———, and G. B. Harrison (eds.), *A Companion to Shakespeare Studies*. New York: 1934.

> A collection of essays on various topics, each by an authority.

Harbage, Alfred, *As They Liked It: An Essay on Shakespeare and Morality.* New York: 1947.

———, *Shakespeare's Audience.* New York: 1942.

Interesting discussions of Shakespeare's audiences and how they affected the action and outcomes of the plays. Pleasantly written.

Hazlitt, W. C., *Shakespeare's Library* (2nd ed., by J. P. Collier). 6 vols. London: 1875.

A collection of the romances, novels, poems, and histories (except Holinshed) used by Shakespeare in writing his plays.

Knight, G. Wilson, *The Crown of Life.* London: 1947.

———, *The Imperial Theme.* London: 1931.
———, *The Shakespearian Tempest.* London: 1932.
———, *The Wheel of Fire.* London: 1930.

A series of interpretive volumes, excellently written and challenging, but not to be accepted without question.

Lawrence, W. W., *Shakespeare's Problem Comedies.* New York: 1931.

Probably the best approach to the bitter comedies.

MacCallum, M. W., *Shakespeare's Roman Plays and Their Background.* New York: 1910.

On Shakespeare's use of classical materials.

Marriott, J. A. R., *English History in Shakespeare.* New York: 1918.

An attempt to explain the underlying themes of the history plays.

Murry, John Middleton, *Shakespeare.* London: 1936.

A very readable volume.

Nicoll, Allardyce, *Studies in Shakespeare.* New York: 1928.

Comment on four tragedies.

——— (ed.), *Shakespeare Survey.* London: 1948, and yearly thereafter.

An annual survey of Shakespearean study and production.

BIBLIOGRAPHY 207

Nicoll, Allardyce, and J. Nicoll (eds.), *Holinshed's Chronicle, As Used in Shakespeare's Plays.* ("Everyman's Library.") New York: 1927.

An easily accessible volume for those wishing to study the sources used by Shakespeare in writing his histories.

Parrott, T. M., *Shakespearean Comedy.* London: 1949.

A carefully done, scholarly work.

Ralli, Augustus, *A History of Shakespearian Criticism.* 2 vols. London: 1932.

A summary of aesthetic criticism from Shakespeare's time to 1925.

Raysor, T. M. (ed.), *Coleridge's Shakespearean Criticism.* 2 vols. London: 1930.

The most complete and accurate collection of Coleridge's criticism.

Robertson, J. M., *The Baconian Heresy.* New York: 1913.

An intelligent refutation of the Baconian theory.

Schücking, L. L., *Character Problems in Shakespeare's Plays.* New York: 1922.

An example of the post-Romantic criticism.

Smith, D. Nichol, *Shakespeare Criticism: A Selection.* ("World's Classics.") London: 1916.

A selection of critical writings from Shakespeare's day to Carlyle.

———, *Shakespeare in the Eighteenth Century.* London: 1928.

——— (ed.), *Eighteenth-Century Essays on Shakespeare.* Glasgow: 1903.

The best critical articles of the eighteenth century gathered in one volume.

Smith, Logan P., *On Reading Shakespeare.* New York: 1933.

A delightful little volume; recommended for undergraduates.

Spencer, Theodore, *Shakespeare and the Nature of Man.* New York: 1942.

A consideration of Shakespeare in the light of certain Renaissance ideas.

Spurgeon, Caroline F. E., *Shakespeare's Imagery and What It Tells Us.* New York: 1935.

    An important contribution to Shakespeare studies; conclusions open to question.

Stoll, E. E., *Art and Artifice in Shakespeare: A Study in Dramatic Contrast and Illusion.* London: 1933.

———, *Shakespeare and Other Masters.* Cambridge, Mass.: 1940.

———, *Shakespeare Studies: Historical and Comparative in Method.* New York: 1927.

    These and other books and articles by Professor Stoll illustrate a modern interpretation of Shakespeare; important examples of the modern trend in Shakespearean criticism.

Swinburne, A. C., *A Study of Shakespeare.* London: 1880.

    One of the best essays in the romantic tradition.

Tillyard, E. M. W., *Shakespeare's History Plays.* New York: 1946.

———, *Shakespeare's Last Plays.* London: 1938.

———, *Shakespeare's Problem Plays.* London: 1949.

    Illuminating commentaries by a sane scholar.

Wendell, Barrett, *William Shakspere.* New York: 1894.

    Somewhat outdated, but recommended for certain illuminating comments.

Wilson, J. Dover, *The Essential Shakespeare.* London: 1930.

    A pleasant little volume; highly recommended for beginners.

———, *What Happens in Hamlet.* London: 1935.

    Excellently written, but very uneven commentary on *Hamlet.* To be read after considerable acquaintance with the play.

BOOKS ON STAGECRAFT AND THE THEATER

Albright, Victor E., *The Shaksperian Stage.* New York: 1909; new ed., 1926.

    An early but still valuable book on the subject.

Adams, J. C., *The Globe Playhouse; Its Design and Equipment.* Cambridge, Mass.: 1942.

Adams, J. Q., *Shakespearean Playhouses: A History of English Theaters from the Beginnings to the Restoration.* Boston: 1917.

> Includes a history of the playhouses with which Shakespeare was connected.

Baker, G. P., *The Development of Shakespeare as a Dramatist.* New York: 1907.

> Still valuable on Shakespeare's dramatic development, his theater, and so forth.

Baldwin, T. W., *The Organization and Personnel of the Shakespearean Company.* Princeton, N. J.: 1927.

> The result of much scholarly work; some parts conjectural, but highly valuable, though hardly the book for the young student.

Campbell, Lily B., *Scenes and Machines on the English Stage during the Renaissance.* London: 1923.

> A scholarly work on a special subject.

Chambers, E. K., *The Elizabethan Stage.* 4 vols. London: 1923.

> A storehouse of reference; the outstanding work on the subject.

Davies, W. R., *Shakespeare's Boy Actors.* London: 1939.

> A readable study on a specialized subject.

Feuillerat, A., *Documents Relating to the Office of the Revels in the Time of Queen Elizabeth.* Louvain: 1908.

> An important early work, but hardly for the general reader.

Greg, W. W. (ed.), *Henslowe's Diary.* 2 parts. London: 1904, 1908.
——— (ed.), *Henslowe Papers.* London: 1907.

> These books throw a great deal of light on theatrical methods in Shakespeare's time.

Kelly, F. M., *Shakespearian Costume for Stage and Screen.* London: 1938.

> Useful for producers; of some interest to students.

Lawrence, W. J., *The Elizabethan Playhouse and Other Studies.* Stratford-upon-Avon: 1912; 2nd series, 1913.

Lawrence, W. J., *The Physical Conditions of the Elizabethan Public Playhouse*. Cambridge, Mass.: 1927.

———, *Pre-Restoration Stage Studies*. London: 1927.

———, *Those Nut-Cracking Elizabethans; Studies of the Early Theater and Drama*. London: 1935.

These various volumes are not difficult to read; they provide useful information on the theater and audiences of Shakespeare's time.

Lee, Sidney, *Shakespeare and the Modern Stage*. New York: 1906.

Linthicum, M. C., *Costume in the Drama of Shakespeare and His Contemporaries*. London: 1936.

Matthews, Brander, *Shakspere as a Playwright*. New York: 1913.

A good general treatment.

Murray, J. T., *English Dramatic Companies, 1558–1642*. 2 vols. London: 1910.

An important early consideration of the subject; useful for reference.

Nungezer, E., *A Dictionary of Actors and Other Persons Associated with the Public Representation of Plays in England before 1642*. New Haven, Conn.: 1929.

A scholarly reference work.

Odell, G. C. D., *Annals of the New York Stage*. New York: 1927 *et seq*.

———, *Shakespeare from Betterton to Irving*. 2 vols. New York: 1920.

These two volumes contain the fullest and best treatment of Shakespearean actors and productions.

Sprague, A. C., *Shakespeare and the Actors*. Cambridge, Mass.: 1944.

———, *Shakespeare and the Audience*. Cambridge, Mass.: 1935.

Useful for the student who wishes to understand Shakespeare's environment.

Tannenbaum, S. A., *The Forman Notes on Shakspere*. New York: 1933.

Tannenbaum, S. A., *More about the Forged Revels Accounts.* New York: 1932.

———, *Shakspere Forgeries in the Revels Accounts.* New York: 1928.

On the authenticity of records, by a handwriting expert.

Thorndike, A. H., *Shakespeare's Theater.* New York: 1916.

A summary of matters relating to the stage, the playhouse, and dramatic companies.

Winter, William, *Shakespeare on the Stage.* (1st, 2nd, and 3rd series.) New York: 1911, 1915, 1916.

Comment on the chief Shakespearean actors and actresses.

THE AGE, BACKGROUND, AND ENVIRONMENT

Allen, J. W., *A History of Political Thought in the Sixteenth Century.* New York: 1928.

Black, J. B., *The Reign of Elizabeth, 1558–1603.* (*The Oxford History of England*, Vol. VIII.) New York: 1936.

Boas, F. S., *An Introduction to Tudor Drama.* London: 1933.

Easy to read; useful for the beginner.

———, *Shakspere and His Predecessors.* New York: 1896.

Superseded by later works, but still useful.

Brooke, C. F. Tucker, *The Shakespeare Apocrypha.* London: 1908; reissued, 1918.

A collection of plays sometimes attributed to Shakespeare.

———, *Tudor Drama.* Boston: 1911.

A discussion of the drama of Shakespeare's time; good.

Bush, Douglas, *Mythology and the Renaissance Tradition in English Poetry.* Minneapolis: 1932.

A scholarly work on a restricted topic; valuable for the mature student.

Byrne, Muriel St. C., *Elizabethan Life in Town and Country* (2nd ed.). Boston: 1934.

Craig, Hardin, *The Enchanted Glass: The Elizabethan Mind in Literature.* New York: 1936.

> On the intellectual background.

Davis, W. S., *Life in Elizabethan Days: A Picture of a Typical English Community at the End of the Sixteenth Century.* New York: 1930.

> How the typical family lived in Shakespeare's day.

Fripp, S. S., *Shakespeare's Stratford.* London: 1928.

> An attempt to reconstruct Shakespeare's native town.

Green, A. W., *The Inns of Court and Early English Drama.* New Haven, Conn.: 1931.

> Useful to the mature student.

Harrison, G. B., *The Elizabethan Journals: Being a Record of Those Things Most Talked of During the Years 1591–1603.* New York: 1939.

> A revised, single-volume edition of three volumes issued previously. A happily inspired work; good reading.

Innes, A. D., *England under the Tudors* (3rd ed.). (*A History of England,* 7 vols., Vol. IV.) New York: 1911.

Lee, Sidney, *Stratford-on-Avon from the Earliest Times to the Death of Shakespeare* (rev. ed.). Philadelphia: 1907.

> Contains a great amount of valuable information; superseded in some respects.

Madden, D. H., *The Diary of Master William Silence.* London: 1897.

> A study of Shakespeare and Elizabethan sport.

Neale, J. E., *Queen Elizabeth.* New York: 1934.

Oman, Sir Charles, *The Sixteenth Century.* New York: 1936.

Schelling, F. E., *Elizabethan Drama, 1558–1642.* 2 vols. Boston: 1908.

> A standard work, dealing with the drama of Shakespeare's age.

———, *Elizabethan Playwrights: A Short History of the English Drama from Medieval Times to . . . 1642.* New York: 1925.

Shakespeare's England: An Account of the Life and Manners of His Age. 2 vols. London: 1916.

A monumental work, with chapters on many subjects by various authors.

Stopes, Charlotte C., *Shakespeare's Environment.* London: 1914.

———, *Shakespeare's Warwickshire Contemporaries* (new ed.). Stratford-upon-Avon: 1907.

Taylor, H. O., *Thought and Expression in the Sixteenth Century.* 2 vols. New York: 1920.

A work that will reward the persevering student.

Thompson, E. N. S., *The Controversy between the Puritans and the Stage.* ("Yale Studies in English," XX) New York: 1903.

Ward, A. W., *A History of English Dramatic Literature to the Death of Queen Anne* (2nd ed.). 3 vols. New York: 1899.

Still valuable as a reference work.

Welsford, Enid, *The Fool; His Social and Literary History.* London: 1935.

Wilson, F. P., *The Plague in Shakespeare's London.* London: 1927.

Wilson, J. Dover, *Life in Shakespeare's England.* London: 1911.

Wright, Louis B., *Middle Class Culture in Elizabethan England.* Chapel Hill, N. C.: 1935.

INDEX

INDEX

Actes and Monuments (Foxe), 141
Adams, J. Q., 31 n, 49 n, 53 n, 66, 70, 78 n, 82, 84, 89, 126, 127, 158
Agriculture, 9, 10
Alexander, Peter, 74
All for Love (Dryden), 128, 143
All's Well That Ends Well, 118–119, 120
Amphitruo (Plautus), 78
Antony and Cleopatra, 128–130, 155
Antwerp, destruction of, 11
Apollonius of Tyre, 78, 134
Apuleius, Lucius, Golden Ass, 92
Arcadia (Sidney), 124
Arden, Robert, 27, 28
Ariosto, 2, 83
Armin, Robert, 48, 183
Arraignment of Paris, The, 44
As You Like It, 106–108, 109
Aspley, William, 61, 62
Aubrey, John, 30, 32
   biographical reference to Shakespeare, 175–176
Audience, the Elizabethan, 54

Bacon, Francis, 13
Baconian heresy, 190 ff.
Baker, G. P., 158
Baldwin, T. W., 48 n, 49 n, 57 n
Bandello, 102, 108
Barnfield, Richard, praises Shakespeare, 161–162
Barry, Elizabeth, 185
Barrymore, John, 189
Bartholomew Fair (Jonson), 141
Bartlett, Henrietta C., 59
Basse, William, poem on Shakespeare's death, 165
Battle of Alcazar, 45
Beaumont, Inner Temple, 141
Beaumont and Fletcher, Philaster, 136
Beeston, William, 32
Belleforest, 102, 108, 113
Belott, Stephen, 35
Benson, F. R., 188
Bentley, G. E., 143
Betterton, Thomas, 184

Bishop of Worcester, 31
Black Death, 9
Blackfriars Theater, 35, 52, 53, 141
Blount, Edward, 61
Boccaccio, Decameron, 119, 136
Booth, Barton, 185
Booth, Edwin, 188
Boswell, James, 29, 148
Bracegirdle, Anne, 185
Bradley, A. C., 158
   Shakespearean Tragedy, 150
British Museum, 59
Brooke, Arthur, 189
Bubonic plague, 9
Burbage, Cuthbert, 52
Burbage, James, 49
Burbage, Richard, 48, 52, 182
Burleigh, Lord, 43

Cabot, John and Sebastian, 4
Cambises, 41
Cambridge edition of Shakespeare, 150
Camden, William, reference to Shakespeare, 164
   Remaines, 131
Campaspe (Lyly), 43
Capell, Edward, 147, 148
Capital, new uses of, 10
Carey, Henry, Lord Hunsdon, 34, 48
Casina (Plautus), 111
Cavendish, Life of Cardinal Wolsey, 141
Caxton, William, 3, 176
Census of Shakespeare's Plays in Quarto, A, 59
Cervantes, 2
Chambers, Sir Edmund, 31 n, 49 n, 52 n, 62 n, 66, 70, 80 n, 82, 84, 93, 105, 118, 124, 133, 134, 136, 158, 161, 173
Changes, economic and religious, of sixteenth century, 5
Chapman, George, translation of Iliad, 117
Characters in Shakespeare's Plays (Hazlitt), 149
Chaucer, Geoffrey, 69, 93

217

Knight's Tale, 142
Troilus and Criseyde, 116
Chester, Robert, 71
Chettle, Henry, 33, 34
Children's companies, 46 n
Chronology of Shakespeare's plays, 64 ff.
Church, Stratford Parish, 22
Church of Rome, England's break with, 7–8
Cibber, Colley, 185
Cinthio, Giraldi, *Epitia*, 120
   Hecatommithi, 120, 121
Cleopatra (Daniel), 128
Clopton, Hugh, 21, 22, 23
Coaches, introduction of, 11
Coleridge, Samuel, 148
Colet, John, 3
Columbus, 4
Comedy of Errors, The, 64, 78–79, 88, 127
Condell, Henry, 48, 61, 62, 63, 134, 169–171
Confessio Amantis (Gower), 134
Copernican theory, 4–5
Coriolanus, 130–131
Coryat, Thomas, 52
Coutances, Bishop John de, 21
Coventry plays, 33
Cowley, Richard, 48
Craig, Hardin, 82 n, 158
Critics, twentieth century, 151
"Crueltie of Gernutus, The," 97
Curtain Theater, 49, 53
Cushman, Charlotte, 188
Cymbeline, 136–137

Daniel, Samuel, 90
   Cleopatra, 128
Dates of Shakespeare's plays, table, 66–67
Davenant, William, Shakespeare producer, 184
David and Bethsabe, 45
Davies, John, poem to Shakespeare, 164
Davies, Richard, note about Shakespeare, 177
Davis, W. S., 18, 158

De revolutionibus orbium coelestium, 4
de Witt, Johannes, 50, 52
Decameron (Baccaccio), 119, 136
Delius, Nikolaus, 151
Democracy, growth of, 13
Diana Enamorada (Montemayor), 85, 93
Digges, Leonard, 104, 105, 144, 183, 189
   poem to Shakespeare, 168
Discovery, world, 4
Doran, Madeleine, 74
Dowdall, reference to Shakespeare, 177
Dowden, Edward, *Shakespeare: His Mind and Art*, 150
Drake, Francis, 4, 11
Dramatic companies, organization of, 46 ff.
Drayton, Michael, 38, 105
   on *Lucrece*, 161
Dress, Elizabethan, 18
Droeshout, Martin, 62
Dryden, John, 144, 184
   All for Love, 128
   comment on Shakespeare, 143
Dyce, Alexander, 150

Economic features of England in sixteenth century, 9
Editions, single volume, 151
Education in sixteenth century, 3
Edward I, 45
Edward II, 44, 91
Edward III, 71
Edward VI, King, 14
Eighteenth-century Shakespearean actors, 185 ff.
Elizabeth, Queen, 6, 13, 14–15, 16, 24
   her policies, 10
Endymion, 43
English Renaissance, 1
Epitaph, Shakespeare's, 37
Epitia (Cinthio), 120
Erasmus, 2, 3
Eschenburg, Johann, 149
Essay of Dramatic Poesy, An (Dryden), quoted from, 145

Essex, Earl of, 100
Euphues, 43, 44
Evans, Maurice, 189
Every Man in His Humour (Jonson), 107, 111
External evidence, 64

Faerie Queene (Spenser), 123
Famous Victories of Henry V, The, 98, 99
Faucit, Helen, 188
Faustus, 44
Feminine ending, 65
Field, Richard, 34
Fiorentino, Giovanni, 97
First Folio, 60 ff.
First period, plays of, 73 ff.
Five Hours' Adventure, The (Tuke), 144
Flatter, Richard, 56, 63 n
Fletcher, John, 58, 140
Fletcher, Laurence, 48
Folger Shakespeare Library, 59
Folio, list of plays in, 61
Food and eating, 18
Forman, Simon, 136, 137
  allusion to *Macbeth*, 126
Fortune Theater, 50, 51, 53
Four periods of Shakespeare's career, 66
Fourth period, plays of, 133 ff.
Foxe, *Actes and Monuments*, 141
Freeman, Thomas, poem to Shakespeare, 164
Friar Bacon and Friar Bungay (Greene), 44
Fuller, Thomas, notes on Shakespeare, 173–174
Furness, H. H., 150
Furnivall, F. J., *Shakespeare Quarto Facsimiles*, 151

Gama, Vasco da, 4
Games, Elizabethan, 17
Gammer Gurton's Needle, 42 n
Garrick, David, 185, 189
"Gatherers," 50
Gesta Grayorum, 64
Gesta Romanorum, 134

Gielgud, John, 189
Gl'Ingannati, 108
Globe Theater, 35, 52, 53
  burning of, 140
Goethe, Johann von, 148
  Wilhelm Meisters Lehrjahre, 149
Golden Ass (Apuleius), 92
Gorboduc, 42 n
Gorgeous Gallery of Gallant Inventions, 16 n
Gower, John, 135
  Confessio Amantis, 134
Grammatica Latina, 30
Granville-Barker, Harley, 158
Gray, H. D., 86
Gray, J. W., 31 n
Great Fire of 1666, 25, 26
Greene, Robert, 4, 33, 34, 42, 44, 49, 73, 85, 112
  Pandosto, 138
Greet, Ben, 188
Greg, W. W., 74
Groatsworth of Wit (Greene), 33
Grocyn, William, 3
Guild of the Holy Cross, 21, 30
Guild plays, 39
Guilds, craft, 6
  break-up of, 6–7
Gunpowder Plot, 123

Hall, Edward, *Chronicle*, 74, 77, 95, 98, 100, 141
Hall, Elizabeth, 36, 37, 38
Hall, John, 36
Hall, William, on Shakespeare's epitaph, 178
Halliwell-Phillips, J. O., 150
Hamburgische Dramaturgie (Lessing), 149
Hamlet, 60, 63, 112–115, 122, 125
Hampden, Walter, 189
Handful of Pleasant Delights, 16 n
Hanmer, Sir Thomas, 147
Harrison, G. B., 158
Harsnett, S., *Declaration of Popish Impostures*, 123
Hart, Joan Shakespeare, 38
Hart, William, 38

INDEX

Harvey, Gabriel, reference to Shakespeare, 163
Hathaway, Anne, 31
Hathaway, Richard, 31
Hawkins, Sir John, 12
Hazlitt, William, 148
 Characters in Shakespeare's Plays, 149
"Heavens," or shadow, 51
Hecatommithi (Cinthio), 120, 121
Heminges, John, 48, 52, 61, 62, 63, 134, 169–171
Henley Street house, 27
Henry IV, 98–100
 Part I, 60, 64
 Part II, 60
Henry V, 60, 65, 100–102, 110
Henry VI, Parts I, II, III, 59, 73–76
Henry VII, King, 6, 13
 policies of, 13–14, 15
Henry VIII, King, 6, 8, 14
Henry VIII, 53, 140–141
Henryson, Robert, *Testament of Cresseid*, 117
Henslowe, Philip, 73, 79, 112
Heptameron (Whetstone), 120
Hero and Leander (Marlowe), 106
Heywood, Thomas, 56
Higgins, John, *Mirror for Magistrates*, 123
Histoires tragiques (Belleforest), 102, 108, 113
Historiae Danicae (Saxo Grammaticus), 113
History of Felix and Philiomena, The, 85
History of King Richard III (More), 74, 77
Holinshed's *Chronicles*, 74, 77, 91, 94, 98, 100, 123, 126, 136, 141
Hope Theater, 53
Horace, 30
Hudson, H. N., 150
Humors, Elizabethan, 107
Hundred Years' War, 5
Hunt, Simon, 30
Huntington Library, 59
Hystorye, Sege and dystruccyon of Troye (Lydgate), 117

Il Pecorone (Fiorentino), 97
Illegitimate editions, 58
Inner Temple and Gray's Inn Masque (Beaumont), 141
Inns of Court, 25
Inns used as theaters, 50
Interludes, 40
Internal evidence, 65
Internal-external evidence, 64–65
Inventions, 2
Irving, Sir Henry, 187

Jaggard, Isaac, 61
Jaggard, William, 61, 62, 71
James I, King, 48
James IV, 44
Jenkins, Thomas, 30
Jew of Malta, The (Marlowe), 44, 97
Johnson, Samuel, 29, 147, 148
Jonson, Ben, 4, 29, 38, 44, 61, 62, 72, 86 n, 104, 105, 107, 111, 143, 144, 171, 172
 Bartholomew Fair, 141
 Oberon, 137
 poem to Shakespeare, 166–168
 Poetaster, 116
 Silent Woman, 130
Julius Caesar, 39 n, 104–106

Kean, Charles, 187
Kean, Edmund, 187, 189
Kemble, J. P., 186
Kempe, William, 52, 102, 183
 Nine Days' Wonder, 126
Killigrew, Thomas, Shakespearean producer, 184
King John, 64, 94–96
King Lear, 60, 123–126, 155
King's Men, 48, 57
Knight, G. W., 158
Knight's Tale (Chaucer), 142
Kyd, Thomas, 4, 42, 43, 78, 80, 105
 Spanish Tragedy, 112

Lamb, Charles, *On the Tragedies of Shakespeare*, 148
Lancaster, House of, 13
Landed nobility, 5
Lawrence, W. W., 158
Lee, Sidney, 151

INDEX 221

Legend of Good Women (Chaucer), 69
Legitimate editions, 58
Leicester, Earl of, 33
Leire, Chronicle historye of, 123
Leland, John, 22
Lessing, Gotthold, Hamburgische Dramaturgie, 149
Lewis, B. R., 31 n, 62 n
Liberty, a, 49
Life of Cardinal Wolsey (Cavendish), 141
Life in Elizabethan Days (Davis), 18, 158
Linacre, Thomas, 3
Literary drama, growth of, 16
Lodge, Thomas, 42, 44, 45, 106
  Wit's Miserie, 112
Lollards, 7
London, in Shakespeare's time, 23 ff.
Lopez, Dr. Roderigo, 96
Lord Chamberlain's Men, 34, 48, 57, 112
Lover's Complaint, A, 70
Love's Labour's Lost, 60, 64, 71, 86–88
Love's Labour's Won, 64, 118
Love's Martyr, 71
Lucian, 132
Lucy, Sir Thomas, 32
Luther, Martin, 7
Lydgate, John (Hystorye, Sege and dystruccyon of Troye), 117
Lyly, John, 42, 43, 85, 87
Lyly, William, 30

Macbeth, 63 n, 126–127
Macklin, Charles, 185
Macready, W. C., 187
Magellan, 4
Malone, Edward, 147, 148
Mankind, 41 n
Manningham, John, 108
Mantell, Robert, 188
Manufacturing, growth of, 10–11
Marlowe, Christopher, 4, 33, 42, 44, 74, 76, 91, 97, 105, 106
Marlowe, Julia, 189
Mary Tudor, 14
Maxims of Cato, 30

Measure for Measure, 119–121
Menaechmi (Plautus), 64, 78
Menaphon (Greene), 112
Merchant of Venice, 60, 64, 94, 96–98
Meres, Francis, 69, 76, 80, 82, 84, 86, 87, 89, 91, 92, 94, 96, 98, 100, 102, 104, 106, 118, 144
  list of Shakespeare's plays, 64
  Palladis Tamia, quoted, 162–163
Merry England, 15–19
Merry Wives of Windsor, 60, 109–111
Michelangelo, 2
Middle class, rise of the, 13
Midsummer-Night's Dream, A, 60, 64, 88, 92–94, 144, 155
Millington, Thomas, 73
Milton, John, poem to Shakespeare, 171
Mirror for Magistrates (Higgins), 123
Mirror of Martyrs (Weever), 104
Miscellanies, Elizabethan, 16
Modjeska, Helena, 188
Montaigne, 2
Montemayor, Jorge de, 85, 93
Montgomery, Earl of, 62
Morality plays, 40
More, Thomas, 3, 74
Mountjoy, Christopher, 35
Much Ado about Nothing, 60, 102–104, 109, 121
Munday, Anthony, 71, 97
Music, interest in, 17
  Italian influence, 17
Musica Transalpina, 17

Nashe, Thomas, 33, 42, 44, 45, 73, 112
Neilson, Adelaide, 188
New Learning, 3, 14, 16
New Place, 35
New Variorum, 150, 151
Newes out of Purgatorie (Tarleton), 111
Newington Butts Theater, 49
Nine Days' Wonder (Kempe), 126
Norton, Thomas, 42 n

Oberon (Jonson), 137
Odell, G. C. D., 182 n
Old Wives' Tale, The, 45

Olivier, Laurence, 188
Oman, Sir Charles, 8
On the Tragedies of Shakespeare (Lamb), 148
Organization and Personnel of the Shakespearean Company (Baldwin), 48 n, 57 n
Othello, 58, 60, 102, 103, 121–122, 125, 144, 155
Ovid, 30, 68, 69
Oxford, Earl of, 43

Painter, William, 89
Palace of Pleasure, 89, 119, 132
Palladis Tamia, list of Shakespeare's plays, 64
Pandosto (Greene), 138
Paradise of Dainty Devices, The, 16 n
Passionate Pilgrim, The, 71
Patterne of Painefull Adventures (Twine), 134
Pavier, Thomas, 73
Peele, George, 33, 42, 74, 94
Pembroke, Earl of, 62
  Epistle to Earls of Pembroke and Montgomery, 169 ff.
Pepys, Samuel, 144, 184
Pericles, 58, 60, 61, 133–135
Petrarch, 2
Phelps, Samuel, 188
Philaster (Beaumont and Fletcher), 136
Phillips, Augustine, 48, 52
Phoenix Nest, The, 16 n
"Phoenix and the Turtle, The," 72
Platter, Thomas, 104
Plautus, 42, 78, 111
Players, Earl of Leicester's and others, 33, 49
Plutarch, 93
  Lives, 105, 128, 130, 132
Poetaster (Jonson), 116
Political backgrounds, English, 12
Pollard, A. W., 59
Pope, Alexander, 146, 184
Population, sixteenth century, 9
Porter's Hall Theater, 53
Printing, invention of, 3
  effect of, 16

Professional writers, 4
Promos and Cassandra (Whetstone), 120
Protestant Church, established in England, 8
Publication of plays, methods of, 57 ff.

Quartos, Shakespeare, 58–60
Quiney, Richard, 37 n
Quiney, Shakespeare, 36 n
Quiney, Thomas, 36
  son, 37 n

Rabelais, 2
Rape of Lucrece, 34, 68 f.
Raphael, 2
Ravenscroft, Edward, 80
Recuyell of the Historyes of Troye (Caxton), 116, 176
Red Bull Theater, 53
Reed, Isaac, 147
Reformation, 2, 7
Religious changes of sixteenth century, 7, 14
Remaines (Camden), 131
Renaissance, 1, 2
Restoration, Shakespeare as acted in period of, 184
Restoration attitude toward Shakespeare, 144
Revels Account, record in, 119, 121
Revival of Learning, 1, 2
Richard II, 59, 64, 90–92, 96, 98
Richard III, King, 13
Richard III, 59, 64, 76–77, 88
Riche, Barnabe, *Riche His Farewell*, 108
Roads and travel, 9
Roche, Walter, 30
Romantic Period, criticism in, 148 ff.
Romeo and Juliet, 60, 64, 88–90, 128, 154
Ronsard, 2
Rosalynde (Lodge), 106, 107
Rose Theater, 49
Rowe, Nicholas, 30, 145, 146
  sketch of Shakespeare, 178–181
Royal Exchange, 11, 25
Run-on line, 65

INDEX

Rymer, Thomas, *Short View of Tragedy*, 144
Tragedies of the Last Age Considered, 144

Sackville, Thomas, 42 n
St. Paul's Cathedral, 25
Saunderson, Mary, 184
Saxo Grammaticus, *Historiae Danicae*, 113
Schlegel, A. W., *Über dramatische Kunst und Literatur*, 149
School, Stratford Grammar, 30
School drama, 42
Second period, plays of, 88 ff.
Seneca, 42, 43
Sententiae pueriles, 30
Shadwell, Thomas, 184
Shakespeare, Hamnet, 35, 94
Shakespeare, Henry, 27
Shakespeare, John, 27 ff.
  children, 28
  death, 36
  fined, 27
  glover by trade, 28
  marriage, 28
  town official, 28
Shakespeare, Judith, 32
Shakespeare, Mary Arden, 28, 36
Shakespeare, Richard, 27
Shakespeare, Susanna, 31, 32, 36, 37
Shakespeare, William, 27 ff.
  affiliation with dramatic company, 48–49
  ancestry, 27–28
  attacked by Greene, 33
  baptism, 29–30
  buys New Place, 35
  children, 32
  death and burial, 37
  epitaph, 37
  growing wealth, 35
  interest in drama, 32–33
  last will and testament, 194–197
  in London, 33 ff.
  long poems, 34, 68, 69
  marriage, 30–31
  one of Lord Chamberlain's Servants, 34
  popularity on Elizabethan stage, 182–183
  schooling, 30
  sonnets, 69–70
Shakespeare Documents, The (Lewis), 31 n, 62 n
Shakespeare: His Mind and Art (Dowden), 150
Shakespeare Quarto Facsimiles (Furnivall), 151
Shakespearean Playhouses (Adams), 53
Shakespearean Tragedy (Bradley), 150
Shakespeare's England, 10
Shakespeare's Marriage (Gray), 31 n
Shakespeare's Producing Hand (Flatter), 56
Short View of Tragedy (Rymer), 144
Shottery, 31
Siddons, Sarah Kemble, 186, 189
Sidney, Philip, 16, 62
  Arcadia, 124
Silent Woman, The (Jonson), 130
Sir Thomas More, 71, 77
Sixteenth Century, The (Oman), 8
Sly, William, 48
Smethwick, John, 61, 62
Smith, Logan P., 158
Smith, Lucy Toulmin, 22
Snitterfield, 27
Somers, Sir George, shipwrecked in Bermudas, 139
Songs and Sonnets (Tottel), 16
Sonnets, Shakespeare's, 69 f.
Sothern, E. H., 189
Southampton, Earl of, 34, 68
Spain, Armada destroyed, 12, 16
  threat of war with, 12
Spanish Tragedy, The (Kyd), 43, 112
Spencer, Hazelton, 158
Spenser, Edmund, 29
  Faerie Queene, 123
Sports, Elizabethan, 17, 18
Stage, Elizabethan, 51–52
Stationers' Register, 57, 62
Steele, Richard, 184
Steevens, George, 147
Stevenson, William, 42 n
Stoll, E. E., 158

INDEX

Stowe, John, *Chronicle*, 74, 98, 100
Stratford-on-Avon, 20
   description of by Leland, 22–23, 27
   location, 20
   origin, 21
   Shakespeare in, 35–36
   trades and industries, 21
Stratford Grammar School, 30
Stratford Parish Church, 22, 37
Stubbs, Philip, 12
Surrey, Earl of, 16, 70
Swan Theater, 50, 52, 53

Table of dates of plays, 66–67
Tamburlaine (Marlowe), 44
Tarleton, *Newes out of Purgatorie*, 111
Taming of the Shrew, The, 82–84
Tate, Nahum, 184
Tempest, The, 139–140
Temple Grafton, 31, 32
Tenant farming, 10
Terence, 42
Terry, Ellen, 188
Testament of Cresseid (Henryson), 117
Theater, the, 49, 50, 53
Theaters, closing of, 34
   description of, 50–52
   Elizabethan, 49
Theobald, Lewis, 147
Third period, plays, 112 ff.
Thorndike, Sybil, 189
Thorpe, Thomas, 69
Timber (Jonson), 144
Timon of Athens, 131–133
Titus Andronicus, 59, 64, 79–81, 122
Titus and Vespasian, 80
Tobacco introduced, 12
Tonson, Jacob, 145, 146
Tottel, Richard, 16
Trade, growth of, 10–11
Tragedies of the Last Age Considered (Rymer), 144
Travel, foreign, increase in, 12
Tree, Beerbohm, 187
Troilus and Cressida, 60, 69, 115, 116–117, 120, 131–132
Tudor, house of, 5, 13

Tuke, Sir Samuel, *The Five Hours' Adventure*, 144
Twelfth Night, 108–109
Twine, Lawrence, *Patterne of Paineful Adventures*, 134
Two Gentlemen of Verona, 64, 84–86, 88
Two Noble Kinsmen, The, 58, 141–142

Über dramatische Kunst und Literatur (Schlegel), 149
University Wits, 42, 44
Unwin, George, 10

Vega, Lope de, 2
Velasquez, 2
Venus and Adonis, 34, 68, 69
Vinci, Leonardo da, 2
Virgil, 30

Warburton, William, 147
Ward, John, 37
   diary reference to Shakespeare, 174
Wars of the Roses, 5, 21, 74, 77
Weakest Goeth to the Wall, The, 118
Weever, John, *Mirror of Martyrs*, 104
West, E. J., 93 n
Whetstone, George, 120
White, Richard G., 150
Wieland, Christoph, 149
Wilkins, George, 133, 134
Wilks, Robert, 185
William Shakespeare (Chambers), 31 n
Wilson, J. Dover, 92 n, 158
Winter's Tale, The, 137–139
Wit's Miserie (Lodge), 112
Woolen manufacture, 11
World discovery, 4
Wotton, Sir Henry, letter about Globe burning, 140
Wyatt, Sir Thomas, 16
Wycliffe, John, 7

Yonge, Nicholas, 17
York, House of, 13

Zelauto (Munday), 97